GW01071959

**Old Story Time
and other plays**

Also in this series

Old Story Time
and other plays

Trevor D. Rhone

Longman

Longman Group Limited
Longman House,
Burnt Mill, Harlow, Essex, UK

© Trevor D. Rhone 1981

First published 1981

ISBN 0 582 78532 4

Typeset by Computacomp (UK) Ltd.,
Fort William, Scotland.
Printed in Great Britain by
Richard Clay (The Chaucer Press) Ltd,
Bungay, Suffolk

Contents

Dedicated to
my daughter Traci,
who likes all the characters in
this book, especially Pa Ben

Introduction

Theatre in Jamaica has a long history; but, on the evidence available, Jamaican theatre is young. From at least the eighteenth century until the 1930s there is evidence of mainly foreign, often visiting, theatre; the amusement of 'the very thin upper crust'. Amusements of the poor and black – 'the bulk of the population',[1] African slaves and their descendants – are broadly described, but they do not yield a convenient wealth of documents for the chronicler. The work of Richardson Wright in *Revels in Jamaica 1682–1838* has been supplemented by other historians of theatre, such as Henry Fowler, Ivy Baxter, Errol Hill,[2] who also take us beyond Emancipation.

In 1911 George Bernard Shaw, on a visit to Jamaica, remarked: 'you want … a theatre, with all the ordinary travelling companies from England and America sternly kept out of it; for unless you do your own acting and write your own plays, your theatre will be no use; it will, in fact, vulgarise and degrade you …'[3] The trend continued nevertheless: plenty of touring companies doing Shakespeare and English trivia. But popular entertainment was beginning to work through institutions of which there is convenient record. The Christmas Morning Concerts, for example, began early this century and gave the stage to people such as 'Cupes and Abes' (Cupidon, an impersonator, and Ableton, his performing partner) and, late in the 1930s, the young Louise Bennett who recited her early dialect verses and sang folk songs. At Edelweiss Park, concerts arranged under the auspices of Marcus Garvey's United Negro Improvement Association projected talents such as that of the comedian Ranny Williams, who both performed and wrote.

With the growth of Jamaican nationalism in the 1930s

there were more and more attempts to write a Jamaican drama which might engage with Jamaican realities: Fránk Hill's *Upheaval*, Archie Lindo's *Under the Skin*, Una Marson's *Pocomania* – the very titles suggest some of the developing concerns. In 1941 the Little Theatre Movement was founded; and it soon became a national institution, responsible for at least two or three major productions a year, including a pantomime which runs annually to good houses from Boxing Day until March or April. But the first LTM pantomime was an English transplant; and, as Ivy Baxter has noted, the lead actor and actresses were, at first, from the expatriate community of Kingston or from Jamaicans of very light skin. By the third year there was a Jamaican script, *Soliday and the Wicked Bird* by Vera Bell; and there has been 'the gradual merging of shade and the reversal of the proportion of dark to light in the cast.'[4] Steadily the 'pantomime' has been transformed into an annual Jamaican musical, often drawing on Jamaican history and folklore, most frequently with the trickster spider Anancy as a central figure.

Trevor Rhone was born in Kingston the year before the LTM was founded. On 24 March 1940, he was born into a large black family – twenty-one children in all (his father married twice). Rhone grew up in Bellas Gate, a village in St Catherine. From an early age he enjoyed the concerts at which members of the audience would, in good humour, show approval or disapproval by paying small sums to take a performer off or to put him on again. 'Before I had seen a play,' he has said, 'I knew pretty well what my life's work should be.'[5] At the age of about nine he had decided; he was going to be an actor. After primary schools in St Catherine he had his secondary education (1952–57) at Beckford and Smith's (now St Jago High School) in Spanish Town. He was heavily involved in the Secondary Schools' Drama Festival and, later, in the annual LTM pantomime. After leaving school he took various jobs and, with the beginning of the Jamaica

Broadcasting Corporation, began to write radio plays. About that time, when he had been thinking seriously of going abroad to study, he happened to meet the Trinidadian actor Edric Connor who suggested the Rose Bruford College in Kent, England, and also cautioned, 'Whatever they teach you, forget half of it!'[6]

At Rose Bruford (1960–63) Rhone learnt a great deal about the history and development of theatre, stage-craft, how to make optimum use of slender resources; about mime, the use of the body, the voice, and so on. His one important reservation about the experience was that he was being forced, in that ambience, to deny his own roots and to acknowledge the roots of England instead. 'That, I think, was the real hazard of the place – that they tried to make you into somebody that you were not, or make you into what *they* were.'[7]

Full of hope, he returned to Jamaica and had to go into teaching, for which Rose Bruford had also trained him. But he was distressed at the low salary and the fact that little seemed to be happening in theatre. Competent ventures such as Jamaica Playhouse or The National Theatre Trust were yet to come. Rhone found the whole climate 'sort of desert-like'.[8] After nine months he travelled to England again. But in London he was unhappy with the type of role available to the black actor; so in 1965 he left for Jamaica again. This time he and seven associates decided that they would *make* something happen in Jamaican theatre. They called themselves Theatre '77, giving themselves twelve years to establish something worthwhile. The beginnings were difficult. For one reason or another, many of the original people fell away. Two of those who stuck it out were Trevor Rhone and Yvonne Jones (-Brewster). A variety of plays, Caribbean and non-Caribbean, were presented at what they called the Barn Theatre, the adapted garage of a private home. Phase by phase, the garage was converted into an intimate theatre, adequately equipped, seating 150.

In the early years of the Barn Theatre, Rhone earned a living by teaching in various schools. Wishing to produce a pantomime for one of them, St Andrew Technical, he found that the English scripts available did not fully engage the interest of his students; and, with the astute encouragement of the headmaster, he took time off from classes in order to write a Jamaican adaptation. The show went well, and next year Mr Rhone was expected to produce another pantomime script. A year later he produced a third. But in 1969, sitting in a staff room contemplating his paltry salary and the dispiriting conditions – preparing, had he known it, for *School's Out* – Rhone decided to resign from teaching and attempt to write full-time.

His first play was *The Gadget*, written in 1969; a relationship in it, between peasant mother and educated son, points forward to *Old Story Time*. In 1970–71, a very productive year, Rhone co-authored *The Harder They Come* (a feature film directed by Perry Henzell), threw off *Music Boy* (a script for the LTM pantomime), and wrote *Smile Orange*. *Comic Strip* (1973) and *Sleeper* (1974) were followed by *School's Out*, first performed in 1975. Scripted and directed by Rhone himself, a film version of *Smile Orange* was completed later that year.

At a time when, in Jamaica, productions other than the LTM pantomime did not normally get beyond a couple of dozen performances, the play *Smile Orange* (in a small theatre, admittedly) ran for 245. It was Rhone's first big success. Rhone thought he was taking a big risk, writing largely in Jamaican dialect. But the way had been prepared: by – for example – Louise Bennett in her dialect writings and performance, by the LTM pantomime as it developed, by comedians Bim and Bam in their topical shows, by a popular radio serial scripted by Elaine Perkins.

Smile Orange is funny, and it is serious. It is a devastating comment on tourism and on attitudes the industry harbours or can breed. 'I will touch di ground,' says Joe, 'if I can find a dollar bill down dere.' 'A will go further than dat,' says Ringo. 'A will bury my head in di san!'

Everything is put into service in pursuit of what the tourist can provide, whether money or a chance to emigrate. 'I not givin away my pearl for nutten,' says Miss Brandon. 'Is all I have. It have to work for me.' Rhone lays bare some of the sordid motivations of tourists and of the smiling workers who seem so willing to oblige. 'White people must pay dem way ... Exploit de exploiter.' Under the skilful tutelage of Ringo (an Anancy figure), the awkward Cyril learns the lucrative routines. A Jamaican cautionary tale (no doubt invented by the owners of orange trees to discourage larceny) is recalled at a critical moment. When the busboy Cyril – a fool becoming a knave – accepts the orange, the moment suggests that he has grown beyond former simplicities, but also that he will now accept emasculation. Smile. Orange.

'If you is a black man and you can't play a part, you going to starve to death.' Play-acting is a recurrent metaphor. The blacks, including Assistant Manager O'Keefe, are playing roles to which they have been assigned by the tourist industry and the realities of power. The lifeguards are exposed; there is a tragedy. The difficulties for Ringo, Joe and O'Keefe are overcome when they recognise the possibilities of a new performance – Ringo as selfless hero, with supporting cast. A little help from the press, and they can act themselves out of trouble.

The success of the original production owed much to the direction of Dennis Scott and to the vivid performances throughout. Some of the pleasures of the play as performed could be missed by a reader. Ringo hiding in the garbage bin is a strong scene, and lucidly symbolic. Ringo's instruction of Cyril involves details which have greater impact when seen: Cyril's clumsy reaching across the body of the 'guest', his armpit directly in her face. Miss Brandon's insolent hostility to Mr O'Keefe is registered in her body-language, and the sarcastic malice in her voice.

The voices, of course, and what they signal about class and role-playing, beg to be actually heard; none more so than that of the telephone operator Miss Brandon switching between her precious on-duty manner and the vulgar relaxation of the gossip sessions with Maisie. Like other good playwrights, Rhone is acutely sensitive to the sound, the tone, of voices; he has an excellent ear; and he makes full use of the continuum of Jamaica talk.[9] His characters in these three plays range between those who, for all the variations in accent, speak versions of 'standard' – O'Keefe, Pat Campbell, Mica McAdam, Russ Dacres, Len Tomlinson, Lois Tomlinson, Margaret Greaves, George McFarlane – through the ceremonious rural Jamaican speech of Pa Ben, Miss Aggie, Pearl, to the racy dialect of Ringo and Joe. There are special cases, such as Miss Brandon's 'Mocho Beach Hotel. Good afternoon. May I help you?', or Cyril's lisp, or Ringo's wheedling sycophancy as he cons O'Keefe, or Ringo teaching Cyril ersatz-American, or Hopal Hendry doing 'voilent' battle with English pronunciation and grammar. The differences should be apparent to the reader; but of course when heard – and, in the theatre, associated with physical characterisation – they communicate more fully.

As indicated in the script of *Smile Orange*, recorded sound is used to suggest a world beyond the immediate playing areas: planes are heard arriving and taking off; that Mocho Beach Hotel is third-rate we know at once from the 'enthusiastic and off-key version' of a Jamaican song (itself ironic: 'Nobody's business but mi own.').

The clever use of sound effects added a similar dimension in the original production of *School's Out*, admirably directed by Yvonne Jones-Brewster. Scenes were linked with the sound of children happily at play, in song and chatter that sounded innocent. These, we were reminded, are the potential victims, young people being damaged in our schools.

In the performance of *School's Out*, an unignorable

symbol is the malfunctioning lavatory, door set Up Centre to dominate the stage. Staff members continually refer to the stench; and at the beginning of Act II a sign is posted on the door: OUT OF ORDER. Like that staff room, clearly; like that school; like the education system. The school has an absentee headmaster, a fact visually registered by an imposing door Down Right which is never opened, though from that quarter, and to the sick delight of the Reverend Steele, is heard the sound of caning. This appalling institution is a church school, we are often told. When the eager new member of staff, Russ Dacres (his name an imperfect anagram of Crusader) comes to clean up the mess, he disturbs those already in possession. The waggish Rosco Callender tapes together two rulers in the shape of a cross which he affixes where Russ Dacres has been sitting. At one moment in the Brewster production that cross is held against the crusader Dacres, as though to ward off an evil power. When the character assassination ('susu') begins to develop, some of the conversations seem like carefully formulated temptation sequences.

Rumour is of critical importance to the action in *School's Out*; and in the other two plays it is also very much present. The hotel staff in *Smile Orange* know far more about Mr O'Keefe's private difficulties than he would wish. In *Old Story Time* Miss Aggie is terrified that embarrassing news might spread.

'I can spread rumours,' says Hopal Hendry. Even Mr Josephs joins in, hinting, with a hypocritical show of fair-mindedness, that Dacres might be communist. ('This student, a thinking student, simply expressed a view.') The aging conservative, Mr Josephs, is an important figure. Attention is focused on him by his tendency to brood in silence, while remaining highly visible on stage. When he explodes at the end of Act I ('Somebody over-reacted,' says Mica), he speaks vigorously for academic standards which have fallen. But he is evidently nostalgic not only for the higher academic standards of the past but also for the old social arrangements. ('Folks knew who they were, Mr Dacres; they knew their place, they were happier for it.') He remembers with pride a time when the school 'had a reputation and a tradition', when people like Hendry could have found no place in the school: 'Not as a teacher, not as a student.' Russ Dacres charges that the school in those days was 'A little corner for the elite and a few lucky blacks with pretension'. The discussion is nicely poised: if the former social exclusivity was to be decried, so is the erosion of academic standards in these more egalitarian times. A man like Hopal Hendry, whatever his virtues, is a certificated incompetent in the schoolroom. Academically, Mr Josephs is surely justified in fearing 'a never-ending stream of Hendrys yet to come'; and, indeed, when the wicked triumph and Russ resigns, Mr Hendry goes to the telephone to let a classmate know of the vacancy. The stage directions at the end emphasise Hendry's triumph. He takes over Russ Dacres' place at the table; and he, who has been casually dominated by Rosco Callender, can now, his power on the rise, blow smoke in Callender's face; for Callender has lost ground, having aligned himself with decency and defeat.

'People disappoint you,' says the hypocritical Chaplain. Indeed they do. None more so than Mr Josephs to whom Callender looked for principled help. 'I am not your brother, and never will be,' is Mr Josephs' anguished rejection of Hendry's familiar address. But the disclaimer is of strictly limited application, and it comes too late. Himself 'a contradiction' – a charge he has made against Russ Dacres and the like – Mr Josephs, by lending support to the conspiracy, has helped to strengthen the Hendrys of this world. *School's Out* is alert to complexities. People are not safely categorised. The Reverend Mr Steele, officially a man of God, is probably the most evil person we see. The idealistic Russ Dacres may be on the side of the angels, but he is also irritatingly self-righteous and pushy. Rosco Callender, the humorist, intelligent and irresponsible, is ultimately shown to have firm moral standards which he is willing to assert.

Goodness is under-represented in *Smile Orange*: there are rogues and victims; amorality triumphs. *School's Out*, on the other hand, is a very moral play; good contends with evil and seems to be defeated. *Old Story Time* is not only moral; it is a deeply religious work. 'We bind ourselves together with strength and trust and confidence, and there was no doubt between us, no enmity in our hearts, for we knew that the one force that could counteract all evil was there, and that force was love.' In their moving ritual of love, Pa Ben, Lois and Len repeat the twenty-third psalm and they struggle through the valley of the shadow. There is silence as the circle is bathed in a rich warm light and Miss Aggie, saved at last, liberated from the consequences of her own hatred, breathes, 'My children, my children.' At this stage we are in the world, essentially, of religious parable. 'All well. All well.' All's well that ends well.

Pa Ben is the main storyteller; others tell episodes within the larger story he narrates. He is a treat. 'What A don't know as a fact, A will make up as A go along, and if A can't do it by miself, mi friend here will help mi. [*Indicating his rum bottle.*]' A rich character in himself, he is also a clever dramatic device. Rhone has explained in an interview[10] that only when he hit upon the storytelling form did he solve the problem of how to present the forty-year span he wished the play to travel. Rhone has consciously tried to use a form of Africa-based Jamaican tradition, though he does not disclaim awareness also of Brecht.

Details of the presentation style, so flexible and economical, were developed partly in rehearsal in Bahamas, while preparing for the première in 1979. As director, Rhone got the cast to agree that in Act I whenever an object was actually needed it would be supplied, and that in Act II what had been used in Act I would be recycled. The process culminated in the absolute minimum of clutter, and in the confident advice of the stage directions and his note on 'The Setting'. In the first Jamaican production, directed by Rhone himself at the Way Out Theatre in July 1979, the transitions – from place to place, and between past and present – seemed almost cinematic in their easy flow.

The play travels the journey of Jamaican society in the last forty years or so, from a time when colour discrimination was the norm and was accepted by its victims, into the era when a few blacks slipped through the net into further education; and on to the period when those educated blacks, in the new political climate, begin to be appointed to positions of power. But they are creatures of their past; they may remember hurts; the PhD will acknowledge obeah; the roots go deep. Their parents, some of them, resist new attitudes. Miss Aggie rejects the proffered comforts of comparative affluence; she retains old customs and her old beliefs – among them, an absolute conviction that 'anything black nuh good'. With her own lot she is content, but she covets some thing better for her son. 'Black was good enough for me. It not good enough for him.' A powerful single mother, she will, if necessary, batter him into improvement; Len must advance through further education and aspire to Margaret, 'the nice brown girl with the hair down to her back'. Profoundly subservient to fairer skins, Miss Aggie is slow to recognise that George McFarlane might be a crook. Her animosity is directed against her own colour; against Lois, the black girl who, she fears, must have captured Len by obeah; against the woman who, in the end, will so generously forgive.

But villainy, it seems, is really brown. In Pa Ben's story, the mulatto George McFarlane is ubiquitously evil: assisted by Margaret, he has been cruel to Len at school; he is largely responsible for a painful episode in Lois's past; he has tried to swindle Miss Aggie; and he has attempted to blackmail Len. George is a sinner whom the play does not redeem.

Attitudes to colour[11], of major concern in *Old Story Time*, are important also in the other two plays. They surface in *School's Out*, for example, when Mica is accused by Rosco Callender of liking white men only and of feeling herself superior to other blacks; and when Rosco expresses resentment of expatriate allowances: 'Ah, white is beautiful.' In *Smile Orange* the black social director is deliberately neglected by a waiter. Ringo accuses blacks of being mean tippers whom he is not keen to serve. But Ringo, who is ready to cheat his black brother, does not hesitate to invoke the concept of black solidarity when he needs it. 'Dat's why black people will never get anywhere – we don't stick together.'

Pa Ben is a black man in whose scale of values colour is not critical. He associates Africa with savages and cannibals, but to him colour is not important. He deplores Miss Aggie's prejudice. When they quarrel, however, he is ready to forgive; and he is patient enough to wait until Miss Aggie, after more than a year, begins to acknowledge him again. He is the soul of love; and he is ready to tackle obstacles to love. He senses that Len's antagonism to George McFarlane has deeper roots than a righteous concern about Miss Aggie's money. ('Piece o' dat story missin'.') Through times of adversity he remains constant, the faithful friend, the good man, the instrument of peace.

Emotionally *Old Story Time* is Trevor Rhone's deepest play. It is capable of moving audiences not only in the concluding scenes of repentance, forgiveness, love; but also in the moments such as Miss Aggie's rhythmic beating of Len for playing with a 'little dutty black gal', the enactment of Len's sexual humiliation at school, and, most harrowing of all, the moment when Dr Len Tomlinson, newly returned from abroad, gives a handout of money to Pearl (the name ironic), the devastated, perennially pregnant relic of his childhood girlfriend who remained deteriorating in the village.

In the Jamaican production the acting was

extraordinarily expert. In particular, Charles Hyatt (Pa Ben) and Leonie Forbes (Miss Aggie) played to and against each other with all the authority of well trained actors in roles they know to be authentic. Trevor Rhone speaks with equal warmth of the work of Winston Saunders and Pandora Gomez in the Bahamas première production. Cyrene Tomlinson who, in Jamaica, for a time took over the role of Miss Aggie has also been highly acclaimed. The fact is that Pa Ben and Miss Aggie are great Caribbean roles.

Old Story Time has been put on in more countries than any other play by Rhone. It has been performed in Nassau, Grand Cayman, St Thomas and St Croix (in the Virgin Islands), Trinidad, Miami and Toronto. In Jamaica it has taken a rest after more than 200 performances. It seemed it could have run forever.

MERVYN MORRIS

Notes

[1] Richardson Wright, *Revels in Jamaica 1682–1838*, Benjamin Blom, New York/London, 1937, reissued 1969, p. 228.
[2] Henry Fowler, 'A History of Theatre in Jamaica', *Jamaica Journal*, ii, I, March 1968, pp. 53–59.
Ivy Baxter, *The Arts of an Island*, Scarecrow Press, Metuchen, N.J., 1970, pp. 248–286.
Errol Hill, 'The Emergence of a National Drama in the West Indies', *Caribbean Quarterly*, xviii, 4, December 1972, pp. 9–40.
[3] Quoted by Errol Hill, p. 17.
[4] Ivy Baxter, p. 261.
[5] Trevor Rhone interviewed by Mervyn Morris, 24 October 1980.
[6] *Ibid.*
[7] *Ibid.*
[8] *Ibid.*
[9] See Frederic G. Cassidy, *Jamaica Talk*, Institute of Jamaica and Macmillan, London, 1961, second edition 1971; and F. G. Cassidy and R. B. Le Page (eds) *Dictionary of Jamaican*, Cambridge University Press, 1967; second edition 1980.
[10] Trevor Rhone interviewed by Mervyn Morris, 24 October 1980.
[11] See Madeline Kerr, *Personality and Conflict in Jamaica*, Collins, London, 1963; first published 1952; Fernando Henriques, *Family and Colour in Jamaica*, MacGibbon & Kee, London, second edition 1968, reprinted for Sangster's, Kingston, 1976; originally published by Eyre & Spottiswoode 1953; Katrin Norris, *Jamaica: The Search for An Identity*, Institute of Race Relations and Oxford University Press, London, 1962; Rex M. Nettleford, *Mirror Mirror: Identity, Race and Protest in Jamaica*, Collins, London, and Sangster, Kingston, 1970.

Glossary

bangarang	noise, confusion
bruck	break; be short of cash; broken down clothes
buck	stub (one's toe)
drudge	wear (shoes) habitually
fluxy	flawless on the outside but rotten on the inside (i.e. liable to cause the flux)
gas	garçon (waiter)
grounds	unpretentious, trustworthy
hex	curse
jeyseyears	filthy person (literally, a person with dirty ears)
nyam	eat; be fussy; become agitated
primp	preen oneself, show off
quabs	friends
quattie	penny, ha'penny
sheg	botch
sheg-up	uncooperative, standoffish

skid	make a mistake
su-su	gossip, slander
toto	small round brown cake (made of flour and brown sugar)
trace	become abusive
wutliss	worthless

Old Story Time

Old Story Time

First performed in Nassau at the Dundas Centre for the
Performing Arts by the Bahamas Drama Circle on 19
April 1979 with the following cast:

PA BEN	– Winston Saunders
GEORGE	– John Trainer
MAMA (MISS AGGY)	– Pandora Gomez
LEN	– Calvin Cooper
LOIS	– Gwen Kelly
PEARL	– Joan Vanderpool

Directed by:	– Trevor D. Rhone

The Setting

Three frames and some very basic wooden furniture against a black back-drop and black wing flats make up the simple setting. Up Right two frames joined together, one angled Down Right, and the other running toward Up Right Centre, suggest the exterior-interior of MAMA's house, and later the interior of LEN's house. A sliding door, not in use when the area is used as MAMA's house, fits into the frame angled Down Right. A picture of Jesus hangs on the wall. During 'Change the house round', the picture is reversed to reveal LEN's college diploma. Reversible panels hang on either side of the door. For MAMA's house they are painted to suggest peeling wattle-and-daub walls; for LEN's house they are painted to suggest a marble finish.

Supports and cross-pieces serve as shelves on the frame running toward Up Right Centre. An old curtain hung in the centre of the frame reflects MAMA's poverty. The curtain is removed during 'Change the house round' to reveal books, candle-holders, a vase, etc.

The third frame Down Left suggests PA BEN's old house. It stands on a six-inch raised level which serves as his verandah. A practical window in two halves opens out towards the audience. The open door is cut into the frame. This area remains constant throughout.

The area in front of the stage – that is, between the stage and the first row of chairs (normally reserved for the orchestra pit) – serves as part of the playing area.

Furniture

MAMA's house:
  (i)   An old bureau
  (ii) A low bench
PA BEN's area:
  (i)   Two old wooden chairs on his verandah
  (ii) A piece of furniture Up Left that serves as
        storage for his tobacco, etc.
LEN's house/GEORGE's office in the bank:
The areas are freely interchangeable.
  (i)   A coffee table
  (ii)   Four wooden chairs; three serve as a sofa Centre
         Stage behind the coffee table.
  (iii) A small table and the fourth wooden chair serve
         as the office furniture in GEORGE's bank, and as
         part of LEN's living area.
  (iv)   The piece of furniture Up Left and the wooden
         stool serve as a bar in LEN's house.

With proper design and construction, the same piece of
furniture serves as the bureau in MAMA's house, as well as
the table in LEN's house/the Bank. Also, the coffee table
covered with matting serves as the low bench in MAMA's
house.

Costumes

Thorough research will help in the accuracy of the designs. It is important to reflect the dress styles of the past.

I suggest a simple device to help the flashbacks in the play, which is the use of *red* coloured accessories, e.g. when MAMA (Miss Aggy) in Act I re-enacts the scene in which Mr Mac encouraged her to buy a house for her son, she replaces her black hat with a red one, removing it at the end of the sequence.

LEN, as a boy, dresses in the style of thirty-odd years ago. As an adult he dresses in the mode of the successful banker in today's world. A red school cap helps the transition in Act Two – Scene One.

PA BEN: Old baggy pants, a time-worn shirt, along with an old-fashioned jacket. An old felt hat completes him.

PEARL, as a teenager, dresses in the style of thirty-odd years ago. Her clothes are well worn, however.
As pregnant PEARL in her early twenties, her dress is even more tattered.
As old PEARL, she is literally dressed in rags. Though only in her forties, she looks much older.

THE REAL ESTATE DEVELOPER: smart and modern.

MARGARET: dresses expensively in the style of thirty-odd years ago, and, most importantly, a flowing hairpiece.

LOIS: expensively modern.

MAMA: market-lady attire, head-tie, apron, old shoes, etc. Her torn clothes are simply cut from inexpensive material.

GEORGE: expensive-looking suits, ties, etc.

When the actors sit round PA BEN as the villagers, they wear street clothes that facilitate quick changes to the roles they will play, e.g. the actress playing MAMA needs only to add an apron to become the market lady.

All the characters are black except GEORGE, a high brown man, and MARGARET, a fair-skinned girl. The same actress plays PEARL, the REAL ESTATE DEVELOPER and MARGARET. Ideally, a fair-skinned girl should play the part (it is easier to make her look black than to make a black girl look fair-skinned).

ACT ONE

SCENE ONE

[*The stage and auditorium go to black. In the darkness we hear the actors singing a quiet, lyrical folk song. Very soon we see the glow of* PA BEN'S *lantern.*]

PA BEN: [*Over the song, sings*] Old Story Time. Old Story Time.

[*As he enters the auditorium, the lights come up fully on him.*]

[*Speaks*] Evening, one and all. Everybody hearty? What happen, you people mouth join church or what? You don't have voice to answer me? Everybody hearty? [*The actors respond* 'Yes, Pa Ben'.] That's better. [*To the audience*] Make yourselves comfortable on them nice chairs. You people lucky, years ago when A was a boy and A use to go to listen to story, it was never in no fancy place like this, with all them pretty fandangles, pretty lights and whatnot. No, sir.

[*The actors in the play start appearing from various directions and start moving to the Storyteller's area, where they will become* PA BEN'S *immediate audience.*]

On an evening in the district, we would gather at the village square, everybody gather round the shop piazza, some sit 'pon old drum, others 'pon the old crocus bags filled with salt, everybody chatting, some meddling in people's business, others giving remembrance to who dead the week before, who saw the ghost and what not, and my father was the chief Storyteller when him feel in the mood. [PA BEN *leaves the auditorium and goes up to his storytelling area.*] But A tell

8

you, give him a bottle of whites, an' two twos him was slap bang in the mood. He hem.

VILLAGERS/ACTORS: Him clear him throat.

PA BEN: And that was the signal to launch into a story. Who present would run go call the rest.

ACTRESS WHO WILL PLAY LOIS: [*Running to call off*] Pa Ben ready! Run come! Story time!

PA BEN: An' mi father would wax warm, him mind 'pon the story an' one eye 'pon the young gal them. Ah boy, those were the days. Yes, A can still hear the bamboo clarinet, and the fife a whistle, and the drum a lick, an' A can still see miself dress up in all mi finery stepping into the dance yard. [*He re-enacts the memory.*] And in those days they had a new fancy dance called the 'corkscrew', and A was the champion corkscrewer. [*He dances, much to the delight of his audience who tease him,* 'Watch your back, Pa Ben, careful, Pa Ben,' *etc.*] If any of you young gals here don't believe me, then meet me when the story done! Yes, those were the days. Good times and bad times, no opportunity for us black people, no water, no road, no 'lectric light. Sweet-mouth politician promise to bring down the moon, cut it up and hang it 'pon stick so we could read bible when night come. Ah boy, sixty years later, they don't even cut the stick yet. Ah well, that is another story.

ACTOR WHO WILL PLAY GEORGE: So how you use to read?

PA BEN: With mi bottle lamp. And in war days when oil short, A catch two firefly, put them in a bottle, light up the place same way. Ah boy, war days, no flour, no saltfish, no soap, the shops empty, but that too is another story.

ACTRESS WHO WILL PLAY PEARL: Howdy, Pa Ben [*As she comes on.*]

PA BEN: All well. All well. Come sit down. A ready for you. Open this for me. [*Giving her his bottle of white rum.*] The tongue nuh fully oil yet, but A going to begin. [PEARL *returns the opened bottle to* PA BEN. *He takes a big swig, to more*

9

comments from his audience, 'Mind you rotten out yuh liver', 'Him don't have no liver', *etc. The over one hundred per cent proof rum makes him temporarily lose his voice but he quickly recovers. He signals to the actress who will play* MAMA. *They whisper momentarily and she goes off.*]
A did live in a certain big yard, next door to some a the people who the story concern, so you see A have first-hand knowledge. What A don't know as a fact, A will make up as A go along, and if A can't do it by miself, mi friend here will help me. [*Indicating his rum bottle.*] Now how the tune go again?

ACTRESS WHO WILL PLAY PEARL: Me know, me know. [*She jumps up and immediately starts to sing a very uptempo blues version of the folk song, with much body gyration.*]
> Once upon a time
> There was a merry ol' time
> The monkey chew tobacco
> And he spit white lime.

[*The actors/villagers listen to the version of the song, bemused.*]

PA BEN: That is not the tune.

ACTOR WHO WILL PLAY GEORGE: No, but it sound nice. [*They all join in.*]
> The bull frog jump from bank to bank ... [*They start going off.*]

PA BEN: An' he never touch water. [*He chants.*] Ol' Story Time. Ol' Story Time. [*As he goes into his house.*]

[*The lights come up on the rest of the stage as* MAMA, *endearingly called Miss Aggy by* PA BEN *and Miss G by the others, enters, dressed in her market wear. A basket sits on top of her head; she carries another in her hand. She looks tired as if at the end of a long journey. She comes on, sets her baskets down on the bench, then calls ...*]

MAMA: Len! [*pause.*] Don't tell me him not here. Lennie! [*pause.*] Watch me an' him today. Lennard! After I tell him to stay in the house an' study him book [*She starts looking around the yard for him.*], him make me come back 'an don't find him in the yard.

[*She calls out once more.*] Lennard! [*Pause.*] Lennard! Pa Ben, Pa Ben! [*She calls across the yard.*]

PA BEN: Oi.

MAMA: You see Lennard?

PA BEN: A think him went to market wid you.

MAMA: No. A left him here to study him book.

PA BEN: Him about. So how was the market?

MAMA: Couldn't be worse this week. A had to give away half of the things, jus' so A never had to carry them back. An' like a bad luck, the damn jackass foot go lame up on me, an' me had to trot the ten mile come home.

PA BEN: Lawd.

MAMA: What to do? Anyway, A bring something for you.

PA BEN: Is what?

MAMA: Wait, nuh. [*She digs into her basket. He cleans his hands in his clothes in anticipation. She hands him a big hymn book.*]

PA BEN: For me? Thank you. [*He opens the book.*] Nice print. [*A hymn catches his eye and he sings.*] 'Rock of ages cleft for me ...'

MAMA: So you going to service tomorrow?

PA BEN: A not too make up mi mind yet. [*He goes into his little house.*]

MAMA: Is fourth Sunday, so Reverend Greaves should come up.

PA BEN: Then I have to try an' go.

MAMA: [*As she watches him go off*] Try. Old devil! A going down the road to look see if A see the one Lennard. [*She takes the market basket offstage.*]

PA BEN: [*He opens his window and looks out at her.*] Buy penny oil, hapenny salt, an' quattie bread for me. See the money here. [*Taking out a handkerchief. The money is securely knotted in it.*]

MAMA: All right. Where A leave the switch? [*As she hunts around for it.*]

PA BEN: Nuh worry beat him.

MAMA: If him can't hear him mus' feel. [*As she is going off*] Is you help spoil him.

PA BEN: Lawd! Harass the poor boy so!

MAMA: [*As she is leaving she sees a switch on the lower level.*] Ah, see it here. Wait till A catch up with him, A going to scour his behind for him this evening.

PA BEN: [*Speaking directly to the audience*] If A had mi wits about me, A would save the boy a licking that evening. A should tell him mother that is me send him out. A have to find him before she catch up with him. Lennie! [*As he goes off calling,* MAMA *can also be heard calling off stage,* 'Lennard!']

[LEN *chases* PEARL *on from Up Left. He catches up with her and touches her on her bosom.*]

LEN: Touch. [*Both laughing like mad.*] Okay, your time.

PEARL: All right.

LEN: Come on then. [*He presents his pelvic area for her to touch.*]

PEARL: [*Feigns at touching, then suddenly lunges at him.*] Touch!

LEN: You never touch.

PEARL: Touch.

LEN: I finish play.

PEARL: You have to go home?

LEN: No.

PEARL: Yuh mother must be soon come from market.

LEN: So?

PEARL: I know what will happen if she come home and don't find you.

LEN: She can't do me nutten.

PEARL: Except tie you to the bed-head and murder you.

LEN: Tie who?

PEARL: You same one. Go on like you is a big man.

LEN: Big man, yes.

PEARL: In yuh pants.

LEN: You want to see it? [*He chases her threateningly.*]

PEARL: You too rude. Play bad when yuh mother not

around. Is only because she gone to market why you
manage to t'ief out.

LEN: I don't have to t'ief out.

PEARL: So you say, but everybody notice how since you get
to go to the high school, how she strict with you more
than ever, like she don't want you to mash ants. You
mus' just primps. Is like you turning into a real high
posh. Hoititoity. All drudge shoes!

LEN: You see me have on shoes?

PEARL: You hide them up the road man; when is time to
go home, you put them on. Go home.

LEN: I go home when I ready.

PEARL: All right. Come we go down by the river. [*As she
walks and stands directly in front of him. Their bodies are very
close. They are both laughing.*]

LEN: So come we go.

PEARL: A don't want yuh mother to beat you, you know.
[*As she pushes herself even closer to him.*]

LEN: Last one reach is a dead dog! [*They race off, then freeze
on the spot. When they break the freeze they are in the river,
playing away, commenting on how cold the water is, accusing
each other of wetting each other's hair, etc.* MAMA *appears
behind them.*

MAMA: Jesus Saviour, pilot me. [*The playing ceases
immediately.* PEARL *scampers off.* LEN *attempts to run away.*]
Don't bother to run. If you run A murder you
tonight. Come here. [*He comes slowly and tentatively
towards her. She grabs him.*] Don't A tell you not to leave
the house? Don't A tell you to stay in the house an'
study yuh books?

LEN: A was studying all morning, Mama. A just came out
for a little breeze.

MAMA: Well then, feel the breeze! [*As she beats him*] Don't A
tell you ... Don't mix up ... Don't carouse. Who is di
gal?

LEN: Is Miss Esmeralda daughter, Pearl, Mama.

MAMA: Pearl? An' what you is to she?

LEN: She is mi friend, Mama.

MAMA: Miss Esmeralda frowsy-tail, jiggerfoot, jeysey ears, board head gal is your friend? Where is yuh ambition? You don't have any ambition? After A struggle out mi soul case to send you to big shot high school, you come home come mix up with that little dry-head gal? How much time A must tell you, don't mix up with the little dutty black gal dem in the district? How much time A must tell you, anything black nuh good? She is no advancement. It look like A will have to beat it into you. [*She drags him up.*] A will hang you, you know. Them little dry-head gal will drag you down! [*As she pushes him to the ground again.*] You think A want to treat you like this? A only want what is best for you. Trust Mama. Mama knows best. Leave out the dutty black gal them, concentrate on yuh books, for life is hard when you black, but with a little education you still have a chance. When time come for you to have girlfriend, A have a nice girl pick out for you. Miss Margaret, Reverend Greaves daughter, a nice brown girl with tall hair down to her back. She is advancement, you hear me. [*She picks him up.*]

LEN: Yes, Mama.

[MAMA *shoves him off home. As they are going she continues*]

MAMA: Miss Margaret. You hear what A tell you? Miss Margaret. Miss Margaret.

LEN: Yes, Mama. [*As she hits him a series of blows going off.*]

PA BEN: [*Coming on to his area.*] Miss Margaret. Miss Margaret. That's all could ring in the boy's ears, year after year. Miss Margaret. Like a drum. [*He comes directly down to the audience.*] You have to understand Miss Aggy. She wouldn't even have a black chicken in her yard. One chop, off with the head. Miss Margaret was like an obsession with her. The years went by, and the boy study him books, day and night, an' him pass all him exams with flying colours, yet still him couldn't get a job in the bank. But later for that. One day A happen to be in a next district about three miles from here, and A happen to see the boy with a pretty black girl. We two eyes make four, an' him beg me not to say anything to him mother, and A kept him secret. In fact, A became him confederate, carry message, arrange meeting, dat sort a thing, till one day the boy announce say him get scholarship to go to foreign to further him studies. Three or four weeks after him leave the pretty black girl send to call me, Miss Lois was her name, an' she give me a letter from Missa Lenny, telling me thanks for everything. One thing him beg me. Don't tell him mother say A hear from him. It was a hard secret to keep, but A couldn't bruck it. As the months went by Miss Aggy still got no proper word from the boy. She worry till she all take in sick. [MAMA *enters through the door Up Right looking sick and forlorn. She sits on the low bench with her back to the audience.*] But still A had to hold mi tongue. Why was he carrying feelings for her? All A could do was to try and comfort her.

[*He leaves the lower area and goes towards his house, calling out to her.*] Miss Aggy!

MAMA: How you do, Pa Ben?

PA BEN: All well. All well. [*He continues into his house to get a basket of peas and returns almost immediately.*] How is the feeling an' you?

MAMA: So so, thank God. [*She leaves her area and comes over to him.*]

PA BEN: You went back to the doctor? [*He sits on a chair beside his little house and starts to shell the peas.*]

MAMA: Waste mi money an' go. Him say is all in mi mind.

PA BEN: Worrination. Yes, is a bad sickness. Stop fret yuhself. Missa Lenny soon write.

MAMA: A convince more an' more say something bad happen to him. [*She sits on a stool beside him and starts to help him shell the peas.*]

PA BEN: No. Nutten nuh happen. Me sure a dat.

MAMA: How you so sure?

PA BEN: Me just sure.

MAMA: Den why him nuh write? Is over a year now since him gone, an' all A get is one postcard say him reach. Lawd a mercy!

PA BEN: Nuh cry.

MAMA: A worry, A fret, A pray.

PA BEN: Is all right.

MAMA: Mass Len wouldn't neglect me so. Him know I would be worried. All sorts of things going through mi head. A wonder if him dead?

PA BEN: Nuh think dat.

MAMA: The only other thing left to think is that. Lawd!

PA BEN: What now?

MAMA: Say that somebody in the district burn a candle on his head.

PA BEN: Miss G, shame on you! Who in the district would do a thing like that? [*He goes to the little storage area by his house to look for his tobacco.*]

MAMA: Plenty a them right here, smile up with me to mi face, but in they heart they malice me off, jealous say mi son doing too well. Me nuh forget the time when him did win the scholarship to the high school. Now him get scholarship again gone to University, they will do anything to bring me down. Me nuh trus' them.

PA BEN: You suspect anybody in particular?

MAMA: Everybody. Them will do it.

PA BEN: Me too?

MAMA: Excep' you.

[*The girl* PEARL *whom we saw as* LEN's *playmate goes by the house. She is now no longer young and lively, but a broken-down shell of her old self, pregnant, and very laden down. She crosses the stage on the lower level during her conversation with* MAMA.]

PEARL: Howdy, Miss G.

MAMA: Is who that now?

PA BEN: A don't catch the voice.

16

PEARL: Howdy, Pa Ben.

PA BEN: All well. All well.

PEARL: How the feeling an' you, ma'am?

MAMA: Bearing up.

PEARL: [*Stopping to ask*] An' how Missa Lenny when you hear?

MAMA: Oh, couldn't be better. Got a letter from him only last week. Doing well with him lessons. Say to tell everybody howdy.

PEARL: Thank him, Ma'am, an' when you write, say we all proud a him, an' him mus' take care a himself.

MAMA: A will tell him.

PEARL: All right then, Ma'am, me gone again.

MAMA: Walk good. [*As* PEARL *goes,* PA BEN *looks at* MAMA *in amazement.*] It hurts mi soul case to tell lie, but what else me can do? Me nuh want them to spread it around the district say him dash me 'way. Me just have to keep up the pretence.

PA BEN: Me understan'. Is who the person?

MAMA: Miss Esmeralda daughter. The one they call Pearl.

PA BEN: She? A thought the face look familiar, like somebody me know, but what a way she mash up! Nuh young somebody?

MAMA: Bad life.

PA BEN: Enh?

MAMA: Batter batter, she batter batter. Me nuh know why she asking me for Mass Len. After them nuh quabs.

PA BEN: She mash up bad. Nuh person the same age as Missa Lenny?

MAMA: Few months apart. She nuh more than twenty you see her there. So the ol' careless boy them lash her, is so she breed. A five children she have so far, an' it look to me as if she going up again.

PA BEN: Yes, it look to me as if she taking spring. The young girls of today don't know when to lock them leg. [*He rests his hand on* MAMA*'s thigh. She looks at him, then removes it.*]

MAMA: When me look on her, an' think say if me never

17

did fight an' struggle with the one Mass Len, all now him would be knocking 'bout the district a turn wutliss like the rest a them.

PA BEN: You put him in the right direction. You finish? [*Taking the basket with the peas.*]

MAMA: Aye. [*He takes the basket into his house.*] The one thing leave to complete him now is for him to married to the nice brown girl with hair down to her back that me pick out for him.

PA BEN: [*Opens the window and looks out at her.*] Yuh mind still set on the Reverend daughter, eh?

MAMA: Is mi dream. What an excitement that would be in the district. Banquet upon banquet. Is then the people in the district would malice me off.

MAMA PA BEN: [*Returns and stands by his open door.*] Missa Lenny did intimate anything about Miss Margaret before him leave?

MAMA: Me did pry him, but him never say much.

PA BEN: What him say exactly?

MAMA: Well, when me pry him, all A could hear him say was, 'Arrr y say Mama'.

PA BEN: Say what Miss G? [*As he walks towards her.*]

MAMA: A so me hear, a so me tell you. [PA BEN *repeats it as well.*] I put it down to say him was concentrating so hard on him books. 'Member how him use to lock up all day, all night a study? Most o' the times A didn't want to disturb him, so I would keep mi distance.

PA BEN: [*Sitting beside her*] I can understand that, but him was a little too withdrawn, too quiet. It wasn't natural.

MAMA: Come to think of it, I agree with you. Maybe he over-concentrate on him lessons that him mind was like ... Pa Ben?

PA BEN: Yes, Miss Aggy.

MAMA: A wonder if the books fly up in him head and mad him? Is that!

PA BEN: Come now, Miss Aggy.

MAMA: [*Repeats* LEN'*s inarticulateness* 'Arrr y say Mama'.]

That nuh the first sign of madness?

PA BEN: Yuh mind playing tricks on you.

MAMA: No! Nice quiet dutiful loving boy. [*As she cries.*]

PA BEN: Think about something else. Don't forget is Pa Zaccy nine night tonight.

MAMA: Is eight days already?

PA BEN: Come, we going to sing Sankey tonight. [*He starts singing and dancing.*]
    Rice an' peas
    Rice an' peas
    An' coconut oil
    Hard dough bread
    An' johnny cake
[*He tries to get her involved in the little song till she gives in. They sing for a little while, till she breaks.*]

MAMA: A don't feel up to it.

PA BEN: You mus' be forget how Pa Zaccy was cantankerous when he was living, quick to take umbrage at any little slight. Now him dead, him duppy going to be miserable. You better go pay yuh respects an' give him a good send-off. If not, you know him will take up residence on yuh door step an' haunt you for the rest a yuh days. And anyway is a good opportunity to send a message to the boy.

MAMA: Send message with who?

PA BEN: Pa Zaccy. You forget he was a ol' time postman. [PA BEN *laughs at his joke.*] As a matter of fact, I better give him a tot to sweeten him up. [*He drops a few drops from his bottle to the ground.*]

MAMA: Lawd, Pa Ben, you too bad! Take bad things make joke. What I would do without you, all the same? Take mi mind off the boy. A going to tie mi head and come.
[*She gets up to go into her house.*]

PA BEN: Yes, I have to go spruce up and sweeten up miself to.
[*He resets the stage, putting the chairs back in place.* PEARL *is heard calling off.*]

19

PEARL: Miss G?

PA BEN: Come, sweetheart.

PEARL: Postmistress send this for Miss G. [*He takes the letter and examines it.* PEARL *is curious.*]

PA BEN: Thank you, sweetheart. [*She goes.*] Miss Aggy! Miss Aggy! [*With great excitement.*]

MAMA: [*Off*] Pa Ben, what's all the excitement?

PA BEN: A letter come.

MAMA: From foreign?

PA BEN: Air mail, an' the king picture 'pon the stamp.

MAMA: [*Coming out with great speed and in much flutter*] Mass Len! Holy fathers in heaven! Thank you, Jesus! [*She kisses the letter.*] You answer mi prayer.

PA BEN: Thank you, brother Zaccy. [*Sprinkling a little of his rum on the ground*] Open it, nuh, Miss G?

MAMA: A too nervous. Open it for me. [*Handing him back the letter*] Woi, woi, woi!

PA BEN: Calm down. Calm down.

MAMA: Say is good news. Is good news? Him hearty? Him 'member me? What him say? Mi heart! [PA BEN *opens letter very gingerly.*] Quick, man!

PA BEN: A coming. Give me a little time. A nervous too, you know. [*He gets it open.*]

MAMA: A can't read it. Read it for me.

PA BEN: But you know mi eyes dark.

MAMA: Tell me what it say.

PA BEN: If A had mi spectacles …

MAMA: Try an' make it out.

PA BEN: All right. Mek A see. [*As he unfolds the letter, a pound note falls out.*] Money!

MAMA: Money?

PA BEN: Him send money.

MAMA: Where him get money sen' for me an' him not working? [*She puts the money away in her bosom.*] What him say?

PA BEN: The right-hand corner up the top say 'At school' an' the date. The lef'-hand corner say 'Dear …

MAMA: Mama.

PA BEN: No. 'Mother.'

MAMA: 'Mother?' Go on.

PA BEN: 'I am fine.'

MAMA: Praise the Lord!

PA BEN: 'Hope you are well.'

MAMA: A feel better already.

PA BEN: 'Enclose see pound sign. One. Busy. Len.

MAMA: Aye. Mi son remember me. Thank you, Jesus. [*She is lost in reverie and joy, till slowly she realises that the letter is finished.*] Dat's all? [*He shows it to her.*] Him don't even ask how you do. For nobody. Him don't tell me not even love. Just 'Len', dry so.

PA BEN: Him busy, as him say, with him books.

MAMA: Yes, is dat. At least him not dead.

PA BEN: An' him send money.

MAMA: The money is no comfort to me. After so long this is all me get. 'I am fine. Hope you are well. Busy. Len'. [*She goes to* PA BEN *and gives him the letter.*] No, Pa Ben, something definitely wrong. Somebody or something turning mi son against me.

PA BEN: No, Miss Aggy. Don't think that.

MAMA: I am convinced of it. Evil forces at work.

PA BEN: Put that thought out yuh head.

MAMA: Sweet loving boy when him leave Jamaica. Woi! Them light candle 'pon him head. Woi!

[*As she bawls,* PA BEN *becomes aware that* PEARL *is watching.*]

PA BEN: Miss Aggy. [MAMA *looks to see* PEARL *disappearing.*]

MAMA: Lawd a mercy! If the news get out, me done for. Come, we have to buy her silence.

[*As they go chasing after* PEARL, MAMA *goes into her bosom for the pound note. Lights go down, then up almost immediately.*]

PA BEN: So said, so done. It wasn't easy, 'cause the one Pearl was carrying feelings in her heart against Miss Aggy. But A counsel the chile an' she keep her mouth shut. If that news did get out, it would spread like bush fire, an' if somehow people did learn that the boy was in contact with me, then them would say is me obeah him, so that night A write to Missa Lenny an' beg him to make the peace with him mother. Him listen to me an' the letters start to come more frequent, an' Miss Aggy start to feel better in herself, the colour come back into her cheeks, and as the years went by, letter come from all over the place, as far as Africa. A nuh little fret we fret for him, for we know say if lion or tiger never eat him raw, the savages in the bush would catch him, cook him up as stew an' devour him. Praises be, him escape. Some photo him send we, native with face paint up an' just one little piece a cloth wrap aroun' them private, but as to the woman them, woi, the whole a them titty out a door, naked as day. Miss Aggy turn her eye, but me look. Me nuh know what me would do with miself if me was to go to all them places. The thought of them eating me! Anyway as luck would have it, Missa Lenny never tarry too long on the dark continent. Two twos him was back in England, an' we gave thanks for his deliverance, an' there was no further cause for alarm or concern, till one evening …

MAMA: Woi. Pa Ben?

PA BEN: Oi.

MAMA: Come quick.

PA BEN: What happen? Is what?

MAMA: [*Holding her belly and bawling*] Woi!

PA BEN: What happen?

MAMA: Now A know. Yes, A know.

PA BEN: Know what?

MAMA: A know is who obeah mi son.

PA BEN: Say what?

MAMA: A have the proof.

PA BEN: Say what!

MAMA: See her there [*Handing* PA BEN *a photograph.*]

PA BEN: Mass Len, married?

MAMA: Is the gal in the picture. Is she.

PA BEN: Miss Lois.

MAMA: Miss who?

PA BEN: Ahm ...

MAMA: You know her?

PA BEN: No, me nuh know her.

MAMA: Then how come you call her name?

PA BEN: How me mus' call her name if me nuh know her? What name me call?

MAMA: You said Miss Lois.

PA BEN: Miss Lois? No, me said 'Jesus Christ!'

MAMA: Me could swear you say 'Miss Lois'.

PA BEN: You must open yuh ears when me talk.

MAMA: Me nuh care what she name. Me nuh want her beside mi son. [*She tears the photograph in two, throwing the part with* LOIS *on the floor.*]

PA BEN: Shame on you, Miss Aggy. Before you happy for the boy, you come with yuh nonsense. [*Picking up the torn photograph.*]

MAMA: Nonsense. Shut yuh mouth. A know what A talking about. After I drum it into him head that anything black nuh good, I know is no way him could pick up *that* of him own free will. [*Pointing to the torn photograph in* PA BEN'S *hand.*]

PA BEN: The boy daddy was a black man. Is obeah you did obeah him?

MAMA: Black was good enough for me. It not good enough for him. There was better for him. [*To herself*] What happen to Miss Margaret?

PA BEN: The boy make him own choice.

MAMA: What happen to Miss Margaret? [*She continues bemoaning the loss of Miss Margaret.*]

PA BEN: Times changing, Miss Aggy. You have to move with the times. Stop living in the past. Any black woman that did marry the boy, you would jump to the same conclusion. You nuh see that don't make nuh sense. You nuh see that is ignorance.

MAMA: Is who you calling ignorance? Is who? Kirrout! Is my son and it don't concern you, so mind yuh own business and leave mi property.

PA BEN: You have to face up to the truth.

MAMA: What more truth I need? Me nuh forget the years when the boy did cut me off!

PA BEN: Examine yuhself.

MAMA: Leave mi property!

PA BEN: Miss Aggy?

MAMA: Get off!

PA BEN: What's so wrong if the boy just want to marry somebody who look like him own mother, eh? Put that in yuh pipe an' smoke it! [*He storms out, but storms right back.*] An' before you make yuh next move an' go set evil forces at work to try an' hit back at the chjle, consider the one chance you might be wrong, an' when you done consider that, consider the consequences.

[*He storms out again.*]

MAMA: [*Pause. Quietly to herself, bewildered*] But I only wanted what was best for him.

PA BEN: [*Pushing out the windows of his house, he speaks to the audience.*] Is years now I never had occasion to lose mi temper, but she make me so mad.

[MAMA *sits with her back to the audience and starts to change her scarf.*]

PA BEN: [*Coming through the door of his little house*]
A year go by, and not a word pass between us. One piece a malice she keep up on me. A try to talk to her. [*He walks over to her space.*] Morning, Miss Aggy. [MAMA*'s head flashes around only to flash back again. She does not return the greeting.* PA BEN *returns to the audience.*] It hurt mi soul case how she was going on. [MAMA *changes her scarf again.*] After all, she was mi best friend. A had to keep trying, for me is not one to keep up malice. [*He goes across to her space again.*] Evening, Miss Aggy.

MAMA: [*Turning very slowly to him*] Evening.

PA BEN: [*He is stopped in his tracks and needs his chair for support.*]

A frighten till A almost faint when she answer me, an' is so we start up again till we start exchange two, three words, but never 'bout the marriage or anything to do with Mass Len, but A know she never go to the obeah man to go hit back at the girl. A guess the one chance that she could have been wrong make her stay her hand. Is a terrible thing when you go to the obeah man to seek vengeance, an' it turn roun' an' come back at you, but A know that in her heart of hearts she was still carrying feelings for the chile. The months turn to years, then one day out of the blue …

[LEN *enters, dressed in a three-piece suit, carrying a small box.*]

LEN: Mama.

PA BEN: Missa Lenny?

LEN: Hello, sir.

PA BEN: Wo yoi! Miss Aggy, come look. [*To* LEN] Is Missa Lenny?

LEN: Yes, sir.

PA BEN: Wo yoi! [*As he holds him, kisses him, dances with him.*] You 'member me?

LEN: How could I forget you, sir?

PA BEN: Nuh worry with nuh 'sir' business. I is Pa Ben.

LEN: Pa Ben.

MAMA: Pa Ben, what you was calling me for? [*Then she sees her son.*] Lord have mercy [*very quietly*].

LEN: Mama! [*They hug each other tightly.*]

MAMA: Mass Len! [*She cries.*] Mi heart!

LEN: You okay, Mama?

MAMA: Joy, Mass Len. Joy. How you do?

LEN: Fine, Mama.

MAMA: Mi one son.

LEN: How are you, Mama?

MAMA: Give God thanks to set eyes on you again.

LEN: You look well, Mama, not a day older.

PA BEN: Me take care a her, son.

MAMA: [*good naturedly*] Get out a mi life. [*To* LEN] Son!

LEN: Mama.

PA BEN: Then let him go now, nuh, Miss Aggy?

MAMA: [*good naturedly*] Come out a mi life.

PEARL: [*entering on the lower level*] Morning, Miss G.

MAMA: Morning, Miss Pearl. Miss Pearl, look who come!

PEARL: But stop, is Missa Lenny?

PA BEN: You nuh have eyes to see!

MAMA: You 'member Miss Pearl?

[*They look at each other for a little while.* PEARL, *who is again heavily pregnant, looks twice her age. Her foot is bandaged.*]

LEN: How are you?

PEARL: Me hearty.

LEN: And the children?

PEARL: Them hearty too.

LEN: How many you have now?

PEARL: Is eleven me gone. This one will make the dozen.

PA BEN: She all have two called Paul.

PEARL: Me like the name. [*They all laugh, except* LEN *who laughs a little embarrassedly.*] Well, me on a little haste, so me gone again. Is nice to see you, Mass Len.

LEN: Take care of yourself.

PEARL: All right, sir. [*As she is going.*]

MAMA: Give her something, nuh, Mass Len? [*Calling after her*] Miss Pearl!

LEN: Here you are, for the baby when it comes.

[PA BEN *and* MAMA *hug each other excitedly.*]

PEARL: Thank you, sir, the Lord will bless you.

[LEN *watches her go.*]

PA BEN: Me a run down by the bush, see if A can get a few starapples for you. A don't forget how you did love them when you was a boy.

LEN: True, sir. I brought something for you as well, sir.

PA BEN: When A come back, man. Miss Aggy. [*As he points a finger at her.*]

MAMA: Come we go inside so we can private. [*They go in.*]
  Mass Len?

LEN: Yes, Mama.

MAMA: Mass Len, A don't know where to start. [*She starts to cough.*]

LEN: You have a bad cough, Mama.

MAMA: Yes, it been worrying me.

LEN: Maybe you should go see a doctor.

MAMA: I was waiting till you come.

LEN: [*Laughs*] I am not that sort of doctor.

MAMA: What you mean?

LEN: I am not a medical doctor.

MAMA: So what kind a doctor you is?

LEN: Well I, ah, I have a Ph.D.

MAMA: A wha'?

LEN: I, ah, am an economist. Banking. I deal with money
  matters.

MAMA: Money doctor? Cooyah! What you saying to me? I
  never know money could sick. Explain yuhself.

LEN: Another time, Mama.

MAMA: No. A been boasting off on everybody how mi son
  graduate as big doctor. Now you making me to
  understand you can't even cure fresh cold. Don't tell
  nobody you is not a true true doctor, you know. You
  hear me.

LEN: Okay.

MAMA: What a distress! Then tell me, you wear white coat
  an' trumpet to sound the money? [LEN *laughs.*] What
  you laughing for? Is foolishness me ask you?

LEN: Another time we'll talk about it, okay?

MAMA: An' me did so glad to see you.

LEN: Me too. This is yours. [*Giving her the box he brought on.*]

MAMA: Thank you. [*As she opens it*] Every time you send a
  parcel for me, excitement in the district. They come
  down on me like vulture, for what they can get.
  Lawd, what a pretty frock! Watch me an' them
  people when I dress off an' go to church. [*She swings
  the frock in front of her.*] I can just hear them – 'Lawd,

Miss G, you look nice. Give me a borrows nuh', yet behind mi back – 'Nuh ol' bruck she get from 'merica'. Ol' hypocrites! Leave them to God, after them never help me struggle? Is nuh one or two times A went to bed hungry so you could eat, you know.

LEN: I haven't forgotten, Mama. [*Slight pause.*]

MAMA: It really nice. You pick it out for Mama?

LEN: No. Lois did.

MAMA: Oh! A don't think it going to fit me. [*She tosses it aside, not too carefully.*] We have a lot to talk about Mass Len.

LEN: Yes, Mama.

MAMA: Anyway, you just come, but you know what you could help me with in the meantime? A paid down on a house in town for you.

LEN: For me?

MAMA: Yes. A knew that one day you would come home, an' would want a nice place to live.

LEN: But what money I sent was to fix up this place for yourself.

MAMA: I soon dead. Where A put the documents? [*She looks for them in the bureau drawer.*] Is a good thing you come. Is over a year now. The house should have been finished, but only last week a letter come asking for more money. Ah, these must be the papers. It is yours so take charge. [*Handing him the documents.*]

LEN: In the meantime we have to fix up this place, get you a little gas stove.

MAMA: Gas? Me 'fraid a gas, come blow me up.

LEN: It is quite safe, Mama, and a little inside bathroom.

MAMA: So what wrong with mi pit toilet?

LEN: You deserve to be comfortable, Mama.

MAMA: I comfortable as it is.

LEN: More comfortable then, Mama.

MAMA: I too old to change. Me 'custom to mi pit toilet, an' as a boy you never complain. Is only now that you expose. Nuh fret yuhself 'bout that. Next thing people malice me off, then come lick me down say me live in big house. No, sir! There is more important an' urgent matters we have to discuss. Sit down. [*He does.*] Now about the woman you married. ... [LEN *is up like a flash.*]

LEN: Now look here!

MAMA: Sit down! [*She stands over him commandingly. He sits, as the lights start to fade on the area.*]

PA BEN: The two a them lock up in the little house for hours. A wonder what they was chatting 'bout, till mi curiosity got the better a me, and A put mi ears to the walls. She was right at him 'bout the woman he married, an' how she obeah him. When Missa Lenny leave that day, it look like he had one helluva headache, and the headache travel with him right back to town, so ...

[*He starts the song 'Change the house round'. The other actors join in, singing the song as a 'round' as they change the set around.*]

> Change the house round
> To the house in town
> So change the house round
> To the house in town
> Wall to wall carpet on the ground
> Big TV set and Frigidaire
> Big stuffed sofa and chandelier
> Big gramophone with latest sound
> But his headache still going round
> and round.
> So change the house etc ...

[MAMA *turns the picture on the Down Right wall round, then helps* LEN *to turn the old bureau round so that it now serves as* LEN's *desk. Then she goes over to* PA BEN, *sits beside him, all the time singing the song.*

GEORGE *comes on with the telephone and sets it down on the desk/table set Down Right by* LEN *and* MAMA. *Next he sets the*

29

coffee table in place, moves Up Centre, strikes the pelmet and takes it off, then positions himself by the Up Right door, receiving the chairs from the Stage Manager and passing them on to PEARL. GEORGE *closes the door behind* LEN *as the change is completed.*

PEARL *comes on from Up Left, removes the matting that covers* MAMA'S *bench and takes it off-stage, returning immediately to set the stool beside the bar, then moves Up Right to collect the chairs from* GEORGE, *setting them behind the coffee table.*

LOIS *follows* PEARL *on with three bottles, three glasses and a box of tablets, sets up the bar and goes off.*

LEN *helps* MAMA *to turn the bureau around, then strikes the right panel from* MAMA'S *house.*

All through this PA BEN *sings lustily.*

The Stage Manager strikes the left panel from MAMA'S *house, receives the pelmet from* GEORGE, *hands chairs to* GEORGE, *and sets book and headache pad Stage Right for* LEN'S *entrance.*

The set change happens in a half light. As it is done, LEN *sits round about Centre Stage.* LOIS *applies a wet rag to his head. The lights come up to full as the singing dies away.*]

LOIS : [*Soothing* LEN'S *troubled brow*] How come you're so tense? Relax.

LEN : I am relaxed, except for this headache.

LOIS : Reading won't get rid of it.

LEN : It's the only thing that helps. You know I don't take aspirin.

LOIS : Oh yes, I forgot. What do you take for gripe? *The Reader's Digest?*

LEN : Funny. Ha ha!

LOIS : You think it's funny, eh?

LEN : Very.

LOIS : I guess if I don't laugh, I'll cry. Put the book down and talk to me, Len.

LEN : My head is splitting. [LOIS *tosses the ice pack down on the coffee table.*] I really have a bad headache.

LOIS : Ah well, another weekend with the four walls staring at the back of your head! I wonder what I'll tell the judge? Women lose their husbands for diverse reasons Your Honour: to another woman, occasionally to another man, although that's becoming increasingly more so nowadays, but has a woman ever lost her husband to a book? A book! I name them all as correspondent. [*She goes to him and attempts to caress him sensuously.*] 'Cepting of course anything written on the theme of 'Tender Love', 'Hot Romance', 'Tales of Passion'.

LEN: Lois, please. [*As he pushes her away*] Your endless squawking is creating havoc with the sensitivity of my ear drums.

LOIS: None of you is sensitive, Len.

LEN: Your mind is between you legs.

LOIS: So that's why you don't stimulate me intellectually!

LEN: [*Rising angrily*] One of these days I am going to plug that mouth of yours with a fist or a foot.

LOIS: [*Shouting back at him*] That's what I need you to do. Let some blood ... Get this marriage out of its menopause!

LEN: Thank your lucky stars I am not a man given to physical violence.

LOIS: You're not given to affection either. I'm off to the beach.

LEN: Two women got raped there last week.

LOIS: Something to look forward to.

LEN: Okay, get my trunks.

LOIS: [*Comes storming back*] And after the beach, what? Back to bionic bliss with the bionic book man. Back to making whoopee in seventh heaven on a choo choo train that's going no place.

LEN: You always had a flair for the dramatic, eh?

LOIS: Why not? Our lives are totally theatrical.

LEN: Sweetheart ...

LOIS: So that's it for today, folks. Join us again later today for another chapter in this unending life drama. Will Lois Tomlinson find true happiness with the Bionic Black, or will she be forever ... [*As she is going off*]

31

MAMA: [*From off*] Hold dog!
　　[LOIS *stops, turns, looks at* LEN *who suddenly becomes very alive, looks in the direction of the* 'Hold dog', *then towards* LOIS. *He rushes towards the latter.*]

LOIS: I wish you would impress upon your mother that we do not have a dog.

LEN: Lois.

LOIS: Unless of course she is referring to me, which in fact she is.

LEN: Lois, please.

LOIS: Excuse me.

LEN: At least stay and say hello.

LOIS: Hello.

LEN: Lois!

MAMA: [*By the door*] Hold dog!
　　[LOIS *barks like a dog.*]

LEN: Lois! It's opened, Mama. [*He pleads non-verbally with* LOIS *as he goes to meet* MAMA *who has entered.*]

MAMA: Mass Len.

LEN: Mama.

MAMA: Mass Len.

LEN: Mama.

MAMA: How you do?

LEN: Oh fine, Mama. How are you?

MAMA: Give God thanks.

LEN: Yes. You looking well.

MAMA: But you don't look too good. A can feel your ribs like something cutting into me. You eating well?

LEN: Three meals a day.

MAMA: If you eating three meals as you say, an' yuh face look so haggard, then you must be under stress.

LEN: Aw, come on, Mama.

MAMA: Then look on yuh head. Every time A see it, it look like you grey up a little more.

LEN: The girls like it, say I look distinguished.

MAMA: [*Hiss*] Nonsense. [*She starts to inspect and clean the furniture.*]

LEN: Mama [*very discreetly and surreptitiously*], tell Lois hello.

MAMA: Ah, Miss Lois.

LOIS: Miss Simmons. How are you?

[MAMA *picks up the ice pack, holds it up disdainfully.*]

MAMA: As well as can be expected under the circumstances.

LOIS: I see. Now you must excuse me as I have to clean the shit out of the doghouse. [LOIS *smiles.* MAMA *smiles back.* LEN *cringes.* LOIS *goes off.*]

MAMA: Vulgar wretch! What she smiling with me for, after she not mi friend?

LEN: Mama, you promised.

MAMA: I promised to keep the peace. I never promised to be nice to her. It hard to play the hypocrite.

LEN: Okay, okay.

MAMA: Tar baby. Every time A come here A come with a heavy heart. When A think of that lovely brown girl with hair down to her back that you could have married. What a distress. [*She shouts off.*] Topsy!

LEN: Mama!

MAMA: All right, I will shut mi mouth, but it not easy to bottle it up inside me.

LEN: Let me get you a drink.

MAMA: So you is the manservant.

LEN: What can I get you?

MAMA: A not thirsty.

LEN: Actually I am glad you came into town, as I wanted to talk to you rather urgently about the house.

MAMA: You have some good news for me?

LEN: Not so good, Mama.

MAMA: Lawd, don't tell me say A going to lose all mi money.

LEN: There's a chance we could get some, if not all of it back.

MAMA: Try yuh best, mi son.

LEN: How did you hear of this housing scheme? Was it advertised in the papers or what?

MAMA: No. Is Missa Mac encourage me to buy.

LEN: You mean George McFarlane?

MAMA: I only know him as Missa Mac.

LEN: How did this Mister Mac encourage you?

MAMA: I was in the bank one day, the same bank A had the little savings in. [LEN *faces Up Stage and freezes.* MAMA *removes her hat, goes into her bag, takes out a red one and puts it on, then faces Up Stage and freezes.* GEORGE *enters.*]

GEORGE: What a thing, eh?

MAMA: What?

GEORGE: The new round of price increases.

MAMA: Things dear, eh, Missa Mac?

GEORGE: And they going to get worse.

MAMA: Don't say so. How poor people going to manage?

GEORGE: Don't ask me, Miss G. Remember in the good old days? You go to the shop with a shilling and you know what you could buy?

MAMA: Bread.

GEORGE: Lard.

MAMA: Salt beef.

GEORGE: And you get back change. Now salt beef is three dollars a pound! [*Pointing it out to her as she holds paper.*]

MAMA: Things can't get no worse.

GEORGE: Don't fool yourself, Miss G. Next year this time, salt beef could be four dollars a pound.

MAMA: Hush yuh mouth.

GEORGE: The hard facts of life. Five years from now, who knows?

MAMA: These are the last days. [*Returns paper.*] Praise God I won't be here much longer.

GEORGE: [*Returns to the table and sits on it.*] It may be cheaper to try and stay alive, I tell you. I buried my father-in-law a few weeks back. Cost me the earth, thousands of dollars. Old Reverend Greaves must be turning in his grave when he realise the expense he put me to.

MAMA: Reverend Greaves who used to be the Minister at Sandilands?

GEORGE: You knew him?

MAMA: Mi Minister. Good and generous man he was to me and my son. Lord rest his soul. So you got married to Miss Margaret?

GEORGE: That's right.

MAMA: Oh, that's all right. I don't feel so bad now.

GEORGE: Eh?

MAMA: Just a little something with miself. How is she?

GEORGE: Very well.

MAMA: I could see her now. Lovely brown-skin girl with her hair down to her back. She still pretty?

GEORGE: She is.

MAMA: She wouldn't remember me now, but tell her howdy for me, from an old friend, and tell her say A sorry to hear about the Reverend. We all did love him.

GEORGE: He lived with us when he retired. He had to. The little pension he got, with the cost of living as it is today, wasn't enough to buy him food for the week.

MAMA: Lord, for a man who saved so many souls.

GEORGE: He was always a thrifty man, mind you. Had put by his few pennies for a rainy day. How was he to know that he would have to cope with this pile of price increases? I warned him; if he had only taken my advice. I was tired of telling him that money in the bank is no use. Let it work for you. Invest. And that is my advice to you too, Miss Simmons. You have too much money in the bank sitting down doing nothing.

MAMA: But it earning interest.

GEORGE: Five per cent when the cost of living jumping forty per cent every year?

MAMA: Advise me.

GEORGE: Example. If you were to pay down on a little house, three or four years from now you double your money, so when the salt beef go up to five or six dollars a pound, you right up there with it.

MAMA: I see yuh point. But the money is for mi son.

GEORGE: Oh.

MAMA: Him livin' in England. A get word only last week say he graduate as doctor.

GEORGE: Nice, nice. You must be proud, eh?

MAMA: If A proud. One day A know he will come home, and whatever in the bank book belongs to him.

GEORGE: But think of it, Miss G, and I am not one to put pressure on you, but let's say yuh son come home some time in the future. He goin' to need a nice place to live. Why not use the money to pay down on a place for him? You could rent it out till he come if you don't want to live in it. The rent pays the mortgage. It's a solid investment, no risks.

MAMA: I know you wouldn't give me bad advice.

GEORGE: Come to think of it, right at this moment I know of a really good buy going. Nice reasonable price. I know the fellers who are building them. Good honest boys. Go home and think about it. Next week you can let me know if you are interested.

MAMA: Is God send you here to guide and look after me, you know. Lord, yes, a house for mi son. Lord, yes! Thank you, Missa Mac, thank you. [*Shaking his hand vigorously.* GEORGE *goes.*]

[*The action returns to the present.*]

MAMA: Missa Mac help me to fill out the papers an' I paid the money. August coming is two years. No money, no house. I been trying to find Missa Mac but him not working at the bank no more.

LEN: I'll find him.

MAMA: Yes, he will help you to straighten it out.

LEN: Leave it to me. But you and this Mr Mac seem to have been quite good friends, how come?

MAMA: At first I thought it a little odd miself, Mass Len, because is years A been going to the bank and we never had occasion to talk, and anyway I am a lady who know mi place. One day I was in the line and Missa Mac call me out, make the lodgement for me,

invite me into his office, offer me refreshment, an'
started to talk to me nice, nice. I was surprised,
couldn't figure out what this high posh white
gentleman wanted with the likes o' poor little me.
Anyway after a few weeks is like we did know each
other for years.

LEN: I think I am beginning to understand, Mama.

MAMA: Is in your hands, all right?

LEN: All right.

MAMA: I have to be going. [LEN *gets up really fast.*] I mustn't
overstay mi welcome.

LEN: You are always welcome here, you know that.

MAMA: Take care a yuhself. Lawd, every time A look at
you water come to mi eye. Look at you. Favour
somebody who could be mi husband.

LEN: [*Hustling her out*] As soon as I have some positive word
on the house I'll come and look for you.

MAMA: Oh Lord, me a leave an' me nuh even give you
what A brought for you.

LEN: Thank you, Mama. [*Taking the parcel which is rather oily.*]

MAMA: An' I have two nice pigs. One is yours, but I don't
suppose you could keep it up here. Mind you, the way
Topsy keep the place ...

LEN: Keep him for me.

MAMA: The pigs friendly, you see! One night A come
home from market and A couldn't find them. A look
everywhere. Not a sign. I say somebody gone with
them. Is when A ready to go to bed, A go to use the
chimmy an' see the pigs under the bed fast asleep.
[MAMA *laughs.* LEN *laughs embarrassedly and goes to open the
door for her. She, however, is caught up with her memory and
continues, unaware that he is no longer beside her.*] A never
see pigs friendly so. Them is mi company. [*She becomes
aware that he is no longer listening. She covers the slight and
goes to the door.*] So you will check with me?

LEN: Fine.

MAMA: All right. [*She is going, stops, turns.*] The dog tie?

LEN: Mama!

[*The lights go down, then come up almost immediately.* LOIS *in the nice new frock is sitting, reading. A knocking is heard off.* LOIS *opens the door and calls out.*]

LOIS: Hello.

GEORGE: Are the dogs tied?

LOIS: We don't have a dog. Do come. [*Pause.*]

GEORGE: [*Getting closer*] I saw the sign on the gate.

LOIS: We just haven't bothered to take it down.

GEORGE: [*As he arrives at the door*] Afternoon.

LOIS: Hi.

GEORGE: I am here to see. … Lois! [*Pause.*]

LOIS: Mr McFarlane?

GEORGE: Surprise, surprise! [*Long pause.*] Aren't you going to invite me in?

LOIS: Come in. This is a bit of a surprise. What are you doing here?

GEORGE: Actually I am here to see a Dr Len Tomlinson. Am I at the right house?

LOIS: Yes. [*Very hesitantly.*]

GEORGE: Are you Mrs …?

LOIS: Yes.

GEORGE: Really? I had no idea. It's been a long time. Ten years?

LOIS: Thereabouts.

GEORGE: You're looking as well as ever, though. [*Pause.*] So how are things?

LOIS: I mustn't complain.

GEORGE: No. By the look of things, no.

LOIS: And at the bank?

GEORGE: I'm on my own now. Real estate.

LOIS: I see. My husband isn't here. He called saying he would be a few minutes late.

GEORGE: I'll wait. [*Pause.*]

LOIS: I didn't know you two knew each other.

GEORGE: I'm meeting him for the first time.

LOIS: Oh. Can I get you a drink? [*She starts towards the bar.*]

GEORGE: The usual.

LOIS: Mr McFarlane!

GEORGE: No need for us to be formal with each other. George.

LOIS: I ah ... [*Pause.*]

GEORGE: Yes?

LOIS: It's just that ... I'd appreciate if you didn't let on to my husband that we ever knew each other.

GEORGE: [*Pause*] Reasonable.

[*The telephone rings.* LOIS *goes across and answers it.*]

LOIS: That may be Len again. Hello. ... Yes, he's here. Hold, please.

GEORGE: Hello ... Bertie ... say what? What you hear? That is true. I went back [*He notices* LOIS.] I can't talk now. [LOIS *sees his distress and goes off.*] Yes, I went back to the bank begging for time. I drew blank. The man say it's out of his hands. Calm down, Bertie. I tell you what, call me at home. No need to panic. ... What you think I been doing all day, man, sitting on mi ass? Listen to me, let's not make a decision till I have spoken with this man. Jesus Christ, Bertie, man, calm down. ... I know that. The valuator is a buddy of mine. He will hold off on his report for at least two weeks. The man owe me a favour, man. Two weeks is all the time I will need to raise the money. You know doors always open to me, Bertie! I'll get you out. [GEORGE *notices* LEN *who has come on some time earlier.*] We will talk later. [*He hangs up. The two men stare at each other.*] Dr Tomlinson?

LEN: Len.

GEORGE: George McFarlane.

LEN: I hope I didn't keep you waiting for too long.

GEORGE: Not at all. Nice place you have here, man.

LEN: Thank you. You didn't have any trouble finding it?

GEORGE: I live up the road, number 34.

LEN: We are neighbours. Imagine that. Nice place you have there too.

GEORGE: Thank you.

LEN: I thought we'd meet here. For what I have in mind it makes it more discreet.

GEORGE: I read you.

LEN: Drink?

GEORGE: Scotch.

LEN: On the rocks?

GEORGE: Straight.

LEN: So we finally meet.

GEORGE: Well, here we are.

LEN: You are a hard man to find.

GEORGE: Always on the go.

LEN: Or under pressure.

GEORGE: Bit o' both.

LEN: So I've been hearing. I have my contacts. I bet you checked me out too, didn't you?

GEORGE: You are the new man at the Development Bank.

LEN: Is that all?

GEORGE: So far.

LEN: [Smiles] And you are the Managing Director of ABC Homes.

GEORGE: That is correct.

LEN: I hear you been having a bit of ill luck.

GEORGE: It's more than that, man.

LEN: Explain.

GEORGE: I think I have an enemy.

LEN: Don't we all? Ha, ha!

GEORGE: No, I am convinced somebody is out to get me. I was Bank Manager for Barclays, and a few months ago I was in line for a promotion. I was the best man for the job, but no, I am passed over for some feller with very little experience, so I told Head Office where to get off and resigned. I had a loan or two out with them. You know the spiteful sons of bitches called them in without notice?

LEN: Other banks would be happy to do business with you, I'm sure.

GEORGE: Yes, but somebody has put the word out on me.

It's like an orchestrated plan to ruin me. Malicious, insidious lies are being spread around.

LEN: I've heard one or two.

GEORGE: Don't believe a word they tell you. What you heard?

LEN: If they are lies as you say, why repeat them?

GEORGE: True, true. [*He laughs foolishly.*] Something you might have heard that could have some truth to it is that I do need a bit of refinancing.

LEN: I represent a group of investors. They suggested that I talk to you.

GEORGE: Who are these boys?

LEN: They want to keep a low profile for the time being. In the event that you and I get to first base, then they'd want to get into the picture.

GEORGE: I see.

[LEN *takes* GEORGE's *glass to get a refill.*]

LEN: What would you give as the rough estimates of the assets of ABC at this time?

GEORGE: About three million.

LEN: Dollars?

GEORGE: Give or take a thou or two.

LEN: Let's get a valuation. [GEORGE *dips into his briefcase and comes out with some papers. He hands them to* LEN.] I see you came prepared.

GEORGE: For any eventualities.

LEN: Estimated profit, twenty-five per cent. Who worked out these figures?

GEORGE: My appraisers.

LEN: I'll get one of my appraisers to do a valuation. [GEORGE *dips into his briefcase again and hands another set of papers to* LEN.] You've been anticipating me. Estimated profit down to ten per cent on this one.

GEORGE: Your valuators always undervalue.

LEN: One or two things.

GEORGE: A recognised auditor to go over the cash flow. [*He dips into his briefcase again for another set of papers.*]

LEN: Profit margins down to only five per cent now. Looking at these figures I'd say, off hand, that my group wouldn't be willing to offer you more than eight hundred thousand dollars at the most; if you had to sell, that is.

GEORGE: What? At that price I would come out with less than nothing.

LEN: I appreciate your position. If you don't get refinanced, chances are the bank will put this place up for auction, and where would that leave you?

GEORGE: Shit! Eight hundred thousand ... [*Pause.*] Maybe we could work something out between us, personal.

LEN: What you have in mind?

GEORGE: How about a piece o' my action?

LEN: How big a piece, and what do I have to do for it?

GEORGE: Finance me through your bank for thirty per cent of the profits.

LEN: Hmm. Tempting.

GEORGE: With financing, ABC could be a gravy train, a money machine. For example, here is a list of prospective purchasers willing to purchase at an escalated price.

LEN: And the people who bought already?

GEORGE: They pay the escalated price, or get their money back.

LEN: Let me think about it.

GEORGE: I don't have much time.

LEN: I know that. I am going to need some more information on ABC, how it is structured, that sort of thing.

GEORGE: First thing in the morning.

LEN: Beautiful. Another Scotch?

GEORGE: Yes, sir. [*Breathing easier.*]

LEN: George, you know I am sure I know you from some place.

GEORGE: I don't think so.

LEN: From where? Let me think. Canada?

GEORGE: No. Never been to Canada.

LEN: I never forget a face. Munro old boy?

GEORGE: Yeah.

LEN: '41?

GEORGE: That's right. You went to Munro?

LEN: You left in '47?

GEORGE: Yeah.

LEN: That's it ! I know you man. Remember me, Len Tomlinson?

GEORGE: Len Tomlinson? Oh yeah. [*He most decidedly has not remembered* LEN.]

LEN: Vague, vague. I was in a lower form. Man, you haven't changed a day. [*Snaps his finger.*] Mongoose!

GEORGE: Jesus! [*laughs*] Look, nuh, man, not a soul's called me Mongoose in years! [*laughs*] Jesus Christ!

LEN: Remember me now?

GEORGE: Yes man. [*He still hasn't.*]

LEN: No matter, no matter. It'll all come back; it's been thirty years. We must talk and talk, roll back the years. To the old school, and those of us who have survived. 'Benedictus benedicat, per Jesum Christum dominum nostrum.' [*They drink.*]

GEORGE: Some say chicken, some say duck, we say matron don't wut a fa, fa, fa, fa ...

LEN: Same old Mongoose! How is the old school? I haven't been back in years.

GEORGE: Place is completely changed. Packed now with a bunch o' riff-raff, scholarship-winners. Sacred walls, man, desecrated. I was there on Sports Day. My boy won the hundreds.

LEN: Chip off the old block, eh?

GEORGE: You remember?

LEN: How could I forget?

GEORGE: Class One champ. On your marks, get set ... Those were the days! God damn it to hell, the good old days! They'll never come back. [*A noise is heard outside.*] What's that?

[LEN *listens;* GEORGE *draws his gun.*]

LEN: I think it's the wife tinkering outside.

GEORGE: Oh boy. I am a nervous wreck. [*Putting his gun back.*] Life has very little pleasure for me today, what with all the fear, the violence, the social upheaval, the economic mismanagement. My house is like a prison, so many bolts on the door. If I lost the key I would have to sell the place! The family alone at home. Jesus! I can use yuh phone?

LEN: Sure. [*Pointing to the instrument.*]

GEORGE: [*On telephone*] Billy? Daddy. Where's your mother? ... Don't worry to wake her. You locked up the house? Lock all the windows. [*Shouting*] I say you must lock all the windows! I soon come. [*He hangs up.*] Can't be too careful these days. They broke into next door 7.30 one evening, lucky nobody was there, ransack the place, rape the maid. You see this, [*taking out the gun*] I declare war! I tell my wife, 'You get diarrhoea at night, wake me up, wake me up!'. For I am going to shoot first and ask questions afterwards. You have one of these? [*Indicating the gun.*]

LEN: No.

GEORGE: [*Getting more and more like a scared trapped animal*] What, man? Get one! An' put some bars on those windows! This place is like a death trap! Not even a dog?

LEN: We should. We should.

GEORGE: Violence. Socialism. Shit! If I wasn't a damn ass I would have been living in Toronto years ago! I tell you, I would rather be a second-class citizen in the first world, than a first-class one in this rat's ass place. I can help myself? [*As he goes to the bottle.*]

LEN: Sure. Stay for supper.

GEORGE: Thanks, but not this evening. The wife would have left supper. Come to think of it, you should know Margaret.

LEN: Margaret? Margaret?

GEORGE: Greaves. Reverend Greaves daughter from school days.

LEN: You and Margaret, married?

GEORGE: Yes, man.

LEN: What a thing!

GEORGE: We been going together from school days.

LEN: I had no idea that you two ... Mmm ... Really! Hey, you remember Blackie?

GEORGE: Blackie? I wonder if it's the same boy I am thinking of, can't remember his name. Bright little boy. Won scholarship.

LEN: Could be.

GEORGE: Must have been as poor as ass, though. Clothes patch, socks have hole. We boys use to give him hell. [*Laughs*] Those days. Blackie. One Open Day ... It wasn't Blackie we called him, though? Anyway, it was Open Day, the other parents came in car an' buggy an' thing, an' when we look through the window, we saw this boy's mother coming up the hill with a basket on her head. The thing full of bananas, yams, cocos, all sort of things for the lad. The boy had a gut, you see, man, could eat! Man, I am telling you, as she was coming through the door, she miss her step an' everything in that basket was rolling all over the place! The headmaster didn't know what to do! At the time I think he was chatting to the Chairman of the Board, and one of the totos rolled right between his legs. When he look down and saw the toto sitting lopsided-like down there; man, the Chairman was just about to look down when the Head's foot ease across and cover the toto. All this time the poor boy an' his mother was busy going around collecting all the foodstuff, the other boys and parents noticing them, but not noticing them, you know what I mean. What a laugh! Weeks afterwards. [*He laughs.*] You remember it?

LEN: I remember it. [*Laughing.*]

GEORGE: The boy didn't know what to do with himself.

From that day, they call him 'Toto'. But wait a minute, that's not Blackie. Might have been the same boy. Was funny, you see?

LEN: You really don't remember me at all, do you, George?

GEORGE: Yes, man.

LEN: Toto. Toto Tomlinson. Who else? Me.

GEORGE: Oh shit!

LEN: That's all right.

GEORGE: I didn't realise.

LEN: How could you? It's been years.

GEORGE: How is your mother now?

LEN: Not too good, George, seeing as how you owe her three thousand dollars on the house deal.

GEORGE: Boy, I hadn't realised.

LEN: Forget it, man, a little joke at my expense. What's a little joke between old friends? Who laughed loudest? Me. Man, it's so damn nice to see you. Ah Lois, come and join us. You met George?

LOIS: Yes, I did.

GEORGE: Hello again.

LEN: Another drink?

GEORGE: Thanks, but actually I have to run. [*Gathering up his papers, briefcase, etc.*]

LEN: First thing in the morning?

GEORGE: Ah, yes.

LEN: Take care. 'Night.

GEORGE: 'Night.

LOIS: 'Bye.

[*As* GEORGE *goes,* LEN *closes the door and he laughs and laughs.*]

LOIS: Len! [LEN *cannot contain himself laughing.*]

LEN: Let's go upstairs and I'll tell you all about it.

[*As they are going,* LEN *stops and turns to the door that* GEORGE *went out through.*]
Son of a bitch!

END OF ACT ONE

ACT TWO

SCENE ONE

[*In the darkness we hear the voices of the actors/villagers questioning who has brought the peanuts, teasing each other, a general hubbub, noisy and carefree. A match explodes in the darkness as* PA BEN *lights his pipe.*]

PA BEN: All right, all right. [*Checking and showing his bottle of rum.*] A ready for you again. Settle off, settle off, while A get mi head together. Where A did reach?

ACTRESS WHO PLAYS MAMA: Where Missa Lenny was laughing.

PA BEN: Ah yes. What a way it did sweet him! Him laugh till him almost wet him pants, but you hear what they say, 'What sweet nanny goat. ...' [*All the actors/villagers join in* – 'A go run him belly'.] Miss Lois anxious to know what sweet him so and what happen between him and the one McFarlane.

ACTOR WHO PLAYS GEORGE: What secret Mongoose carrying for Miss Lois?

PA BEN: Miself want to know.

ALL THE ACTORS/
VILLAGERS: You know, man, you know.

ACTOR WHO PLAYS LEN: Yes, him know.

PA BEN: I don't know, honest, would I tell a lie?

ALL THE ACTORS/
VILLAGERS: Yes.

PA BEN: What I do know is that if Missa Lenny did know, maybe him wouldn't laugh so. Anyway that same night Missa Lenny tell Miss Lois everything about the one Mongoose.

ACTRESS WHO PLAYS PEARL: Everything?

PA BEN: Well not quite everything. Him leave out a very important piece o' the story.

ACTOR WHO PLAYS LEN: What him leave out?

PA BEN: Not just what, but why.

ALL THE ACTORS/
VILLAGERS: So tell us. Tell us. [*They keep demanding.*]

PA BEN: [*He gets up from his storytelling area and walks a little right.*] Patience, everything in its time. Him tell her some of what happen in schooldays. How the boy McFarlane did dunce. Missa Lenny remember it as if it was yesterday. No, Missa Lenny never forget Mongoose and all the other big shot boys them.

[*During the above speech the actor playing* GEORGE *dresses himself in a black and red cape, black on the outside, and dons a flamboyant red cap. Armed with his riding crop he mounts the storyteller's chair and sits on the back, his feet resting on the seat. Two of the actors turn slowly towards the audience becoming the horses to* GEORGE'S *buggy. The actor playing* LEN *dresses himself in a much less flamboyant red cap, then waits Up Right of the storyteller's area. The transition happens smoothly and there is no break in the action.*]

On the one or two occasion that I had occasion to accompany Miss Aggy up to the school, me miself remember seeing the Hi Poshers riding into the school yard in them shiny new buggies with the big black stallions in harness – kippity kop, kippity kop [*The actor playing* LEN *makes the sound of the 'kippity kop' using two coconut shells. The actress playing* MAMA *jangles a chain for the effect of the bridle, etc. All the odd bits of clothes and the effects are brought on in the darkness at the beginning of Act Two.*]

GEORGE: [*On buggy riding away*] Giddy yap!

PA BEN: You should see them, just sneering down on the world, them head way up in the sky, drunk with power and authority.

GEORGE: Whoa. [*He dismounts.*]

PA BEN: But is when they start to strut roun' like peacock, the fat slobs them dress up in they Sunday go-to-meeting. Biggitty, oh so arrogant!

[GEORGE *struts around still dressed in his finery.*]

GEORGE: Here, boy. [LEN *hesitates.*] On the double, boy! Move! [LEN *hurries.*] Clean my shoes, burnish it till you see your big black ugly face in it, boy! [LEN *goes on all fours and starts to polish* GEORGE*'s shoe.* GEORGE *is enjoying himself immensely. He uses* LEN*'s back as a foot-rest for his free foot, his riding crop poised over* LEN*'s backside.*] And boy, don't forget we need you for the Easter play. We have you down for three parts – Judas Iscariot, one of the thieves, and both ends of the donkey. Ha, ha, ha! [*He straddles* LEN, *riding and whipping him.*] Sport, what sport!

[*The action freezes after a little while.*]

PA BEN: Yeah, you hear what they use him for? They beat him black behind till it turn blue, all o' them playing Jesus, and they ride him into Jerusalem! I don't forget them, and Missa Lenny don't forget them either. It live in him memory. [PA BEN *calls the actress who played* PEARL. *He whispers to her and she goes off, excitedly.*] Dere it was, Miss Aggy spend her good money to educate the boy, and he pass good good, but him couldn't get no job in the bank, only manual labour.

[*During the above speech,* GEORGE *dismounts and very haughtily takes off his cape and cap. He hands them to* LEN, *along with his riding crop.* GEORGE *walks into the bank area, which is to the right. On the chair behind the table, his coat and tie have been set during the interval. Back to the audience, he puts them on.* LEN *goes off with cape, crop and cap, returning to put the chairs back in place behind the coffee table.* PA BEN*'s line*

Only manual labour *coincides with this action. The action is continuous, no break.*]

But duncey Mongoose who never pass one subject never had to ask for no job. No, they ask him if him want the job. Him who didn't even know enough to work in Missa Elias cloth shop, and they give him the keys to the vault. In no time at all, him move from Teller to Bank Manager. In a few years him end up rich rich. I couldn't figure it out so I had to ask Missa Lenny to explain it to me, and the way I understand it ... Suppose you want to start a housing scheme, you going to need money to borrow, so you go to George's bank.

[GEORGE *dials a number and is talking quietly on the telephone.*]

GEORGE: Yes, Bertie, up to now the wife is none the wiser. [*He laughs, as the actress who played* PEARL *enters* GEORGE's *office as the* REAL ESTATE DEVELOPER.] Hang on, Bertie. [*To* DEVELOPER] Are you the lady from the Real Estate Development Company?
DEVELOPER: I am.
GEORGE: Let's see the plans. [*She displays them on the coffee table, inadvertently laying the plans upside down.* GEORGE *looks them over.*] Ah ha ... hmm. Yes.
PA BEN: Him only looking. Him don't understand nutten.

[*The* DEVELOPER *seeing the plans upside down turns them round.*]

GEORGE: Oh. [*Laughs foolishly.*] Hmm. Hmm. I see. Not bad, not bad. I'll have to put this up to head office, see what they think. Leave everything and check back with me next week. [*Hustling her out.* GEORGE *resumes his telephone conversation. He is very excited.*] Bertie boy, I am on to something hot, a housing scheme development! It's brilliant! Contact the other boys,

51

we have to meet later. Financing will be no problem.
Contact our lawyer friend, same contract as last time.

PA BEN: Sly. No wonder they call him Mongoose.

GEORGE: Man, we could make a million off this one. I
don't know how I didn't think of it before. I was
sitting here and the thing just flash in front of my
eyes.

PA BEN: Liar.

GEORGE: Now, about a name for this new company,
Bertie. We going to need something really profound,
like ahm let me see. How about A.B.C. Homes?

PA BEN: Damn! I could call it that. A.B.C.

GEORGE: Homes. That's it man, you like it? Good, good.
You see the symbolism?

PA BEN: So when next week come and the woman go back
to see what happening with her plan ...

GEORGE: [On phone] Tell her I am out.

PA BEN: Damn lie.

GEORGE: And head office turned down her proposal.

PA BEN: Wicked brute.

GEORGE: But if she come up with anything else, she must
check with me.

ACTRESS WHO PLAYS LOIS: Him want to t'ief her again.

PA BEN: Now him have the plan, him need to get money
to develop it. Him can't borrow it in him own name
for him is the bank manager, so him go roun' the
corner an' set up him friends to borrow it in their
name; one of the friend name Bertie. At the same
time George draw up papers with them giving
himself seventy per cent of the profit, and the profits
keep rolling in.

GEORGE: [On phone, sits on the sofa, one foot up on the coffee table, a
huge cigar in his hand.] Bertie, contact the lawyers. We
need to set up two more companies, same plan as
before. [He hangs up, then pulls on his cigar, savouring it.]

PA BEN: Greed married to ignorance. Him try it once too
often. The bank find him out. [GEORGE looks around
furtively, puts out his cigar, foot off the coffee table.] The

newspapers hear about it, an' before you know it, Mongoose name gone abroad, [*The actors/villagers sing* 'Sly Mongoose, yuh name gone abroad ... oooh!'] and is panic in a him pants.

[GEORGE *is up and about like a scared mongoose in a cage*.]

GEORGE: Jesus Christ, Bertie, man! All right, all right, don't panic. Advertise them again. We have to sell twelve houses this week or we are in plenty trouble! Yes, I read the article. Somebody should burn down that newspaper. Who the hell could have fed them that information? No matter, if we organise we can come out. Leave it to me, I have an idea. [*As he looks across to the files in the bookcase*.]

PA BEN: And that is when George start to forage into people's bank accounts.

ACTRESS WHO PLAYS MAMA: Forage? You mean t'ief.

PA BEN: Me mean t'ief. Poor Miss Aggy was only one of the people that him trick.

ACTOR WHO PLAYS LEN: Ol' tree card man.

PA BEN: Before you know it, the bank kick him out. Of course they wasn't going to shame one a dem own in public but dem demand back di money him did borrow, and in two twos him start to lose him shirt.

[*The actors/villagers sing* 'Sly mongoose, yuh name gone abroad ... oooh', *as they go off*.]

PA BEN: [*To the audience*] Missa Lenny investigate Mongoose down to the last. Him is a smart boy now, that Missa Lenny. Him got the mongoose in a cage, but A don't like it. When you got a mongoose lock up, is then him dangerous. And that thing with Miss Lois, A don't like it at all. [*He goes into his house*.]

[GEORGE *appears on the lower level down right. He is on the telephone, dressed as he was at the end of Act One*.]

GEORGE: Yes, Bertie, man, the man Tomlinson is a
definite possibility. Is a black man, I can handle him.
Plus, and this is a real plus, I know his wife. Ha, ha!
We will talk. Look up the files on ABC, a Mrs
Tomlinson, tell me where she live. [*Pause*]

[LEN *and* LOIS *come on in their area.*]

LEN: I've been chasing the bugger for months. Ignores
my calls; stroke of genius how I got him to come here
tonight.

LOIS: How did you?

LEN: I put the word out that the new man, Tomlinson, at
the bank was a soft touch for a loan, that I wasn't
unapproachable about making a deal – under the
table, of course. He arrives here tonight with one set
of hocus-pocus information. Where is that list of
people who he says would be willing to purchase at
an escalated price? [*He goes off to get it.*]

GEORGE: [*On phone*] Say what, no Mrs Tomlinson on the
file? There must be, unless … All right, I know how I
can get the information. Any luck with tomorrow's
pay bill? Oh no! You try your uncle? Anybody we
can borrow from? If everything else fails there is a
lawyer who can give me a second mortgage on my
mother's house. Get a message to the office. Tell the
workmen the paybill will be a few hours late an' tell
the office staff half pay till Wednesday. I know we
won't have it on Wednesday, but then we can think
of something else. You have Tomlinson's phone
number on you? Let me have it.

LEN: [*Coming on with the papers*] Here we are. Peter Malcolm;
this man died five years ago. I'd say Mr Malcolm's got
all the real estate he is likely to need. All fictitious
characters.

LOIS: If he's down and out as you say he is, aren't you
wasting your time trying to get your mother's money
back?

LEN: Maybe, but McFarlane is vermin. I have a moral right to rid society of that sort of scum. Come to think of it, you should know McFarlane.

LOIS: Should I?

GEORGE: [*On the phone*] Six, eight ... [*He records the number as he gets it from Bertie.*]

LEN: You didn't run into him when you worked at Barclays?

LOIS: What branch was he at?

LEN: Uptown.

LOIS: I was downtown.

GEORGE: [*On phone*] Tomorrow.

LEN: Were you?

LOIS: Does it matter?

LEN: Not really. Thought you may have known the bum.

[*The phone rings in* LEN'*s house.* LOIS *answers.*]

LOIS: Hello.

GEORGE: Lois?

LOIS: Yes.

GEORGE: Len's mother, is she a Tomlinson as well? Tell me where she live.

LOIS: Wrong number. [*She hangs up. The lights go down very slowly on all the areas. In the darkness,* LOIS *and* LEN *leave the stage.* GEORGE *removes his jacket. As the lights come up again he is walking towards* PA BEN'*s house.*]

GEORGE: [*Calling out*] Hello, hello, anybody at home?

PA BEN: [*From inside his house*] Is who dat now?

GEORGE: Come here, man.

PA BEN: [*Coming out to see* GEORGE] All well. All well. [*He has on his spectacles and there is an open bible in his hand.*]

GEORGE: Miss Agatha Simmons, where I find her?

PA BEN: Simmons, Simmons?

GEORGE: Yeah, Simmons.

PA BEN: Oh, Miss Aggy. You in the right place, but she not here right now. She just gone down by the Baptist Church. If you walk fast you will catch her, straight ahead. [GEORGE *goes*.] Hey man, you forget something.

GEORGE: What?

PA BEN: To tell me thanks.

GEORGE: Oh, sorry, man. Thanks. [*He goes off left on the lower level.*]

PA BEN: Rude, no manners, an' 'manners maketh man'. [*To audience*] No, mi spirit never take to him. Never like the looks of the fellow. A wonder what him want with Miss Aggy. She so cagey nowadays, nuh tell me her business like first time. It strange all the same to see a big white man in these parts an' is nuh election time. A just hope is nuh something bad. [*He looks in the direction* GEORGE *left in, then goes into his house.*]

ACT TWO

SCENE TWO

[*As* PA BEN *goes in the lights come up on* LEN *in his living area. His jacket is thrown over a chair, his shoes are off. Very relaxedly he is going over* GEORGE's *dossier.*]

LEN: Damn crook!

[MAMA *is heard knocking off.*]

MAMA: Hold dog!
LEN: Oh no! Not her with that nonsense again. [*He puts the dossier down and is going towards the door, when he stops, returns fast, puts on shoes, scrambles into his jacket.* MAMA *knocks again.*] Coming, Mama. [*He packs his briefcase quickly and leaves with it to the door. Opening the door*] I wish you wouldn't do that, Mama.
MAMA: Do what?
LEN: That 'Hold dog' nonsense.
MAMA: But you have a sign outside.
LEN: Okay, Mama. [*He checks his watch.*]
MAMA: You going out? [*She walks in and sits on Stage Right chair.*]
LEN: Yes, I have this important meeting.
MAMA: Don't tell me now say you so busy, you don't even have time to tell me howdy and greet me me properly?
LEN: [*Pecks her on cheek.*] How are you, Mama?
MAMA: Thank God for life; I should've been up since yesterday, but I had to go to a funeral. You 'member Miss Pearl?
LEN: Pearl?
MAMA: Miss Esmeralda daughter. She dead yesterday, dead in childbirth. The baby live, though. [LEN *looks at his watch and* MAMA *notices.*] Anyway, I see you in a

57

hurry, so I won't keep you. [*With great pleasure*] So you couldn't come an' tell me that you saw Missa Mac?

LEN: [*Very surprised*] Who told you that?

MAMA: Missa Mac himself come down to see me yesterday.

LEN: Oh? [*He puts down the briefcase and sits on edge of table.*]

MAMA: Yes, sit down off in mi kitchen. Big big Missa Mac, comfortable as anything. Him tell me say he saw you, and how him explain everything to you 'bout the house. How him not working at the bank no more.

LEN: Yes?

MAMA: And say that the people he did recommend to me to buy the house from was one bunch a crooks, let him down bad bad, and since he couldn't sit back and see me lose my whole life's savings, he buy them out, and he managing it now. You should see him telling it to me. [LEN *laughs.*] What you laughing at so?

LEN: It's all right; go on, Mama.

MAMA: Only say that right now him in a little financial difficulty, but give him a little time and everything will be all right, but I explain to him that he don't have to worry 'bout my couple pennies, just straighten out his own business first. Since I know is Missa Mac in charge, I know my money safe.

LEN: Mama. [*She gets up and walks to him.*]

MAMA: You know what is a comfort and a blessing to me now, Len?

LEN: What is, Mama?

MAMA: That it turn 'round that now you can help Missa Mac.

LEN: He said that?

MAMA: Yes, he say how you contact him, offer him help.

LEN: Let me explain that to you, Mama.

MAMA: Is a good opportunity to repay the debt we owe the family. His father-in-law feed you when I was down and out. I remember and I am grateful.

LEN: You heard the rumours about him, Mama?

MAMA: And don't you repeat them. You have more sense

than that. Missa Mac warn me, how people out in the street plotting against him. Scandal and malicious lies.

LEN: No, Mama.

MAMA: Shut yuh ears to wickedness, you hear me?

LEN: Listen to me for a while.

MAMA: No! Black people too wicked and bad. Missa Mac say you could help him. If not for him, then for Miss Margaret. Is God send you this opportunity. Help them for Mama's sake.

LEN: [*Taking papers out of his briefcase*] Read some of this.

MAMA: Some of what? [*She looks at it, then pushes it away.*] Move it from me. Is Miss Margaret father help make you what you is today!

LEN: You damn right about that! [*He throws the dossier on the coffee table.*]

MAMA: Where is yuh gratitude?

LEN: Gratitude for what? For the two scraps from their table?

MAMA: Jesus, Saviour, hold mi hand!

LEN: When they eat and leave they throw it to me in the kitchen, like I was a damn stray.

MAMA: You did want to eat with them 'round the table? You did give dem anyt'ing to put down? They didn't have to give you anything, you know. You should know yuh place. You was always too uppitty.

LEN: Jesus Christ! Is time you stop bow down an' worship them people like them was God.

MAMA: Take this cross, Saviour!

LEN: Them nuh God!

MAMA: [*Sitting*] Oh Lord, forgive him!

LEN: Set them up on pedestal. I tired of it.

MAMA: Shut yuh mouth!

LEN: I've had enough!

MAMA: [*Shouting at him*] Shut it, I say! If it wasn't for Miss Margaret Pa, you wouldn't get to go to Englan' to come back here to spit on my head, and refuse them help.

LEN: Help? If it was a damn drop o' water I had to give them to save they life, they woulda dead. You hear me, dead!

MAMA: You think you too big for me to drop hand on you? [*She grabs him by his jacket and pulls him to her. He breaks her hold, then picks up a chair to hit her, but he stays his hand.*] Ooh. Jesus. Lawd, you see what you come to do? Kill me. Kill me. [*She spins him round.*] You mad? You see what you threaten to do? You realise now say something wrong with you. Woi! The boy pick up chair to kill him ma!

LEN: I'm sorry, Mama. [*As he sits rather disconsolately.*]

MAMA: Sorry? Sorry can't help situation. You always sorry. Like for the years you did barely write to me, tie me out in the wilderness and all you could say is you sorry. Same thing when you married, and is one year after you send come tell me. Why you married her? Is like you married her and you can't say why. Is like one morning you wake up, and plops, you married.

LEN: Jesus Christ, Mama, you coming with that again?

MAMA: I must come up with it again, Len [*As she strides over to him.*] What else you expect me to say? I can't forget the day news come say you married. Black Sambo pose off with you in wedding picture. Lawd, against my better judgement I keep the peace, but after your performance here today, raise yuh hand to kill yuh Ma, there is no power on God's earth could convince me say is not obeah that woman obeah you.

[*During the above it is as if* MAMA *is a woman possessed with great religious fervour. By the end of the scene, the spirits that move her are in total control of mind and body.*]

LEN: Mama! [*He gets up to hold and implore her.*]

MAMA: [*As she holds him with great urgency*] Len, Len, son, listen to me, son. Your soul is in bondage! A have to release you! A have to set you free!

[LEN *stands transfixed. The lights go down on them.*]

ACT TWO

SCENE THREE

[*Ten seconds or so later.* LEN *is with* PA BEN *at* PA BEN's *house.* LEN *is in a great state of agitation. He sits, he stands, he walks, turns, etc.*]

LEN: And so I came right away, sir.

PA BEN: Settle your nerves. Drink one, drink one. [*Gives* LEN *the bottle.* LEN *drinks. The over hundred per cent proof rum throws him into a tizzy.*]

LEN: Ooh!

PA BEN: See what I mean. It take your mind off things.

LEN: [*With hardly any voice.*] Any water, sir?

PA BEN: Don't use it, 'cept to cook with and clean miself. Where Miss Aggy now?

LEN: I left her in town.

PA BEN: Praises be, the sun gone down. She can't do anything till tomorrow.

LEN: Isn't there a man one could go to for protection?

PA BEN: There's one right here in the district.

LEN: That's too close to home. You don't know any a bit further away?

PA BEN: What you want him for?

LEN: Could you go to him for me?

PA BEN: What for?

LEN: To get some protection for Lois.

PA BEN: Is that you come down here to ask me? I thought you come to ask my advice. Is not protection you want. You want to get your mama to stay her hand.

LEN: That's not possible, sir. If you knew anyone you could go to, I'd really appreciate ...

PA BEN: Even if I did know anybody, Miss Lois would have to go for herself. But that's not the answer. You got to soften up your mother and give Mongoose the money.

LEN: No sir. No, no, no, no. [*Pause.*] No!

PA BEN: I heard the first 'no'. I not deaf. Tell me something, you know what will happen if your mama carry out her threat?

LEN: That's why I have to protect Lois, sir.

PA BEN: And what happens to your mother? You goin' to leave her wide open for the boomerang?

LEN: Boomerang? What's that? I never heard about that.

PA BEN: You're a scientist, but you don't study high science yet. Depending on what your mother set off on Miss Lois, whether she just out to get her out of your life or ...

LEN: Or what, sir?

PA BEN: I can't bring miself to say it, boy. This is no joke. You never can tell how the chips goin' fly. Obeah is a serious thing. Don't meddle with it. You have to stop yuh mother!

LEN: How?

PA BEN: I just tell you. [LEN *hesitates*. PA BEN *pauses*.] Is two ladies in yuh life. You love them? Answer me.

LEN: Yes, sir.

PA BEN: Well, then, you can't expose none o' them to this kind of danger. If you don't stop her you have a good chance of losing one o' dem. Now tell me, what more important to you – mashin' up Mongoose life, or would you rather sacrifice one of the women you love? What it is between you and him, anyway?

LEN: What I told you.

PA BEN: No. Piece o' the story missin'. If not, your heart couldn't set so against him. If you pay up before she go to the obeah man it could work out.

LEN: Could!

PA BEN: Is the chance you have to take. Take the pressure off Miss Lois. If yuh mind is that set against the white feller, then you got to think of something else, an' quick.

LEN: You think you could talk to her again?

PA BEN: And say what? The mood you say she in it would be a waste of time. [*Pause*.] Like mother, like son. Two a you stubborn like ol' mule. Supposing ...

LEN: What sir?

PA BEN: No. [*Pause.*] What a dilemma you come lay on my doorstep this day of our Lord! You don't have any idea?

LEN: I'm thinking.

PA BEN: Think fast. [*Pause.*] The other day when me and you had the little argument and you was telling me 'bout the work you do.

LEN: Yes sir.

PA BEN: You did explain to me 'bout a thing name computer, solve all kind o' problem. It couldn't help you with this?

LEN: I'm afraid not, sir.

PA BEN: So you see, you have science and science. [*Pause.*] Miss Lois suspect any of what going on?

LEN: Not about this. Look, whatever we do has to be without her knowledge.

PA BEN: If you don't tell her and you don't stop your mother, confusion.

LEN: There's always the chance Mama might not ...

PA BEN: Don't fool yourself, join hands with Miss Lois. She may have the solution to the problem.

LEN: What could I say to her?

PA BEN: The truth.

LEN: Lois, my mother is ... ahm ... planning to put a hex on you. That's what you want me to say?

PA BEN: Hex? What name hex? It name obeah.

LEN: This is 1980, sir. The whole thing is ridiculous.

PA BEN: What the year have to do with it? Is your roots and they grow deep! Don't be ashamed of them! Miss Lois is roots too. She'll understand. Depending on how much love, trust and understanding there is between you, the greater the chance you have of fighting this thing. You have to stop yuh Ma, boy.

LEN: Till I can think of some way to do that, I have to protect Lois. She is the innocent in all this.

PA BEN: So is your mother.

LEN: No, sir, that's ignorance.

PA BEN: Born and bred of what?

LEN: At this point I just don't care.

PA BEN: Well, I care and you better care too.

LEN: Right now I have to find a way that Lois doesn't go stark raving mad or worse. If you know somebody, give me the name.

PA BEN: You make yuh choice then?

LEN: You know the hell I've been through with Mama.

PA BEN: So be it. I finish. I wash my hands.

LEN: Mama took her chance, she knew the consequences. [*Pause.*] Didn't she? [*Pause.*] Give me a break, sir.

PA BEN: There's a lady in town on Mountain View Road by the almond tree, with a flag in her yard. She name Mother Rachael. [*He goes into his house.*]

LEN: Thank you, sir. [LEN *is going but stops, then returns to knock on* PA BEN's *windows.* PA BEN *opens it.*]

PA BEN: Yes?

LEN: One last favour. Go see her for me, sir?

PA BEN: That you have to do for yourself, boy. [*As he tries to close the window.*]

LEN: [*Hanging on to the window.*] Sir, consider my position at the bank, my reputation. People see a man like me going into a place like that! You want to see me ruined, sir?

PA BEN: You is the one who need protection, from yourself!

[PA BEN *slams the windows shut.*]

LEN: Oh no! [*He goes. In a little while,* PA BEN *comes out again and looks at* LEN *disappearing. He shakes his head sucking in on his teeth, when he hears* MAMA *coming from the opposite direction on the lower level.*]

PA BEN: All well. All well.

MAMA: [*Sullenly*] Hmm. [*She continues walking. He tries all he can to delay her and talk to him.*]

PA BEN: Why you greet me so cold?

MAMA: A tired.

PA BEN: You went out?

MAMA: Hmm.

PA BEN: A was wondering what happen to you. Me know is not like you to make dark catch you on the road.

MAMA: The old bus broke down.

PA BEN: The man who name that bus name it right. 'Surprise'. You surprise when it carry you home. Anyway you reach. You going out tomorrow?

MAMA: A might.

PA BEN: Outside of the district or what?

MAMA: [*Angrily*] What you want?

PA BEN: You have to be so short with me?

MAMA: A say A tired.

PA BEN: Anyway, if you going, let me know, nuh?

MAMA: Hmm. [*She storms off.*]

PA BEN: Somehow I going to have to detain her here tomorrow, play sick or something. [*As he goes into his house.*]

ACT TWO

SCENE FOUR

[*As the lights go down on the storyteller's area, they come up on* LEN*'s living space. 'Beat'.* LEN *enters dressed in a straw hat, oversized dark glasses, outrageous red pants, and a vile sports jacket over an out-of-tune plaid shirt. He carries his briefcase and some flowers along with some bush. He locks the door behind him and charges towards the coffee table, where he rests briefcase, flowers and bush, then takes off dark glasses, straw hat and jacket, resting them on the chair behind the coffee table. He opens the briefcase and takes out two candles, then reaches behind him for the candle holders, sets the candles in, lights them and sets them down rather ceremoniously on the coffee table. Into his briefcase again for a list of instructions, he reads it quickly, then picks up the flowers and the bush. He starts an incantation, waving the flowers over his head, the bush round his waist.*]

LEN: Protect her, protect her from the forces of evil! Search mi heart, hug me close, dead and wake, hug me close! [*He stops abruptly, finds a vase on the bookshelf, sticks the flowers in and places them on the coffee table. From his briefcase he takes out a vial and sprinkles a powdery substance in the four corners of the room, tossing it over his head. As he sprinkles, he cleans. The whole thing has to go at a terrific pace. Done with that, he digs into the briefcase and comes out with a pair of panties and a tape measure. A little unsure how to proceed, he goes to the telephone and dials. Before he completes the dialling, he panics, hangs up, returns to the chair, picks up dark glasses, hat and jacket and very quickly dresses himself. In fact, he is dialling and putting on his jacket at the same time.*]

LEN: [*In a fake accent*] Ah, Mother Rachael. Yes, the gentleman who was in to see you this morning. No. No, not the politician, the tall dark gentleman with the straw hat and the dark glasses ... Yes. Oh very well, I got everything, including the oil of deliverance. There is just one little problem, the

undergarment, does it go at the head of the table or
… Ah, I see … Fine. Thank you. Good spirits to you
as well!

[*He hangs up, removes dark glasses, straw hat and jacket, then
puts the tape measure at the head of the table, and places the
panties on his head. Not turning, he sort of reverses, walking as
if he has a crick neck. He sprinkles the oil of deliverance in the
corners of the room.*]

Oil of deliverance. [*He does a little dance.*] Oil of
deliverance. [*Dances.*] Oil of deliverance. [*Dances.*]

[*A knocking is heard from off;* LEN *is visibly startled, panics in
fact.*]

Is that you, Lois?

LOIS: Your key is in the door.
LEN: Coming.

[*Madly he attempts to stuff the things back in the briefcase,
attempting at the same time to tidy up. A lot of business can be
developed for this scene because as we will later discover that
Mother Rachael is a fraud, so her potions for protection and
deliverance can be as farcical as possible.* LEN *goes to the door,
forgetting to remove the candles and one or two other items. He
remembers the panties when he is half way through opening the
door. He snatches them off, puts them in his pocket, then opens
the door fully.* LOIS *enters and goes directly to the table Down
Right.* LEN *follows beside her.*]

LOIS: Why you smiling so?
LEN: Smiling so? [*Still using the fake accent.*]
LOIS: What you been up to?
LEN: Been up to? Nothing. [*He reverts to his normal speech.*]
LOIS: Must you repeat everything I say?

LEN : Everything you say. I wasn't, was I? [*He checks behind him to discover the candles and whatever other items he has forgotten to clear. He somehow manages to get rid of them without* LOIS *seeing.*]

LOIS : What are you doing home anyway? Aren't you working today?

LEN : I just popped in to see how you were.

LOIS : I'm okay.

LEN : But you didn't look too good this morning.

LOIS : I'm fine.

LEN : But you look so pale, out of sorts, as if something's bothering you.

LOIS : Nothing.

LEN : You tossed and turned all night last night, won't tell you where you kicked me. [*Perspiring, yet relieved that the space is now clear. He goes for a handkerchief to mop his face, but the red panties come out. He is halfway through mopping his face when he realises. Quickly he pushes them away in his pocket.*] Ha, ha! What's the matter?

LOIS : Nothing, Len.

LEN : No pains, aches, dizziness?

LOIS : I'm having a bit of a headache.

LEN : Headache? When did it start?

LOIS : A day or so now.

LEN : That's all right. [*Catches himself.*] Anyway, sit down, I'll get you something. [*He puts her in the seat directly opposite to the flowers.*]

LOIS : What's the ... Who brought these? [*The flowers.*]

LEN : Oh, I thought they'd cheer you up, my love. [*She looks at him in utter amazement.*] Why not, you are always accusing me that ...

LOIS : Something terrible has happened.

LEN : No, it won't. Whatever you do, think positive.

LOIS : What's that you say?

LEN : Oh it was nothing, my love. To bring you some flowers. I said to myself [*he takes the flowers from the vase, and in the moment that* LOIS *looks away, he repeats the business with the flowers over his head*], what can I do to surprise her? So aren't you going to thank me? Give me a kiss.

LOIS: You are behaving most odd. Out with it. What have you been up to?

LEN: Not a thing.

LOIS: You are hiding something from me.

LEN: Goodness gracious, no. Wait till I really surprise you. Close your eyes. [*As he goes directly behind her.*]

LOIS: What are you up to?

LEN: Trust me.

LOIS: You know I don't.

LEN: Just this once, close your eyes, please.

LOIS: Len!

LEN: Please! [*She does.*] And no peeping. [*He makes the sign of the cross over the amulet which he takes from his pocket, pushing back the panties. He puts the amulet around her neck.*] There you are.

LOIS: Len!

LEN: Just a little something to restore your spirits. You look beautiful. Absolutely smashing! Promise me you will wear it always. [*He kisses her passionately on the mouth.*]

LOIS: Wow! Okay, now give me the bad news.

LEN: You'll have to understand what happened to me today.

LOIS: I'll try.

LEN: I was on my way to work this morning, and like Saul going to Damascus ...

LOIS: You were struck by a great light.

LEN: As if in a vision, I had a stunning revelation.

LOIS: The Virgin Mary is with child again.

LEN: No, no, no. [*Searching in his pocket for another of his potions. Desperately he goes for his briefcase, sits himself down on the bar stool, the lid of the briefcase serving as a sort of mask as he digs around till he finds what he is looking for. While searching he continues his speech.*] All my life I've worked, slaved, buried myself. To what end? To no purpose. I was miserable. [*He finds the potion and hides it behind him.*

He puts the briefcase away again, and walks behind the chairs to LOIS.] From now on I am turning over a new leaf. In fact I am throwing away the books, getting a new lease on life. I am. Yes, I am unleashing myself on the pleasure spots of the world. I am going to freak out. [*He gets her up and leads her into a dance, a mixture of quickstep and tango. On each natural break in the dance, he sprinkles the potion behind her back.*] Yeah, drop out. [*He sits her down again, then goes directly behind her, and the action and the words should be so synchronised that as he touches her on the left shoulder, she automatically looks in that direction while he sprinkles the potion to her right.*] It all came to me in a flash, and since morning I've been making decisions right, left, and centre. One major decision is ... Wait for it. [*His body language changes. He is trying to be very sexy. He goes to her, caresses, kisses her on the neck.*] Come, let's go upstairs. [*She is bemused.* LEN *pulls her up; she collects her bag, then he guides her in front of him, gently pushing her off.*]

LOIS: I read somewhere that the world was coming to an end today. I think it has.

[LEN *removes the panties from his right pocket and twirls them around, a look of relief, pleasure, and accomplishment on his face, as the lights fade.*]

ACT TWO

SCENE FIVE

[*As the lights go down on the previous scene, they come up again almost immediately on the lower area.* MAMA *enters Down Left and calls across to* GEORGE *who we can imagine standing at his gate.*]

MAMA: Missa Mac. Missa Mac.

GEORGE: Oh Miss G, how are you?

MAMA: Right here, how you?

GEORGE: Well, not too badly. I would invite you in, but the doctor's inside.

MAMA: Somebody sick?

GEORGE: Miss Margaret.

MAMA: On top a everything else? Don't say that.

GEORGE: Yes, last night one of my workmen phone her up, threaten to kill me if I don't pay him his doggone money.

MAMA: Say what?

GEORGE: Yes, so she is badly shook up, as you can imagine.

MAMA: Lord, yes. You don't deserve this.

GEORGE: The doctor trying to calm her down. Have her under sedation.

MAMA: Poor little thing. Help her, oh Lord, help her!

GEORGE: Imagine, the same workman who I have been helping to put bread in his mouth.

MAMA: Bite the hand that feed them. The whole world gone mad.

GEORGE: It's been a rough couple o' days. I could tell you. Sometimes I just feel as if I could throw in the towel.

MAMA: No. Keep fighting, you hear what I tell you.

GEORGE: Yes, Miss G.

MAMA: I saw Len and I put in a word on your behalf.

GEORGE: Thank you, Miss G.

MAMA: Some good news soon come your way. In fact

everything woulda been all right already if it wasn't for that. … Lawd! [*Beating her breast.*]

GEORGE: What's the problem, Miss G?

MAMA: A little obstacle in mi way.

GEORGE: What obstacle?

MAMA: It sorta private, but anyway the world have to know. Is the woman him married to.

GEORGE: Lois, what about her?

MAMA: She is a distress to me, you see, Missa Mac? But I know her number. She won't know what hit her when I finish with her. Len willing to help, but …

GEORGE: And she said no?

MAMA: She have him under influence.

GEORGE: Lois?

MAMA: She control him. Him mind don't belongs to him.

GEORGE: Tell me more.

MAMA: Leave it to me.

GEORGE: No, I need to know all the details.

MAMA: In a day or two everything will come through for you and Miss Margaret. You just have to trust me.

GEORGE: You certain of your facts?

MAMA: As certain as the night follows day [*confidentially*], but you didn' hear nutten from me.

GEORGE: No, no.

MAMA: Just leave everything to me. A goin' now and tell Miss Margaret say the Lord is on her side.

GEORGE: I'll do that.

MAMA: And cheer up. Things goin' to be all right. [*As she leaves, boldly and positively*] You hear what A tell you.

GEORGE: Take care, and thanks.

[GEORGE *watches her go for a moment, then he too leaves the lower area.*]

ACT TWO

SCENE SIX

[*As the lights go down on the previous scene there is a knocking at the door.* LOIS *answers.*]

LOIS: Hi, George, Len's not here, I'm afraid. [GEORGE *barges through past her.*] Was he expecting you?

GEORGE: Don't ask me no questions, bitch!

LOIS: I beg your pardon!

GEORGE: Beg pardon? After I protect you that's the way you try and pay me back, by screwing me up!

LOIS: What the hell is going on?

GEORGE: Don't play the innocent with me. Your mother-in-law tell me how you set your husband against me.

LOIS: What? Me? She said what?

GEORGE: But I mean to get what I want, you see, and I'll expose you to get it.

LOIS: No George, it's a damn lie. I'd have nothing to gain by ...

GEORGE: You have reason enough to hate my guts.

LOIS: But more reason to protect you. What could I say to Len?

GEORGE: I don't know what lie you cook up; anyway I didn't come here to talk to you. Your husband say the deal is off. When he comes, we reopen negotiations.

LOIS: [*Imploringly*] George! [*She touches him. He pulls away.*]

GEORGE: Don't even bother to try, baby.

LOIS: You son of a bitch! [*She goes to the telephone and dials.*] Dr Tomlinson, please. Has he left for the day? Thank you.

LEN: [*Entering*] Hi yah, beautiful, it's the new me. I got some good news. I called London today. [*She makes him aware of* GEORGE *who is sitting on the sofa.*] Hi ya, George.

GEORGE: Hi, man.

LEN: My secretary gave you a message, didn't she?

GEORGE: Yeah, I got the message.

LEN: I'm sorry things didn't work out.

GEORGE: That's all right, they will.

LEN: Good.

GEORGE: Sit down.

LEN: I beg your pardon.

GEORGE: I am reopening negotiations.

LOIS: Len.

LEN: Yes.

LOIS: George has something to tell you.

[*She moves Upstage, back to the audience, and puts on a jacket which suggests her bank uniform. As soon as she has finished dressing she freezes. In the meantime* GEORGE *gets up and goes across to the desk Down Right. He sits, picks up the phone and dials just one number.*]

GEORGE: Five minutes ago I asked Miss Stuart to come in, where is she? And no calls through to me till I tell you.

[LOIS *breaks the freeze and enters* GEORGE's *office.* LEN *has turned his back on the action.*]

LOIS: You wanted to see me, sir?

GEORGE: What took you so long?

LOIS: I only just got the message.

GEORGE: Oh. Have a look at this. [*Hands her bank cards.*] You handle those accounts, don't you?

LOIS: Well, yes, sir.

GEORGE: I was hoping you could throw some light on the matter.

LOIS: I don't know, sir.

GEORGE: Miss Stuart, you must know. The lady who the account belongs to was in to see me this morning. She says she's been living in England for the last eight years. That last withdrawal was made on the

75

eighteenth of this month, two days before she left England.

LOIS: There has to be some mistake.

GEORGE: I would say it's more than that.

LOIS: I'll go and check the ledger.

GEORGE: Don't waste my time. [*Hiss.*] Tell you what, let me get the police in on this. [*He picks up the phone.*]

LOIS: Sir! [*Pause.*]

GEORGE: Yes, Miss Stuart? You want the cops in on it or not? [*Pause.*]

LOIS: No, sir. [*He hangs up after another pause.*]

GEORGE: I thought I knew every trick in the book, but this is a new one on me. I take my hat off to you. When I found out what you were up to, I had a choice: call the cops, or do what anybody in my position would do, and protect his staff. As luck would have it, the customer we are dealing with wasn't too smart. I managed to sort it out with her; inflation, devaluation, bank charges, that sort of thing. Learn one thing in this life: you can sell anything to people, so long as you package it right! She left happy. Naturally my curiosity was aroused, so I did a little digging.

LOIS: I can explain.

GEORGE: You been playing this game for quite a little while, little bit here, little bit there.

LOIS: Most of it's been repaid, sir, I only ...

GEORGE: The deed is done, my dear: now we must cover your tracks. Damn bad luck on your part. If the woman had kept her tail in England you would have got away with it. Anyway, in future when you are a bit strapped for cash, check with me, I am sure we can come to some arrangement. [*He touches her.*]

LOIS: Thank you, sir, but ...

GEORGE: I know how you girls like to dress up, show off on the fellows. [*He is playing with her blouse.*]

LOIS: The money wasn't for me ...

GEORGE: No?

LOIS: There's this friend ...

GEORGE: Boyfriend, eh, put you up to it?

LOIS: You don't understand, sir. He doesn't know. He's at university, and we have this arrangement; I would work and pay his way, and later ...

GEORGE: You send him away on a scholarship. Good.

LOIS: But since then my father died, and me being the eldest, all the responsibility for the younger ones fell on me. You won't say anything to anyone, will you, sir? [*She cries.*]

GEORGE: This is strictly between us.

LOIS: [*Crying*] I'll pay it all back.

GEORGE: What you crying for? Come, come. On to brighter things, like how you planning to thank me. Tell you what, to show good faith, proof that I won't go back on my word, it'll be my pleasure to drop my signature right here on this card, then nobody can touch you, and who is going to accuse me? I am a citizen above suspicion. But later for that. [*He walks away from her and sits on the sofa.*] Why am I sticking my neck out for you? Two reasons. You are one of the first black girls that the bank employ. Think what it would do for your race if the news was to get out; and secondly, as a man I couldn't sit back and see an attractive girl like you go to waste in some dirty prison, just for a few dollars. No way. Such a nice body, pretty face like that. Come here.

LOIS: Please, Mr McFarlane. No!

GEORGE: Call me George. [*As he goes towards her and touches her again.*]

LOIS: Please, sir, no!

GEORGE: I like you for a long time now.

LOIS: No!

GEORGE: I bet you could feel me looking at you.

LOIS: No! [*As he tries to kiss her*] No! [*She pushes him away.*]

GEORGE: Wait a minute, baby, I am not going to wrestle with you at all. Take your time, think it over. After all the stress you owe it to yourself to have a little relaxation. [*He sits on the sofa.*] The choice is yours, for I can easily put this matter back on a strictly business basis. Come here.

[*She starts removing her jacket. She takes one tentative step towards* GEORGE, *then another. On the third she breaks down crying and runs away from him towards the entrance to the area upstairs.* LEN *runs after her, embraces and consoles her.* GEORGE *is still sitting on the sofa.* LOIS *is crying uncontrollably.*]

LEN: It's okay, it's okay.

LOIS: Oh, Len, I am so sorry. I have ruined everything.

LEN: It's okay, sweetheart, we are in this together now.

LOIS: I'll go away. I'll do anything.

GEORGE: Touching scene.

LOIS: Let me go upstairs. I have this splitting headache.

LEN: Yes, go and lie down. [*He walks with her to the door.*] You son of a bitch! [*To* GEORGE]

GEORGE: [*Showing the withdrawal slip*] The withdrawal slip your wife signed to defraud the bank. Kept a copy as a little souvenir. Never know when these things will come in handy. [LEN *takes it.*] Tear that up, the original's at home.

LEN: [*Looking at it*] This is no longer valid in a court of law.

GEORGE: I know that, but I can use it to damage you, man. A man in your position can't afford a scandal. This is a small town, word travels fast, plus you never know how I will twist the story when I release it. It could even involve you. Who is going to believe you never knew what she was up to? The story might even get around that you put her up to it.

[LEN *grabs him by the collar. Immediately there is an urgent knocking at the door.* LEN *releases* GEORGE.]

LEN: Come in. [PA BEN *enters. He is very agitated.*] Pa Ben!

PA BEN: Missa Lenny. [*He sees* GEORGE] All well. All well.

GEORGE: Fine.

PA BEN: Cry excuse, beg pardon, forgive mi manners. A can talk to you in private?

LEN: Yes, of course. [*They move down left away from* GEORGE.] Is it about Mama?

PA BEN: No, Missa Lenny, is about Mother Rachael.

LEN: What about her?

PA BEN: She is a fraud!

LEN: What! Where'd you get this?

PA BEN: Reliable sources. She is an impostor, a bogus.

LEN: Oh no! Jesus! You know anybody else?

PA BEN: Is too late for that. Talk to your mother. Is yuh last chance. Pray God you not too late.

LEN: We're right back where we started, going around in circles.

PA BEN: How is Miss Lois? Any sign of anything?

LEN: No. Well, she had a headache just now.

PA BEN: Headache? Oh my God! Negotiate with your Mama. In another couple of hours Miss Lois could be of no use to herself.

LOIS: [*Calling from off*] Len, Len.

LEN: Excuse me. [*He goes off to her. There is a pause.* PA BEN *in his nervousness wanders around the space.*]

PA BEN: [*To* GEORGE] All well. All well.

GEORGE: All well.

PA BEN: Aye. [LEN *returns nervously to the drinks table and is getting some aspirins.*] Tablets is of no use if …

LEN: It's just an ordinary headache.

PA BEN: You think. You can't take any chances at this the eleventh hour. Him is your only hope. [*Pointing to* GEORGE.]

LEN: [*Thinks momentarily.*] You know you right. Old man, you are a genius, absolute genius.

PA BEN: But I been telling you that all the time.

LEN: Go find Mama and bring her back here. Whatever you do, don't come back without her.

PA BEN: Oh, I aint go fail you, but it going be hard.

LEN: All right.

PA BEN: All right. [*He is going when he stops and turns.*] Hey, now listen, you have to tell Miss Lois everything.

LEN: Yes, yes, yes.

PA BEN: Thank God you see the light.

LEN: Hurry.

PA BEN: All right. Praise God. I hope we not too late. [*He goes.*]

LEN: [*To* GEORGE] I'll be a little while. While you are waiting, you might like something to read.

GEORGE: I'm fine.

LEN: I insist. After all it's your life story. [LEN *pushes the dossier at* GEORGE. *He takes it rather tentatively.* LEN *goes off with the aspirin to* LOIS.]

PA BEN: [*Appears on the lower level*] Quick as a flash I was on mi way, all the time mi brain going tick tick, like a clock, trying to think up a story to get Miss Aggy to come back with me, but you know I am a storyteller. Before the hour hand had gone around once in mi mind, I knew what I was going to tell her, and A knew she would go back to town with me.

GEORGE: Oh shit! [*Reading the dossier.*]

PA BEN: More or less. [*He travels from Stage Right to Stage Left going off, to reappear immediately with* MAMA *in tow.*] In a flash we was heading back to town on the ol' country bus 'Surprise'. A pray for it to surprise me today and nuh bruck down. The one question A wanted to ask Miss Aggy, A couldn't ask, but A had a feeling I would find out soon enough. Lawd, A hope we not too late. If we is, today going be the day. [*They go off as* LEN *appears in his area.*]

LEN: Not a very pretty picture, is it? Then again, it's not the whole story. There's still a little surprise package I have for you.

GEORGE: Hang on to this, I'll go home and get the original, then we can forget the whole thing.

LEN: Sit your ass down. There are two signatures on this, yours and my wife's. It'll be hard to prove who signed first.

GEORGE: I said I was willing to forget it, man.

LEN: Forget! How many times did you yourself use this same method to defraud the bank?

GEORGE: What?

LEN: You heard me. You knew all the tricks but one. Lois taught you something new, didn't she? In this little surprise package that I promised you, twenty photostat copies of withdrawal slips all signed by you, and some innocent bank clerk. In a couple of cases yours is the sole signature. All within the last seven years, therefore valid in law. It could be ten years in jail or more. The Director of Public Prosecutions should find this very interesting. [*As he goes to the telephone*.]

GEORGE: Wait a minute, man.

LEN: Ten chances to one, you'll get buggered the first night in prison. Then again there's your family to consider. Margaret is principal shareholder in A.B.C., so is your mother.

GEORGE: They didn't know. Leave them out.

LEN: Conspiracy to defraud. Jail again. It's going to be a full house!

GEORGE: Jesus Christ, man, if you want me to beg, I will beg. I beg you, I'll do anything. Please, I just couldn't face it. Have a heart. What do you want me to do, clean your shoes? [*As he goes on his knees in front of* LEN.]

LEN: Okay. When my mother comes, you will tell her how you took her for a ride.

GEORGE: Whatever you say.

LEN: Good. Not just about the house now.

GEORGE: What else is there?

LEN: Among other things, Cassava Nova. Rings a bell? At Munro, by the old bell tower.

GEORGE: [*Pause*] You?

LEN: Tell her what happened that night, George, and the events leading up to it. Leave nothing out. [*Pause*.]

GEORGE: And after that, what you going to do with me?

LEN: This could still go to the Director of Public Prosecutions. It's a chance you'll have to take.

[*There is a knocking at the door.* LOIS *enters from the direction of the bedroom.* LEN *opens the door.* PA BEN *enters, and points to* MAMA *behind him.* MAMA *comes on almost immediately.*]

Hello, Mama.

MAMA: [*Very surprised to see him.*] Len! [*To* PA BEN] But how come you tell me ...?

LEN: We need to talk to you, Mama.
[MAMA *sees* LOIS.]

MAMA: [*To* PA BEN] You trick me. [*Seeing* GEORGE] Missa Mac?

GEORGE: Miss G.

MAMA: What dis mean?

[*The lights go down on all but the Storyteller's area.*]

PA BEN: You see dat boy make me go home and bring him Ma back, I thinking he want to settle up with Mongoose in front of her. But no, Missa Lenny start to replay the story of his youth in the days when Mama drumbeat Miss Margaret so much in him head. Miss Margaret; Advancement; Advancement; till him gone like a fool write love-letter to the girl, and that's when the perpendicular meet the contuberance, which in lay the conbrucksion.

[*During* PA BEN*'s speech to the audience,* GEORGE *goes off; so does* LEN. MAMA *and* LOIS *stand with their backs to the audience. As* PA BEN *finishes his speech he also faces upstage. At the same time* MARGARET *comes on with a letter in her hand. She is calling out for* GEORGE.]

MARGARET: Georgie! Georgie! Georgie! [GEORGE, *wearing his school cap, enters behind her as she is calling. He surprises her, tries to hold and kiss her.*] No Georgie, look what that fellow sent me.

GEORGE: What! [*He takes the letter and shoves it into his pocket, then continues slobbering over* MARGARET.]

MARGARET: It's a love-letter.

GEORGE: Love-letter? [*He breaks his hold on her and gets the letter from his pocket.*]

MARGARET: That black, ugly, little big-lipped ugly ...

GEORGE: You mean Tomlinson, the school mascot? [*He starts to read.*] 'I love you with a love that knows no boundary.'

MARGARET: Not aloud. Give it back. [*As she tries to take it back.*]

GEORGE: 'With a passion that leaves me breathless.' What! 'Helen of Troy, Cleopatra, Margaret, the fairest of them all. Princess, I call out your name and the echoes ring like cathedral bells summoning me to worship at thy feet. Oh goddess!' Shit! [*He gives her back the letter. They sit.*] Your daddy seen this?

MARGARET: He'd have a heart attack. God knows he's a generous man, but he expects those people to know their place. He'd expel the boy ...

GEORGE: I'd say right away.

MARGARET: 'Cept daddy would refuse to believe it's entirely the boy's doing.

GEORGE: So who?

MARGARET: Well, the boy's got a rather ignorant unfortunate dragon of a mother, she must have put him up to it, always bowing and scraping, wheedling her way into father's favour. A real little pest.

GEORGE: But it's the boy who wrote the letter. He should have more sense than that. We have to put him in his place. This has to go up on the school notice-board. [*He starts to go.* MARGARET *runs and stops him.*]

MARGARET: Out of the question, Georgie. Think of my reputation.

[*As she tries desperately to get the letter.*]

GEORGE: Remain silent and see what happens. Next thing you know the rumour gets out with all the nasty innuendoes. We have to nip this in the bud.

MARGARET: No, Georgie, please.

GEORGE: On second thoughts, you know [*he gives her the*

letter with a flourish] pinning that on the notice board is no big thing, it'll be a little laugh. In a couple of days it's blown over and done with. No. We need something that lover-boy will never forget as long as he lives.

MARGARET: [*who has been stuffing the letter in her shoe*] Like what, Georgie?

GEORGE: You have to reply to the letter.

MARGARET: You out of your mind Georgie?

GEORGE: I'll compile the letter. You will tell him you received his letter, and you need to see him, urgent. Tonight in fact. He must meet you after lights-out down by the old fort, next to the cannon. Me and the other boys will be waiting for him. [*As he removes his belt.*]

MARGARET: Oh, it'll be ever such good sport, eh, Georgie?

GEORGE: And you don't know what I am coming up with yet.

[*They go off together in high spirits.* GEORGE *shouts from off,* 'Lights out'. *In the darkness the actors on stage stack the three chairs that make up the sofa, and the coffee table Upstage. In the darkness* LEN *screams, terrible and long. A spotlight picks him up as he appears in the auditorium. A pillow case has been tied over his head, his hands are tied in front of him, his trousers are about his ankles. His screaming, mixed with his sobbing, continues over the taunts of his attackers.* LEN *runs, trying to find his way.*]

GEORGE: That'll teach you, lover-boy! That'll teach you. Next time we cut it off. This was just a rehearsal. Next time it's for real, so let this be a lesson to you, lover-boy. You cassava-nova you. [*He laughs.*] Cassava-nova, yeah, cassava-nova! Breathe a word of this to anybody and you know what you will get, you hear me, boy. Don't forget. [GEORGE *picks up a couple of imaginary stones and throws them after* LEN. *The action freezes momentarily.* GEORGE *removes his red school cap, gives it to*

MARGARET, *who takes it and exit Up Left. The lights come up.* LEN *returns to the stage, dressed as he was before the flashback.*]

MAMA: [*Spinning and charging* GEORGE *with her handbag*] You wicked evil wretch!

GEORGE: What the ...

LEN: Mama! [*Going after her.*]

MAMA: A have to wash mi hand in him blood. [PA BEN *and* LEN *try to restrain her.*] Let me go! Make A kill him!

LEN: All right, Mama.

PA BEN: Miss G.

[GEORGE *escapes through the Up Right door.*]

MAMA: I have to kill him! [*They take away the handbag.*] No, don't make me go to mi grave with mi soul in torment, Lawd, mi spirit in bondage. I have to atone for mi sins. I have to cleanse mi soul. Oh Len, how I going to sleep tonight? How I will sleep ever again? Oh Len, Len, forgive me, please, forgive me.

LEN: Mama, the story is not finished yet.

MAMA: No. I don't want to hear any more.

LEN: I ran away from school that night and stayed away for a week.

MAMA: But you didn't come home?

LEN: No, I didn't.

MAMA: Where you went?

LEN: A good Samaritan and his daughter took care of me till I could go back to school.

MAMA: Who are these people? They living?

LEN: Her father is dead, Mama.

MAMA: Heaven rest his soul! I have to find the daughter to thank her.

LEN: I married her, Mama. [*Pause.*] She was good to me, and I love her.

[MAMA *looks at* LOIS, *and as if hit by a bullet she immediately begins to lose control of mind and body. She tries to escape Down Left.*]

85

MAMA: Help me, oh Lord! Give me the strength to do what I have to do before the sun go down! [*They all four look at the setting sun.*] Miss Lois, I am not begging forgiveness. Just take care of mi son, is all I ask.

LOIS: Miss Aggy!

MAMA: Oh daughter! Child! [*They hug each other.*] The time is going. Pa Ben? [*As she goes to him.*]

PA BEN: Yes, Miss Aggy.

MAMA: A could never have had a better friend, you know.

PA BEN: No. I let you down.

MAMA: No, you tried with me. I took mi chances. I knew the consequences. I do it to miself.

PA BEN: Yes, no, Miss Aggy. [*Deeply overcome with emotion.*]

MAMA: Len, son, I am a foolish old woman.

LEN: No, Mama.

MAMA: Take care o' Miss Lois and find a little happiness for yourself. You hear me.

LEN: Yes, Mama. I love you, Mama.

MAMA: Aye, mi son, let me go. I don't want night to catch me on the road. [*She is going.*] It is going to be a long night.

LOIS: [*Barring the door.*] 'The Lord is my shepherd.'

MAMA: Stop it. [*Turning fast.*]

LOIS: 'I shall not want.'

MAMA: No. No, don't do it. Don't endanger yourself. Pa Ben, warn her, tell her.

PA BEN: Miss Lois!

LOIS: I know the risks.

MAMA: No. Not for me, Miss Lois.

PA BEN: If you willing for a fight, I willing to fight with you.

MAMA: Not for me. Len!

LEN: We need you, Mama.

[*As* MAMA *tries to escape they encircle her. Their hands come together and* MAMA *is trapped in the circle.*]

MAMA: No, no, don't do this to yourselves. No, no!

PA BEN, LEN, LOIS: [*Break into the chant*] Omia n Twi. Mia Kuru. Omia n ani.

[MAMA *screams, wrenched with pain, as the prayer for her deliverance from the evil spirits continues.*]

PA BEN: Omia n Twi. Mia Kuru. Omia n ani.

[*After some time* PA BEN *leaves the circle and goes towards the audience.*]

All night long we pray. We pray for strength in this the vigil of the long night. We bind ourselves together with strength and trust and confidence, and there was no doubt between us, no enmity in our hearts, for we knew that the one force that could counteract all evil was there, and that force was love.

[*All during the above speech* LEN *and* LOIS *hold on to* MAMA *as they repeat the twenty-third psalm. There is a note of real urgency and desperation in the prayer. The struggle goes on for a little while longer, then it quietens, and in the gentlest voice* MAMA *sings* 'Omia n Twi'. *There is a silence as the circle is bathed with a warm rich light.*]

MAMA: My children, my children. [*As she hugs* LEN *and* LOIS.]

PA BEN: [*Sitting in his chair*] A tell you, every time A see the three of them together as a family, the feeling just well up inside, and the eye water ... [*He starts to cry in his joyfulness. He gets up, overcome with emotion, and goes towards his little house. He stops by the doorway, then he turns, looks at the family, and smiles.*] All well. [*The lights go down slowly.*]

School's Out

School's Out

Performed for the first time at the Barn Theatre, Kingston, Jamaica on 3 April 1975 with the following cast:

RUSS DACRES	– Trevor Rhone
MICA MCADAM	– Pauline Cowan-Kerr
MR JOSEPHS (JOE)	– Vin McKie
HOPAL HENDRY	– Vernon Derby
	– Teddy Price
PATRICK CAMPBELL	– Robert Kerr
REV. STEELE (CHAPLAIN)	– Calvin Foster
ROSCO CALLENDER	– Oliver Samuels

Directed by Yvonne Jones-Brewster

The Setting

Peeling dirty walls, old books, dog-eared examination papers, defaced maps, piles of rubbish, used milk cartons, empty soft drink bottles with bent-over straws, etc., suggest a cluttered, decaying, dilapidated staff-room.

Up Right an exit leads to classrooms, laboratories, etc. Dominating the set directly Up Centre is a door that leads to the bathroom.

Down Left another exit leads to the car park, the canteen, etc. Down Right, preferably on a lower level, an imposing door reads 'HEADMASTER'. This door is never opened.

Up Left Centre is a small desk with two chairs facing each other on a platform. MR JOSEPHS sits Left. HOPAL HENDRY Right. MR JOSEPHS' old guitar hangs on a nail within his reach.

Down Left above the exit an old broken-down piece of furniture serves as ROSCO's desk. He has no chair.

A long table that seats four dominates Centre Stage running from left to right. THE CHAPLAIN sits Left facing across Right. PAT CAMPBELL sits on his right facing out. Next to PAT CAMPBELL is MICA MCADAM, also facing out. The fourth chair right of MICA will later be taken by RUSS DACRES.

At Stage Right is an old couch. On the wall directly above is the staff room clock.

Up Right in line with the exit is a bookcase with chalk box, attendance registers, etc.

The Characters

RUSS DACRES idealistic, energetic, compassionate; but also pushy, self-righteously eager to assume the role abdicated by the ever-absent headmaster.

HOPAL HENDRY young, unsure, half-educated, ungrammatical, conspicuously under-qualified to teach.

THE CHAPLAIN vain, lecherous, lazy.

MR JOSEPHS (JOE) the most senior member of the staff, he has been at the school for over 20 years. He's an old failure much given to the sardonic, an aging conservative bemoaning the creeping egalitarianism of our times.

ROSCO CALLENDER intelligent, but has taken to playing games.

PAT CAMPBELL an expatriate.

MICA MCADAM young, very attractive, emotionally fickle.

The language of the characters

MICA, PAT, RUSS, JOE and the CHAPLAIN speak a fairly standard English.

ROSCO uses dialect for effect.

HENDRY attempts to speak the language, but invariably adds an 'h' to words beginning with a vowel, omits it when it is there, and often replaces the 'th' sound with a 'd'.

HENDRY and ROSCO speak dialect much of the time. I have tried to write their speech in such a way that the text may be easily understood by people accustomed to reading Standard English. But the reader or actor is at liberty to articulate in the idiom peculiar to his particular country, provided that the meaning remains intact.

ACT ONE

SCENE ONE

[*Lights up to reveal the new teacher,* RUSS DACRES, *knocking on the Headmaster's door.* MICA MCADAM *is entering the staff-room from Down Left when she sees* RUSS.]

MICA: Hi. Good morning. [*Very warm and friendly.*]

RUSS: Good morning. I wonder if you could help me.

MICA: I'll try.

RUSS: I am supposed to be joining the staff and I've been trying to find the Headmaster, but he doesn't seem to be in.

MICA: He may be by the general office. It's down to your right, left by the brown building, then ... Tell you what, let me take you.

RUSS: Thank you. [*As they are leaving together,* RUSS *is affected by the smell from the overflowing bathroom.*]

MICA: Do excuse the smell. It should have been fixed weeks ago. [*They go out.*]

[*Lights up on* MR JOSEPHS (JOE) *playing his guitar in the staff-room. He too is bothered by the smell. He sprays air freshener towards the bathroom and continues playing his* 'Monday Morning Blues'. HOPAL HENDRY *enters from Up Right and goes directly to his desk.*]

HENDRY: Solicitations on this lovely Monday morning, Mr Josephs. [JOE *pretends not to hear him.*] Mr Josephs!

JOE: Ahm, oh Mr Hendry!

HENDRY: Solicitations on this lovely Monday morning. [JOE *sniffs.*] I see the smell is still smelling strong. [MICA *enters.*] Solicitations to you on this lovely Monday morning, Miss McAdam.

MICA: Yuk!

HENDRY: The smell, eh? One would have thought that

95

after three weeks something would have been done about it.

MICA: Salutations, Mr Josephs.

JOE: [*Laughs*] Good morning, Miss McAdam.

HENDRY: Oh, that is the time? I thought it was later. Never thought I would get here on time, what with all the terrible traffics. The squeeze I squeeze to get on the bus I mashed a lady on her toe who got ignorant and voilent and started to trace me, you see?

MICA: My lungs cannot face another week of this stench.

HENDRY: The smell on the bus was worse than the one we have here in this staff-room. Something really has to be done to effect improvement of conditions in school, to facilitate better learning environments for the children and staff alike. Some of the conditions are really shacking. Don't you think so too, Mr Josephs?

JOE: Yes, yes. Shacking! [*Imitating* HENDRY's *speech.*]

MICA: Things have come to a sorry state, haven't they, Mr Josephs?

JOE: Indeed, my dear.

HENDRY: [*Sniffs*] Take my classroom, for example. It is not spacious enough to accommodate the forty-two pairs of desks and chairs, and, even so, some of my students have no place to sit. The cleaners never clean the place. Mind you, I do think most of the children are happier here in this stench than the one they wallow in in their own environments.

JOE: 'But 'tis a common proof that lowliness is young ambition's ladder' etc., etc., etc.

MICA: 'Looks in the clouds, scorning the base degrees.'

HENDRY: That is exactly what I mean. [JOE *and* MICA *look at each other, not believing his ignorance.*] The rush I rush this morning I leave my tea. I will have to be careful that gas don't take up my stomach. Mind you, with the high gas price, maybe I could open mi own gas station! [*He laughs uproariously at his joke.*] That was a good joke, eh, Mr Josephs? Hilarious! [*No one laughs with him. In fact they are quite stony-faced.* HENDRY *realises that he is laughing on his own, so he quickly breaks off.*] Let me sign the register. I would hate the headmaster to think I was late.

PAT: [*Entering from Up Right*] Don't any teacher move; this is a smell-up! [*A handkerchief covers his face like a bandit.*]

MICA: Jesus Christ, Pat, it is not funny. I suggest we boycott classes till something is done about it. How do you feel about that, Mr Josephs?

JOE: Let me think about it.

MICA: Mr Hendry?

HENDRY: I too need to organise my mental status, weighing the cons and pros. This matter is, after all ...

CHAPLAIN: [*Entering*] Top of the world, fellow members of staff!

MICA: [*Aside to* PAT] Do we have to put up with that on a Monday morning?

HENDRY: Solicitations, Reverend. [*As he pulls out the* CHAPLAIN's *chair.*]

CHAPLAIN: Mr Hendry, good morning. I hope I find everybody well on this lovely Monday morning, fully rested from the vigours of the weekend and rearing to go, eh Miss McAdam? Mr Campbell? [*The* CHAPLAIN *laughs a little dirty laugh at* MICA *and* PAT, *who studiedly ignore him.*] I see the smell is no longer with us.

MICA: Jesus Christ!

CHAPLAIN: Mind over matter. Not a thing.

MICA: Yes. Well if the headmaster doesn't do something about it today ...

CHAPLAIN: My dear, don't quote me, but it is easier for a camel to go through the eyes of a needle than for one to get the headmaster to lift his little finger to do a single thing to effect the proper running of this school. Don't think I am being uncharitable. As a matter of fact, I know you share my views.

PAT: I am for the boycott, Mica.

CHAPLAIN: [*To* MICA] My dear, I must say you're looking

very charming. Pretty dress, pretty dress. [*He touches her.*] What's this material? Lovely, lovely! You don't mind do you, Mr Campbell?

MICA: Cheesecloth.

CHAPLAIN: Yes, I do recognise it. I'm a man of the cloth, after all. Cheesecloth, eh? Watch out for mice.

MICA: I hate rats.

ROSCO: [*Entering, with a gas-mask over his face, and carrying a small plastic bag with books, etc.*] Peace, love, and justice. I come prepared for the smell today.

MICA: From the sublime to the ridiculous.

ROSCO: You like it, Bishop?

CHAPLAIN: It looks good on you. Wear it more often, it improves your image.

ROSCO: Think what it could do for you, Bishop.

CHAPLAIN: Mr Callender, why are always testing my faith? What's this new thing you've taken up, calling me Bishop? I am not flattered. I have no ambitions in that direction.

ROSCO: [*Removing gas-mask*] Boy, the place smell bad!

MICA: Exactly. We have to make a protest. No classes 'til the smell goes. You with us, Mr Callender?

ROSCO: Sure, but I question if there are not more pressing matters that we should protest about.

CHAPLAIN: Hear, hear!

ROSCO: For example, the question of salaries.

HENDRY: Hear, hear!

MICA: It always comes back to that.

ROSCO: The smell don't really bother me. That is minor when you relate it to my total financial distress. Another hundred dollars a month in my pay cheque will make this smell smell like eau de Cologne.

PAT: Come now, Mr Callender, some of us really don't expect to get more money for the amount of work we put in. Some of us are absent more often than we're here.

ROSCO: I know you wouldn't complain or sign a deputation about salaries.

PAT: I can't. I am an expatriate. I'm on contract.

ROSCO: And contracted to get more than me, eh Mr Hendry?

MICA: Naturally, Mr Callender. Pat is a superior teacher, a superior man.

ROSCO: Ah, white is beautiful. Same thing A tell you Mr Hendry. White is beautiful.

CHAPLAIN: Fellow teachers, fellow teachers! [*As he tries to keep the peace.*]

ROSCO: That is the stink we should protest about, Mr Campbell, nothing personal. You don't think so, Bishop?

CHAPLAIN: These are decisions of policy made by the Board and Ministry.

ROSCO: The Board, Bishop? That's the biggest stink of all! Those men don't care about education, Bishop. They climbing the political ladder to glory road – a little pay-off from the party – their own little bit of power. That stink affects the pocket and the intellect. I will sign a deputation to the Prime Minister to get politics out of education. I say get rid of the headmaster. Now, there is an odour! Give me the job, with Bishop as Assistant Head.

CHAPLAIN: Thanks, Mr Callender, but I have no ambitions in that direction either.

ROSCO: Okay, Bishop, you be the Head and I be the assistant.

CHAPLAIN: No thank you, Mr Callender.

ROSCO: You are after bigger stakes, eh Bishop? Like a seat in the senate on the right hand of God.

CHAPLAIN: Mr Callender, you are incorrigible!

ROSCO: Don't forget me, Bishop, when you get into your kingdom. So now, who's going to sign my deputation about salaries? [*The bell goes.* HENDRY *jumps up, picks up a register, and is leaving.*] Mark mine for me, or give it to my head boy. [ROSCO *tosses the register at* HENDRY *who catches it and goes out.*]

PAT: [*Searching around on the table*] Where is my blasted

register? Why I had to get a form master's job, I don't know. The bloody students hate me and I hate them.

ROSCO: Hey, Joe, you see some test papers about the place? [JOE *shakes his head.*] I have to get out some marks for the headmaster this morning and I just can't find the papers.

PAT: Ah, here it is. Bloody hell! It's not bloody bleeding it. Doesn't this belong to what's his name, Hendry? So it is. 2C. Ten chances to one, he's marking his form with my register. Where do I find 2C?

MICA: Upstairs.

PAT: [*He thinks about it.*] I am not climbing those stairs. [*He relaxes in the couch, hiding* HENDRY's *register under the seat.*]

ROSCO: I am tired of how the headmaster hound me for the marks. Where I could put the test papers? I wonder if I leave them down at that girl house.

[*He intrudes on* MICA's *space, and is busy searching among her things. His behaviour is slightly raucous and overbearing, all done deliberately to annoy her. Whether by accident or design, he touches her in a fairly sensitive spot.*]

MICA: Now look here, you! [*In a rage she is up and out of her chair.*] How the hell did you ever get into a school to teach, like all the rest of you! What am I doing here, in a place like this?

PAT: What you upsetting yourself for, girl?

MICA: But Pat, did you ever see such spineless, vulgar, good for nothing ...

PAT: Okay, okay.

MICA: This place gives me the creeps. CREEPS, like bloody stupid Hopal Hendry! Give him time and he'll be the headmaster. And that other slug, can't somebody knot a guitar string around his neck?

PAT: [*who has sat in something rather wet*] Oh no, my, good clean pants!

MICA: Filth! They live in it. Ask them to do something about it and ...

PAT: Don't cast your pearls before swine, to quote the almighty vicar.

HENDRY: [*Enters*] I seem to have picked up the wrong register.

PAT: [*Extending his hand for the register*] Thank you. [*He goes out, as* HENDRY *starts looking around for* 2C*'s register.*]

[*The bell goes.*]

CHAPLAIN: Assembly calls. Coming, Miss McAdam?

MICA: I don't believe in God.

CHAPLAIN: [*Looking her up and down in a most lecherous manner*] I would love to save your soul.

MICA: I bet you would. Excuse me. [*Exit* MICA *outside for a breath of fresh air. The* CHAPLAIN *watches her go. His thoughts are very obvious. As she is out of sight, he turns and goes out to the chapel.*]

ROSCO: Mr Hendry, help me to look for mi test papers.

HENDRY: I am trying to locate my register.

ROSCO: I will help you look. [*As he sits in the couch,* HENDRY *searches, while* JOE *plays his song, getting more and more up tempo in* JOE*'s bad blues fashion.* ROSCO *watches* JOE *and appears to be moved by the music.*] Heavy, man. Heavy. You going to record that one? [JOE *shrugs, his body saying* 'Maybe, maybe not'.] That sort of music don't sell. You have to try it with a reggae beat. Titillate the people. [ROSCO *does a reggae beat to which* HENDRY *reacts.*] Look on Hendry, look how it move him.

HENDRY: It nice. [*As he dances.*]

ROSCO: Reggae is a big seller.

[JOE *sniffs, not at the smell, but at* ROSCO*'s ideas.*] That is your problem, you are a snob. If you want to make money [*taking the music sheet from* JOE] then all these lyrics will have to change. [ROSCO *reads the lyrics in a very British manner, almost an imitation of* JOE*'s speech.*] 'Same old day, going the same old way'. No, no, no, that

101

should be 'Same same day, going di same same way, yeah'. [*He reverts to standard English.*] 'Same old me in the same old bed'. Listen to this version. 'See mi yah, see mi yah in a di same ol' bed, not a ting, not a ting in a mi 'ead'. That's how you have to sing it. [JOE *snatches the music sheet away from* ROSCO.] The School of Music messing up your head, Joe. Black man born to beat drum. [ROSCO *beats out a rhythm on* JOE'*s desk.* HENDRY *joins in.*] All them concertos I hear you singing [ROSCO *imitates a fat Italian singer*], no money in that for you. Try it reggae. [JOE, *tired of the interruption, packs his guitar away.*]

JOE: This is a blues. Monday morning blues. It's an expression of my soul. I feel blue.

ROSCO: You feel blue? Boy, you don't look it. To my mind you look wash-out, and if that is the case, then you should call the song 'Monday Morning Wash-out'. If you personally feel blue, don't take it out on the song, take it out on the students. What you think they come here for? I don't understand you, Joe. You have a mental block against the true sounds. Stop writing the tune as a sonata in G for strings. I bet you don't have a single reggae record in your house?

JOE: You have any?

ROSCO: I look like I could afford to buy record?

JOE: Neither can I.

ROSCO: You have 'Back' and 'Choppin'', though. Waste my time talking to you, all the same. Any luck, Mr Hendry?

HENDRY: No, not yet.

[ROSCO *puts the clock back five minutes, and then sees a packet of cigarettes sticking out of* HENDRY'*s pocket. With deft fingers* ROSCO *removes the cigarettes.*]

ROSCO: I see you start to buy my brand. [*As he puts a cigarette in his mouth he sticks it out for* HENDRY *to light.* HENDRY *strikes a match and lights the cigarette, but not before* ROSCO *shifts the cigarette around in his mouth, making it as difficult as possible for* HENDRY. *When the cigarette is lit,* ROSCO *blows the smoke in* HENDRY's *face.* ROSCO *pockets the pack, ignoring* HENDRY's *protests.*] Now keep looking for the test papers.

HENDRY: If I had some notion where you might have left them.

ROSCO: How I must know that, Mr Hendry? [ROSCO *finds an old exercise book on the table.*] Hey, look! This exercise book, from Queen Victoria times. Mr Josephs, you better take it.

HENDRY: [*Finding the test papers*] Mister Rosco, is these they?

ROSCO: Them, yes. Cool. Tell you what you do now, help me mark them.

HENDRY: I have to go to assembly.

ROSCO: Forget that, man. Just call out the names for me. Where is mi chair? [*Hiss, as he looks around for it.*] Let me just t'ief the old man's chair, you hear. Where him is? Him gone to assembly or what?

HENDRY: He departed on Friday last.

ROSCO: Him dead?

HENDRY: No, he immigrated to Canada.

ROSCO: To do what? To go dead?

HENDRY: No, he gone to take up a teaching position.

ROSCO: The old man? Joe, is true what Missa Hendry say?

JOE: So it is said.

ROSCO: Him can't do dat. Is not one or two times I sit down here and look across on him and say to myself, 'Rosco boy, is no way you stay here and become like him'. All the time he sit down there quiet-like, him was planning to leave the place. Him must be don't know how Canada cold. They will use him balls to play ice hockey. The man gone and leave me him chair. When Missa Hendry tell me he departed, I was about to push mi hand in mi pocket to contribute towards the wreath. I don't want him chair. I will stand up. Missa Hendry, call out the names and I will work out a mark.

HENDRY: Abrahams, H.

ROSCO: Abrahams. Abrahams. Who is Abrahams? Oh, dat boy! Write down 50. No, dat's too much, make it 45. Hold on, when the headmaster see all dem low marks, him will say me not teaching the boys a thing. Make it 60, you hear, sar.

HENDRY: Brown. Well, I think this one is nought.

ROSCO: Which Brown? White Brown or black Brown?

HENDRY: P. Brown – nought.

ROSCO: How you mean nought?

HENDRY: Di boy didn't do di test, just name and subject.

ROSCO: Oh, is dat Brown! Boy, I have to give him 50.

HENDRY: But the boy didn't do the test.

ROSCO: Master, is two tyres I lose last month, and I know is that boy Brown responsible. You see the same test here, Joe. Is borrow the boy borrow a pen to write him name, and when I go to collect the test papers, you know what the boy did? Pull out a ratchet knife an' start to clean him finger nails, an' all the while him looking me up an' down. Boy, come to think about it, I wonder if 50 is really enough. Sixty-five look more reasonable.

JOE: You should have reported the boy.

ROSCO: You report him. Don't you have a car too? I don't see a thing on this scene to risk my neck for. Give me them, Mr Hendry. Go to chapel. [*Exit* HENDRY. ROSCO *looks at the test papers.*] This boy is an idiot. Thirty. No, 40. No, 30. Him is an idiot, even the Headmaster know that. The Headmaster wants marks, and marks he will get. [*He puts the marks down at a furious pace. In the background, the* CHAPLAIN *can be heard preaching.*]

CHAPLAIN: Today's lesson is about the ten virgins. Five were wise and five were foolish, but let me remind the girls of this school that they were all virgins.

ROSCO: Assembly still in progress. Good. One thing about the Chaplain, him can preach. Hey, Joe, I still can't get over how the old man gone. Is three men leave on staff now.

JOE: How you get three?

ROSCO: You, me, Chaplain and Hendry count as one, half each. The expatriate I don't count at all, and the Headmaster ... well, the least said, the better. Three men, and the one woman, she look like an adjectival clause, behave like a past participle, but she is really a common noun. [JOE *sniffs.*] Exactly. [*The bell goes.*] What's that? Assembly over, and I don't finish marking the papers yet. [*He puts the clock forward ten minutes.* MICA *enters to prepare for her class.*] Hey, Joe, what I said about the adjectival clause? Take a good look. [*He laughs.*]

[HENDRY *enters quickly, collects his books, etc. to go off to his class.*]

MICA: Is there any chalk?

ROSCO: My hands are allergic to it, so I don't use it. Where is 4C, Joe?

JOE: I don't teach them.

MICA: Mr Hendry, do you know if there is any chalk?

HENDRY: Look in that box. [HENDRY *is on his way out, as* MICA *looks in the box and screams.* HENDRY *rushes back to the staff-room.*] What happen? What was that noise? [JOE *and* ROSCO *ask* 'What happened?']

MICA: It's a mouse! [*As she climbs atop the nearest chair.* HENDRY, *hearing it's a mouse, begins to look very uneasy; quietly he sidles away from the bookcase.*]

ROSCO: Where?

MICA: In the box.

ROSCO: [*At the bookcase,* ROSCO *pretends to trap the mouse in the box.*] A little mouse can't do you anything.
[MICA, *seeing* ROSCO *with the box, climbs atop the table.* HENDRY *too is now looking quite scared.*] What's the matter, Mr Hendry, you afraid of him too?

[*As* ROSCO *threatens to throw the box at him.* HENDRY *panics and runs away from* ROSCO.]

HENDRY: No, man, me not afraid of them. [ROSCO *throws the box at* HENDRY.]

ROSCO: See him on the chair leg, Mr Hendry. [HENDRY *joins* MICA *on top of the table*.] See him under the exercise book. [ROSCO *searches among the books on the table for the imaginary mouse*.] Aye, catch it! [*His hands are carefully masked, so* MICA *and* HENDRY *are quite convinced that he's caught it*.] Mr Hendry, a big man like you! [MICA *is getting very hysterical*.]

HENDRY: I just don't like them.

ROSCO: What I must do with it, eh?

MICA: Throw it outside, please. Please.

HENDRY: Yes, yes. Dash it away, man.

ROSCO: You want to bet A just ... [*threatens to throw it at* HENDRY.]

HENDRY: Don't do that, man.

ROSCO: What about you, Miss McAdam? [*Edges up to* MICA.]

MICA: I'll kill you! I'll kill you!

ROSCO: All right.

[*As he throws the imaginary mouse at her.* MICA *screams, brushing away the mouse and becoming totally hysterical.*]

HENDRY: Jesus Christ! [*As he leaps from the table onto the couch.*]

PAT: What's going on here?

[ROSS DACRES, *attracted by the screams, runs into the staff room. He stands there transfixed.*]

MICA: I am going to get you! You son of a bitch! [*She picks up a large compass.*]

PAT: Mica!

MICA: Get out of my way, Pat!

PAT: Come, be sensible. Give me the compass. Come on. [*She faints.*] Catch her somebody, quick.

[ROSS DACRES *runs around fast, and along with* JOE, ROSCO *and* PAT, *they catch her in mid-air.*]

PAT: [*To* HENDRY] Get off there. Clear the table. Make some space. [*Just about everything on the table is swept to the floor. Then* MICA *is put down very gently.*] Smelling salts!

ROSCO: Where is the first aid box, Joe?

PAT: I have never seen one.

JOE: There was one here some years ago.

PAT: [*To* HENDRY] Wet this. [*He gives his handkerchief to* HENDRY.]

JOE: Here it is. It's empty.

HENDRY: There is no water in the bathroom.

PAT: Brandy, rum, anything!

ROSCO: Yeah, I have a bottle. [*Getting it quickly from his desk, he opens it and gives it to* PAT *who wets* MICA's *face with it. There is no response.* RUSS, *all this time, is fanning away at* MICA.] She coming to?

PAT: No. Get me a glass of water.

ROSCO: Missa Hendry! [HENDRY *picks up a glass and dashes out, only to collide with the* CHAPLAIN.]

CHAPLAIN: Mr Hendry, what in heaven's name is going on in here?

HENDRY: Is Miss McAdam, Chaplain. She faint away.

[*The* CHAPLAIN *goes quickly to the prostrate* MISS MCADAM. *The sight is almost too much for him, but he controls himself.*]

CHAPLAIN: She needs air. Open all the windows. Let me feel her pulse. Good, pulse is there. Heartbeat? [*He feels her breast.*] Heartbeat is there. Has anybody called a doctor? [*To* RUSS] Are you a doctor?

RUSS: No. I am the new member of staff.

CHAPLAIN: Get a doctor and I'll say a prayer. Mr Campbell, get on the phone. This is an emergency.

ROSCO: The phone's not working.

CHAPLAIN: Oh Lord, look down from heaven, behold, visit, and relieve this Thy servant. Look upon her with the eyes of Thy mercy.

HENDRY: [*Re-entering with the water*] The Bishop is coming.

PAT: Christ! Not now. He's never been in here before.

ROSCO: Head him off, Mr Hendry.

CHAPLAIN: Find some excuse.

ROSCO: Just don't let him come in here. Quick!

CHAPLAIN: Spare us the complications, O Lord, and let Mr Hendry be successful in his mission. How is she?

PAT: The same.

CHAPLAIN: There is just one thing else we can try.

PAT: What?

CHAPLAIN: Mouth-to-mouth resuscitation.

PAT: I don't know …

CHAPLAIN: If I can remember my first aid. Pull her blouse. Pull her blouse, man. This is an emergency! Excuse me. [*He pulls her buttons.*] Close your eyes, everybody. If it wasn't an emergency I wouldn't go this far. [*He is awed by her young body. He takes off his collar and sets it on her, then unbuttons his shirt.*] So young. [*Slowly his lips descend on hers. She wakes before he kisses her. She slaps him.*]

MICA: What the hell! Where am I? Oh my God, what's happening? [*As she discovers her clothes in disarray.*]

CHAPLAIN: It's okay, my dear. We give God thanks. [*The* CHAPLAIN *rescues his collar from between her legs.*]

MICA: Rape! Rape! [*As she feels his hands on her body.*]

CHAPLAIN: [*Clamps his hands over her mouth.*] Shut up! Aaiee! My finger. The little bit … she bit me.

MICA: Rape! [*As she gets off the table.*]

PAT: Mica, love, it's me – Pat.

MICA: Why didn't you stop him?

CHAPLAIN: Don't be ridiculous. Will somebody explain?

MICA: Where is the Headmaster?

PAT: Don't you remember? You fainted.

MICA: Fainted?

CHAPLAIN: Yes. For one moment I thought you were dead, you were so warm.

MICA: The day you ever try that again, Mr Callender!

ROSCO: Try what again? I was playing a little joke with Mr Hendry. [HENDRY *returns.*] Mr Hendry, I trouble her? [*Shaking his head at him.*]

HENDRY: No. You never trouble her.

ROSCO: I wouldn't be running no joke with you.

CHAPLAIN: Fellow teachers, finish it off. [MICA *goes to the bathroom to freshen up.*] Our new member mustn't get the wrong impression. We haven't met officially. Reverend Steele, with two E's.

RUSS: Russ Dacres.

CHAPLAIN: My pleasure, pleased. I hope your stay here will be rewarding and fruitful. Let me introduce you.

PAT: Patrick Campbell. [*Extending his hand.*]

CHAPLAIN: One of our stalwarts. Mr Josephs [JOE *does not shake hands with* RUSS, *but holds his hand up in acknowledgement as he goes out.* HENDRY, *who has been picking up the books, etc., from the floor, now positions himself to be introduced.*], our rock of Gibralter. Been with us for twenty years. [*The* CHAPLAIN *notices* HENDRY'*s antics.*] And Mr Hendry, one of our, ahm, promising young educationalists.

HENDRY: I am pleased to make your acquaintance. [*Hanging on to* RUSS'*s hand. The* CHAPLAIN *breaks the handshake, and tries to push* HENDRY *into the background.*]

CHAPLAIN: Mr Callender.

ROSCO: [*Dashing off the rest of his marks, looks up but does not stop what he is doing.*] Sorry about the first impression, but I don't dig no black woman who only dig white man [*very loudly*]. It's a personal insult to me, my race, my manhood.

CHAPLAIN: [*As* MICA *enters from bathroom*] Ah, and last but not least, Miss McAdam, our rose among thorns. [MICA *nods to* RUSS, *collects her books and she and* PAT *go out.*]

ROSCO: [*As they leave*] Hypocrite! That girl feel herself superior to every black man in this staff-room.

CHAPLAIN: It's a nice place to work in, really.

ROSCO: She go to some university in North America and feel she is some sort of intellectual. As far as I'm concerned, the only genuine intellectual on this staff is me.

CHAPLAIN: We are a happy family, really.

ROSCO: She don't like me, because I speak so badly. Did

you ever hear such assininity? I can use the Queen's English if I so desire, but to me it is no more than an acquisition by the black bourgeois to create barriers and underline the status quo. [*A boy knocks and enters.*] What you want, boy?

BOY: You have us now, sir.

ROSCO: I don't have you now. What form?

BOY: 4C, sir.

ROSCO: Get back to your class. [*The boy hesitates.*] Move, boy!

RUSS: Any idea where I might find the Headmaster?

ROSCO: Boy, I haven't seen him for a month. The man is a hustler. A little politics, a little real estate, a little vegetable garden.

CHAPLAIN: Mr Callender, shame. Ahm, try the canteen. The lady who runs it is very interesting – a divorcee – great favourite with the male members of staff. The Head loves her … er … cooking. Mr Callender never misses a meal. Check the canteen. I'll walk over with you.

[RUSS *looks around for his bag, while the* CHAPLAIN *collects his bible, etc.* ROSCO *gets* HENDRY *quietly into a corner.*]

ROSCO: Hey, not a word to the parson about the mouse.

HENDRY: My lips are seal.

ROSCO: Cool. [*Then sings*]   Hickory dickory dock,
The mouse ran up her frock,
Oh what a shock the mousie got,
Hickory dickory dock!

[*He and* HENDRY *go off to class.*]

CHAPLAIN: [*As he watches them go*] It's a nice place to work in really, apart from the odd gossip, the occasional intrigue, the little undercurrents, that sort of thing, plus there is a fair amount of backbiting, su-su. Good staff. A few bad eggs, naturally, some of them not to be trusted; one or two of them, pathetic. And the things I see some of them wearing to work! Imagine – no bra! Don't ask me how I know these things, but I know. It's not fair ... ahm ... to the boys. Temptation, man, temptation. No wonder there is a breakdown of discipline. The Headmaster does his best, but he's a little bit insecure, nervous. A political appointment, they say. People say all sorts of things about him. Sex maniac, interferes with little girls or some such, most uncharitable, rumours. He is a good churchman. After you. [*The lights go down as they go off.*]

ACT ONE

SCENE TWO

[*The lights come up on* JOE *in his space and* ROSCO *half asleep on the couch.* PAT *and* RUSS *enter the staff-room from Down Left.*]

PAT: The place is as you see it, the staff as you saw them, a bunch of bloody clowns, with one or two exceptions. The students, semi-literate mostly. The smell, it grows on you, conversation piece. Things are bad but we get by. Expect nothing, avoid disappointment. Things won't change, not with jokers around like … Let's not call names, but take a fellow like Callender. He should be banned from the classroom. Does more harm than good. He and the one they call the Chaplain, tongue like a female, mind like a gutter. Money-grubbing capitalistic sex-fiend, bound to go to Heaven.

CHAPLAIN: [*Entering*] Ah, Mr Campbell, I see you are taking good care of our latest addition. You are in good hands. So how is it going, Mr Dacres?

RUSS: Okay.

CHAPLAIN: No trouble with the students?

RUSS: None.

CHAPLAIN: You should have no problems if, like me, you don't spend fifteen minutes to settle your class, like some of the others. You just go in – bang, bang – get some order. If they fool, you run them out. Thirty, if need be. Teach the other five. Many are called, etc. etc. Gospel.

[*The bell goes.* DACRES *collects his things quickly and is on his way out as* MICA *enters. They smile at each other.* PAT *notices, so does* ROSCO.]

ROSCO: Boy, the new man anxious, eh? What a man can

move fast! Him will learn all the same. [*He looks directly at* PAT, *smiles mischievously, then picks up a table-tennis bat.* HENDRY *enters as* ROSCO *begins to play with an imaginary ping-pong ball, each shot giving him a great deal of pleasure. Synchronise his smash with the first stroke of the cane offstage.*]

CHAPLAIN: Ah, the Head. [*As he goes over towards the Headmaster's door.*] Whoever is getting it obviously deserves it. A good licking is like a good tonic. [*Whacking continues.*] Tones up the skin, repels the devils. Never spare the rod. Gospel. Rules are to be obeyed [*whack*]. Each student, boys and girls, should get at least six a week [*whack*]. They thrive on it. Break the law, you'll be punished. Break God's law, you know the consequences [*whack*]. Yes [*whack*]. Yes [*whack*]. Yes. Ahhh! [*Overcome with pleasure.*]

BLACK OUT

ACT ONE

SCENE THREE

[JOE, HENDRY *and* PAT *are in the staff-room.* ROSCO *enters from the bathroom.*]

ROSCO: Hey, Joe, inside that bathroom is definitely not right. I will have to start doing my things at my yard. [*Sniff.*] No paper, no soap, no nutten. What they expect a man to use? Plenty old exercise books about, all di same. Only trouble is dat so much crap on them already.
[*The bell goes and* HENDRY *rises.*]
Where you going?

HENDRY: The bell ring.

ROSCO: I never hear it. Sit down, man. The bell ring, Joe?

JOE: Not to my knowledge.

ROSCO: Sit down, man.

HENDRY: Yes, man, I 'eard it.

ROSCO: Leave me a cigarette. [*Taking* HENDRY'S *pack.*]

[*As* HENDRY *is leaving the* CHAPLAIN *comes on from Down Left.* RUSS DACRES *enters from Up Right with a first-aid kit, books, magazines, etc.* MICA *follows immediately with a tape recorder.*]

RUSS: Ahm, members of staff [*displays first-aid box*], a present for the school.

MICA: And a tape-recorder.

CHAPLAIN: Thoughtful man. Useful thing, eh, Mr Campbell? I have one or two things at home myself. Remind me to bring them in. Is that the time? I must dash. The Prime Minister wants to see me. Ah, Mr Dacres, I should be going to 5B now, but, ahm, could you take charge for me?

RUSS: What shall I do with them?

CHAPLAIN: Just keep them quiet. Thank you. [*Exit* CHAPLAIN. RUSS *prepares to go but* MICA *stops him.*]

MICA: The one day he is never away is pay day.

PAT: Mica. [*She does not respond.*]

MICA: Do it once and you're doing it every day.

PAT: Mica! [*Much louder.*]

MICA: Just a second. [*Without looking back at him.* PAT *is upset by her offhand manner. He leaves the staff room in a huff.*] Don't believe that P.M. rubbish. He's just using that. Self-righteous, power-crazy little bastard!

RUSS: I said I would, so see you at lunch-time. [*He goes.*]

MICA: Pat? Where did Mr Campbell go, Mr Josephs?

JOE: Is he in school today? I haven't seen him. [*Exit* MICA.]

ROSCO: [*laughs*] How you mean is the man in school, Joe? Him in school, yes, and it look like him in bad trouble. Yes man, look like Dacres moving in on the white man girl. [*He goes to the tape-recorder and picks it up.*] Nice. I would love a tape-recorder like this. Why Dacres bring it to school? The boys will t'ief it, you know. Him must be don't know di breed o' boys him dealing with. [*He puts the tape-recorder in his bag and away in his desk.*] I think I have a class, but where the hell is mi timetable? I left it here. The Sellotape is still here but the timetable gone. [*Hiss*] Boy Joe, mi head hurting me. I wonder if any Phensic in this thing. [*He picks up the first-aid kit.*] Hey, Joe, you want a pack? [*Throwing one to him, he pockets two himself.*] What a fat elastic! [*He holds up the rubber band and shows it to* JOE. *Then he starts making a paper shot, at the same time looking around for a fly to fire at. He sees one and quickly makes the rubber band into a sling.*] Watch me and that fly, Joe! [*He pursues it Vietnamese style. Each time he is set to fire, the fly escapes, till eventually it flies through the door.* ROSCO *fires after it, then he panics.*] Jesus Christ, Joe … A shoot the Headmaster!

BLACK OUT

ACT ONE

SCENE FOUR

[*Lights up on* ROSCO *and* JOE, *together sharing a form magazine. They read for a moment.*]

ROSCO: Is not a boy write this. No, sir. Nuances, licentious, dialectic. [ROSCO *walks away.*]

JOE: I think it's terrible. Apart from that one article which seems very verbose and pompous, the rest of it is sheer dialect nonsense. Better use could be found for the paper.

ROSCO: Not really, Joe. The thing have some merit.

[RUSS *enters the staff-room with a stack of form magazines.*]

RUSS: Mr Callender, you might like to see the first edition of 3A's form magazine.

ROSCO: Thank you, man. [*Accepting a copy.*]

RUSS: Mr Josephs. [*Handing him a copy.* JOE *hands him back the one he was reading.* RUSS *is aware of the snub, yet presses on.*] Ah, Chaplain [*as the* CHAPLAIN *enters*], a copy of 3A's form magazine.

CHAPLAIN: Thank you.

RUSS: Mr Campbell — [*As* PAT *enters. He offers him a copy.*]

PAT: [*very cuttingly*] I've seen it. [RUSS *puts a magazine in* MICA's *space, then goes up to* HENDRY's *desk. He is putting a magazine down, when an open book catches his eye. He examines it more closely.*]

RUSS: Jesus Christ! [HENDRY *enters and sees him with his book.* RUSS *senses* HENDRY, *and puts the book down.*] Ah, Mr Hendry, I was just leaving you a form magazine. [RUSS *turns away and goes out.* HENDRY *picks up the book, annoyed, looks after* RUSS, *then flicks the magazine off his desk.*]

CHAPLAIN: [*Who has been reading the funnies in the magazine*] It's a brave effort.

ROSCO: It's all right for a start, but I bet you never see it come out again. Hey, Joe, that Arts magazine you started some years ago, what was the name again? 'Vox'? No, 'Pox', Latin, nuh? Whatever became of it? The boys couldn't dig the classics.

[MICA *enters quickly with a magazine. She is very excited.*]

MICA: Seen the new 3A form magazine, Pat?

[PAT *looks at her, takes the magazine and crumples it very slowly and deliberately, then tosses it away, all the time looking directly at her. The others watch as the lights fade slowly.*]

ACT ONE

SCENE FIVE

[*All members of staff are present, awaiting the Headmaster to have a staff meeting. The* CHAPLAIN *sits in his space,* JOE *has brought his chair down to sit to the left of* PAT. MICA *is in her space beside* RUSS. HENDRY *is Up Stage and* ROSCO *sits atop* JOE's *table.*]

ROSCO: [*Singing in the darkness*] 'Why are we waiting? ... Oh why ...' [*The lights come up.*] So what time this staff meeting going to start? I don't understand the Headmaster, is the second time him call a staff meeting this term and him don't turn up. Is thirty minutes of my life gone down di drain.

CHAPLAIN: And I have a meeting at 3 o'clock. Prime Minister ... [*Mutters.*]

MICA: Waiting here like children. Totally irresponsible.

ROSCO: 'Why are we waiting. ...' etc. [*Sings.*]

PAT: He could at least send some message. [*Pause.*]

MICA: Common decency, that's what's lacking, common decency!

HENDRY: I hope he comes, cause there are one or two tings I have to say.

[*A little boy brings in a message.*]

CHAPLAIN: Out! 'Knowest thou that the ground on which thou walkest is hallowed ground?' Out of bounds! Out! [*The boy scampers away followed by the* CHAPLAIN.] What you want? [*The boy hands him the message. He reads it quickly.*] A message from the Head's secretary. The Headmaster regrets that he has been unavoidably delayed and cannot grace us with his presence. [ROSCO *gets off the table and begins to pack away his books, etc. The other members of staff, excluding* MICA *and* RUSS, *also start making a move to leave.*] He further requests that I deputise for him, so I would like to take this opportunity to remind all teachers that they are expected to attend the services on Sunday. There being no further business, meeting dismissed.

ROSCO: Nice.

[*All, except* MICA *and* RUSS, *are on their way out, when* RUSS *stops them.*]

RUSS: Ahm, Reverend Steele, with your permission, there are one or two things I would like to discuss.

CHAPLAIN: With the Head absent, I don't see much point. [*Again they make to go.*]

RUSS: First thing. This place that we have to work in is a mess. [*Indicates staff-room.*]

MICA: An awful mess.

RUSS: Can anything be done about it?

CHAPLAIN: Well, the Headmaster, you know, hires and fires the cleaning staff. If I was in charge of this place, all the pussy-footing that I see ...

ROSCO: What sort of footing, Bishop? [*Much laughter.*]

RUSS: Be that as it may, gentlemen, I don't think that any self-respecting teacher can work in a place like this.

MICA: Hear, hear. I've been saying that for months.

HENDRY: Can I express a little view?

CHAPLAIN: Yes, Mr Hendry.

HENDRY: They say that when you throw a stone in a pigsty, the one that bawl is him it hit. But I would like all teachers to cast their eyes over to where I sit. I hope you notice it is meticulous.

RUSS: I'm sorry if I offended you, Mr Henry, but ...

HENDRY: Hendry, if you don't mind.

russ: No offence meant, Mr Hendry, I am not being personal.

HENDRY: Why are you always picking on me?

RUSS: Me, Mr Hendry?

HENDRY: You 'tink I don't know that you been spying on me, and passing remarks behind my back?

RUSS: Mr Hendry, I don't understand.

HENDRY: Excuse me. [*As he grabs his books and makes a very dramatic exit. There is much laughter, making of faces, etc. from* ROSCO, PAT, JOE *and the* CHAPLAIN.]

RUSS: Oh, oh.

CHAPLAIN: I had no idea Mr Hendry was so sensitive.

RUSS: What was that all about? Maybe Mr Hendry's imagination is running away with him. However, what can we do about the staff-room? We are the ones who use the place.

MICA: Why don't we stay one afternoon and tidy it up?

RUSS: That is what I was about to suggest; thank you, Mica.

CHAPLAIN: Uh, yes. Those in favour, say Aye.
[MICA *and* RUSS *raise their hands, and say* 'Aye'.]
Those against?

PAT: Abstain.

ROSCO: Abstain.

CHAPLAIN: Mr Josephs?

JOE: Oh, abstain.

CHAPLAIN: I think it's a matter that has to be left up to each member of staff. Reasonable, Mr Dacres?

RUSS: Reasonable. [*Again they start to leave.*] Just one other thing. [ROSCO *looks at his watch.*] I won't be long. What is the position regarding teachers doing duty at the canteen? I'm not patting myself on the back, but I am the only person here who even bothers to check the duty roster and go to the canteen at lunch or break to try and maintain a little discipline.

ROSCO: But, Missa Dacres, you dealing with hooligans, you must expect hooliganism.

RUSS: That attitude is a reflection of this whole ...

ROSCO: Mr Dacres, let me ask you a question. I see you risking your neck in that mess they call a canteen. Things get any better since you start going down there? You achieve anything so far?

RUSS: Nothing.

ROSCO: It's a waste of time, right?

RUSS: Right.

ROSCO: Exactly.

RUSS: Exactly what?

ROSCO: Exactly why I never go down there. If you know you going down there to waste your time, why worry?

PAT: I did duty once, and I thought they were serving pork. It wasn't until some time later I realised they were referring to me. Plus one of them picked my wallet that first day. I am never going down there again.

CHAPLAIN: No, no, no! That is not the attitude at all. Members of staff should never neglect their duties.

ROSCO: It's all well and good for you to say that, Bishop, but I never see you down at the canteen yet.

CHAPLAIN: I'm not on the canteen duty roster.

ROSCO: I don't expect to see your name on it. After all, you make up the roster, but at least you could go down there and bless the soul food.

CHAPLAIN: Callender, you are being trivial and irresponsible. I disregard you.

ROSCO: Say what you want, Bishop. I come here to teach. I never come here as a policeman. Let Mr Dacres or the headmaster get two soldiers to man the place, for when that mob storm the raisin-bread counter, is tear gas alone can bring a little order. You people don't know the scene.

RUSS: I know the scene. The reason I can't get anything done down there is simple. No one else bothers to try, so when the boys see me alone down there, how do you think they regard me? As an oppressor. Until everybody on the staff is willing to co-operate, we are going to have this vicious circle. You say the boys are hooligans, and the boys will be hooligans because the staff won't attend duties.

PAT: This is a matter for the Headmaster. [*As he walks out.*]

CHAPLAIN: I think so too, Mr Dacres. This matter falls within his province. [*He goes.*]

ROSCO: Agreed, agreed. [*To* JOE, *sotto voce*] What the man trying to do? To take over the school. [*Loudly*] The Headmaster don't really care, and I follow the leader.

RUSS: That sort of attitude, Mr Callender, is killing this school. What we see wrong is most times what we contribute to, or what we ourselves could in fact stop. But no, we just walk back to the staff room, shrug our shoulders and blame it all on the Headmaster. Most of these things have nothing to do with the Head, but it is a nice way to rationalise away the fact that we are not accomplishing anything.

MICA: I agree with Russ, let us give it a try.

[*The bell goes. Exit* JOE.]

ROSCO: Wait for me, Brother Joe. [*To* MICA *and* RUSS] So that's it for today, folks, and remember if you can't be good, be careful. [*Exit, laughing.*]

PAT: [*Returns angrily*] Coming with me, Mica?

MICA: Yes. [*Exit* PAT. MICA *goes up to* RUSS, *touches him.*] Well, at least we tried. [*She leaves him and rushes out after* PAT. RUSS *is left alone. He looks around at the state of the room. Very determinedly he picks up a number of books and puts them away on the bookshelf, then he stands for a moment surveying the job ahead of him. He throws up his hands in the air despairingly.*]

END OF ACT ONE

122

ACT TWO

SCENE ONE

[*The stage is in darkness. The bell goes. The lights come up. It is lunch-time.* JOE *sits in his space.* MICA *reads a newspaper. Sound effects of* CHAPLAIN *trying to flush the lavatory. Whatever it is that needs flushing, won't.* HENDRY *enters, goes to his desk, puts his books down, and is going out again.*]

JOE: Mr Hendry, going to the canteen?
HENDRY: Yes.
JOE: Two patties and a pint of milk. [*Taking out money.*]
CHAPLAIN: [*Half appearing from bathroom*] A carton of cherry milk. [*Gives* HENDRY *money.*] Bathroom's a nuisance, just won't flush. [*He re-enters bathroom and closes the door as* PAT *enters.*]
PAT: Ah Mr Hendry, an orange juice and a cheese sandwich for me. Want anything, Miss McAdam? [*Very formal.*]
MICA: Orange juice.
PAT: Then it's two orange juices. Now, where is my newspaper? [*Looking directly at* MICA. *She hands it to him. He takes it and sits in the couch.*]
CHAPLAIN: [*Coming from bathroom*] Ah, Mr Campbell, Miss McAdam, what's new? Where is Mr Dacres? [*Chuckles.*] Bathroom's out of order, won't flush. I'd better put up a sign.

[ROSCO *enters as* CHAPLAIN *starts writing the* 'out of order' *sign.* HENDRY *is just finishing writing the orders in his palm.*]

ROSCO: Ah Mr Hendry, the usual: three coco breads, three patties and two pints of chocolate milk, and put it on mi bill, right? [*Exit* ROSCO *to the bathroom.*]
CHAPLAIN: Anybody seen the paste or some tacks?
ROSCO: [*Reappearing from the bathroom, goes to* JOE] Somebody

do a thing in that bathroom. I better go and tell Mr Hendry not to bother with the patties. Boy, I have to smoke a cigarette. [*Takes* JOE's *cigarette, pulls on it and gives it back to him.* CHAPLAIN *finds a tack, puts up his sign, goes for his lunch inside his briefcase.*] I am as hungry as hell, but I won't be able to eat those patties when they come.

CHAPLAIN: I would offer you a sandwich, but I know you don't eat pork.

ROSCO: It's against my spiritual religion, Bishop, same way I don't eat lobster, steak or caviar, as it's against my financial religion.

CHAPLAIN: Don't take out your frustrations on me, Mr Callender. If there's something you need that's missing from your life, 'ask and it shall be given unto you'.

ROSCO: Who I must ask, Bishop?

CHAPLAIN: God!

ROSCO: Oh, well, him don't like my face, or the way I talk, 'cause him never pay me any attention.

CHAPLAIN: Maybe because, like me, your faith is not strong enough.

ROSCO: Bishop, you're the luckiest man I know.

CHAPLAIN: It's not luck. I heard the word of God and I sought out God and that's how I got my faith.

ROSCO: Sounds reasonable, Bishop; but, Bishop, I don't know where to look.

CHAPLAIN: Didn't you hear about God when you were a little boy?

ROSCO: Sure, and I heard about Hitler, Mohammed, Mussolini.

CHAPLAIN: Mr Callender, I will pray for you.

ROSCO: No, thank you, sir. If your God is the type of God who would dismiss me so, then I prefer to go to hell.

CHAPLAIN: God is a good God, Mr Callender. Think of the rain, the flowers, the food we eat. Thank God for these things.

ROSCO: You don't thank God for the hurricane and the

earthquake, I am not thanking him for the sunshine. I don't understand you, Bishop. Last drought you prayed for rain, then a storm threatened, and you prayed for it to pass.

CHAPLAIN: And it did pass.

ROSCO: Sure it pass.

CHAPLAIN: The power of prayer, Mr Callender.

ROSCO: It pass here, but it smash into Cuba, and you go back to the church and thank God for His mercy. So what happen to the Cubans, Bishop? Don't tell me is because them is communist, and them wicked, I hear that argument from you already. You only pray for yourself. Tut, tut, tut, selfish, Bishop.

CHAPLAIN: The devil comes in many guises, Mr Callender, to test my faith, but I will pray for you in the hope that one day you will be able to do something worthwhile with your life, for now you are in the throes of darkness.

[*He looks around to see that* ROSCO *is now wearing a paper collar.*]

ROSCO: Hey, Joe, heard thou ever of the parable of a young lass who visited a certain physician, and complained thereof of an indisposition? And it came to pass that he [*pointing to the* CHAPLAIN] examined her and found that she was with child. Whereupon, the young virgin [*he bows to* MICA, PAT *sniggers*], for so she termed herself, was much alarmed, and cried, 'Impossible, for as yet I have known no man'. Hearing these words, the physician opened a window and gazed into the heavens, and many hours did he spend there a-gazing. And the young lass, on seeing this, was puzzled, and inquired of him, 'Why dost thou so gaze into the heavens?' And he replied, 'My good woman, the last time this phenomenon happened, a star rose in the East, and I am not going to miss it this time'. [ROSCO *and* PAT *laugh uproariously.*

MICA *chuckles. Even* JOE *manages a smile. The* CHAPLAIN *is stony-faced.*] And there is another one about a Bishop.

CHAPLAIN: We've heard that one before, Mr Callender.

PAT: I haven't.

CHAPLAIN: Don't encourage him, Mr Campbell. [HENDRY *enters empty-handed.*] So Mr Hendry, where is the lunch?

HENDRY: No lunch.

ROSCO: What you mean, no lunch? The canteen staff on strike again?

HENDRY: Is not a strike. Mr Dacres take it upon himself to lock down the canteen.

ROSCO: Lock it down! What you mean?

HENDRY: It was the usual situation where the students storm the place; so Mr Dacres say, if no line, no lunch. [*Non-verbal reaction from the rest of the staff.* JOE *stops playing; the* CHAPLAIN *stops chewing:* PAT *looks up from his paper;* MICA *listens keenly.*] They ignore him, so him lock the door, and is then the riot start. One boy broked a bottle and start to threaten Mr Dacres. [*Exit* MICA *quickly towards the canteen.*]

CHAPLAIN: This situation is becoming very interesting, eh Mr Campbell?

ROSCO: But line don't apply to you, Mr Hendry?

HENDRY: As a member of staff, I thought I had certain privileges so I bored my way through the students and positioned myself at the door. Mr Dacres tell me sorry, he can't let me in, so I explain to him that I am a member of staff and I have certain privileges. Him say him don't business with that – 'no line, no lunch.' What I must do is get the students to form a line. I wasn't staying down there. You should hear the indecent language. The more Mr Dacres defend the door, the more they storm it, the more him push them. Him t'umped a boy in him mouth, blood gash. Is like a riot, I tell you. I have never seen such voilence.

PAT: [*Interpolating throughout with brief exclamations*] And where is the Headmaster in all this?

HENDRY: He is off the premises.

PAT: So who is running the school? Is it Mr Dacres? Is he the new Head? I'd love somebody to tell me. Close the canteen? Can any member of staff, a junior at that, take it upon himself to take this sort of unilateral decision? God knows I'm hungry, but it's more than that, there are principles involved. The man walks in, takes over, what gives him the right? I don't know about you people, but I am not going to sit back here and allow this situation to continue. I am not going back to class until I get something to eat. I am prepared to sit here all day and all of next week if needs be, and if the Head wants to know why I haven't been to class, I will tell him.

[MICA *enters with orange juice and sandwich for* PAT, *cherry milk for the* CHAPLAIN, *and juice for herself. She waits on them.* PAT *ignores food and* MICA.]

MICA: There is a line now. Everything is orderly.

PAT: What's this thing about him punching a boy in his mouth and there's blood all over the place?

MICA: Blood? Oh, he pushed a boy or two, but no blood. Oh Mr Hendry, there is a message for you from Mr Dacres. He says you may now come for your lunch.

HENDRY: I am not hungry. [*Very angrily.*]

ROSCO: I hungry bad. [*He points* HENDRY *towards the canteen.*] Put it on mi bill, don't forget. [HENDRY *is on his way when the bell rings. He stops and returns to his desk.*] What happen?

HENDRY: The bell ring.

ROSCO: I never hear it, man.

HENDRY: I have a class. [*Collects his books and goes out in the direction away from the canteen.* PAT *follows him immediately.*]

ROSCO: Is a good thing I'm not hungry. I better check if I have a class. [*He does.*] I have a class, yes. I going to eat. [*Exit towards the canteen, meeting* RUSS *on the way.*] Hail the man!

[CHAPLAIN *pats* RUSS *on his back*]

CHAPLAIN: Keep up the good work. [*As he goes out.* JOE *too goes out.*]

MICA: [*To* RUSS] I never thought it was possible. Nice.

RUSS: Somebody had to do something. [*They look around the staff-room and decide to have a go at tidying up.* PAT *and* HENDRY *come on, on the lower level.*]

PAT: What's the name of the boy he punched in the mouth?

HENDRY: Ahm, I don't remember his name.

PAT: You could recognise the boy, though?

HENDRY: There was so much confusion that it would be difficult.

PAT: Let him keep it up.

HENDRY: Somebody is going to fix him business. Insult me in front of the students! Some of the rumours I hear about him and some of the girls in this school!

PAT: Rumours, Mr Hendry? What rumours?

HENDRY: I am a man that mind mi own business, so I have nutten to say. But make him fool wid me. I can be a real Mother Long-Tongue. Mi temper short and I can spread rumours.

PAT: Well, Mr Hendry, maybe I shouldn't tell you this, but he's been saying that you are not qualified for this job. [*Pause, as he lets it sink in, noting the effect on* HENDRY.] The Headmaster should know what's going on in this school. Someone should say something to him, and you may be the best person to do it. He thinks a lot of you, I know that. Only the other day I heard him say that you were his right-hand man.

HENDRY: He really said that?

PAT: That's what he said.

HENDRY: Huh! [PAT *guides him over to the Headmaster's door.* HENDRY, *slightly unsure of himself, knocks tentatively.* PAT *offers encouragement from a distance.* MICA *and* RUSS *continue to tidy the staff-room as the lights go down on the scene.*]

ACT TWO

SCENE TWO

[*Lights up on a reasonably tidy staff-room.* ROSCO *enters, and is surprised at the transformation. A look of real mischief crosses his face as he decides to put the place back to how it was before.* ROSCO *sets to work tossing books, paper, etc. in the air and letting them fall where they will. Among the papers he finds a comic. His face lights up with pleasure, but he needs time to read it. The* CHAPLAIN *enters and catches him putting the clock back. Moments later* JOE *comes on.*]

CHAPLAIN: Have you just finished a class, Mr Josephs?

JOE: Yes.

CHAPLAIN: So the bell has gone.

JOE: I don't go by the bell.

CHAPLAIN: Some days it's fast, some days it's slow. I don't understand it. [*Exit.*]

ROSCO: Hey, Joe, give me a hand with this table.

JOE: You joining the Crusader's tidy-up campaign?

ROSCO: What you call him? Crusader! Is a nice name. Joining him? No, man. As Mr Crusader tidy, so I untidy. Is war. The man should be at public cleansing. The place don't feel right tidy, Joe – uncomfortable. Ashtray and all – nice. [*He picks up the ashtray and examines it.*] Boy, this would look good on my bedside table. [*Puts ashtray in his bag.*] Good old Chinese proverb, you know, Joe, 'Ash on floor keep tray clean'. [*Then he gets another thought.*] Hey, Joe, pass me that ruler.
[ROSCO *picks up another ruler and puts them together in the shape of a cross. He uses the masking tape to affix it to* RUSS*'s space.*] If the man was fighting for more salary I would support him, but what him hope to get out of all the things him doing in the school? No promotion in this job, unless is the Headmastership him after. Then him really have no ambition. [*The* CHAPLAIN

enters to look at the time.] Man get to school before day
break, leave after dark. Those little girls in third form
will rape him, you know. Him better watch himself
that them don't start spread some serious rumours
'bout him.

[RUSS, *on his way to the Head's office with* HENDRY's *reports,
meets the* CHAPLAIN *on the way out of the staff-room.*]

RUSS: Ah Chaplain, I am starting a welfare organisation
in the school for the underprivileged children.

CHAPLAIN: Absolutely splendid idea! It's been knocking
around my head for months.

RUSS: How about us organising it together?

CHAPLAIN: Love to, but, ahm … Let me check my
commitments for the rest of this term … ahm … this
term is bad. Pressures of school and church, plus I am
on one of the Prime Minister's committees. How
about next term?

RUSS: I'd like to start right away.

CHAPLAIN: This term is definitely out for me. [*The bell goes.*]
After you. [RUSS *goes to the Head's office.* CHAPLAIN *returns
to the staff-room.*]

ROSCO: I have a class, but where are the books?

[JOE *goes to the bathroom.* ROSCO *puts the clock forward ten
minutes and sits in the couch.* PAT *and* MICA *arrive.*]

PAT: Something must be wrong with the clock. That was
the longest forty minutes.

CHAPLAIN: Something is definitely wrong. Now it's
running fast.

MICA: It's no use reporting it to the Head.

PAT: I don't suppose Mr Dacres knows about it, eh Miss
McAdam? [*Sarcastically.*]

CHAPLAIN: Good man, that Mr Dacres, good man. Now
where do I go next, Heaven or Hell?

RUSS: [*Entering*] Any one seen Mr Hendry?

MICA: I think he's teaching.

RUSS: Have you seen his comments on these reports? [*Shows them to her.*] That is ridiculous. The Head cannot send these to parents. Did you see these, Mr Josephs?

JOE: Yes, but I noticed nothing unusual. [MICA *laughs.*]

RUSS: Listen to this one. Davis – 2C History – 'He his making good progress.' H – I – S!

JOE: That is not unusual for Mr Hendry.

RUSS: What about this one. King – 2C – 'He as not learn his lesson.' These can't go out. How long has this man been teaching here?

MICA: Too long.

RUSS: And the Head?

PAT: 'E his 'is favourite teacher. What can 'e does?

[*Everyone laughs except* JOE *and* RUSS.]

RUSS: And you? [*To* PAT]

MICA: What can we do, Russ? The Head sees it, knows it, does nothing.

PAT: The Head's a sensitive man, Mr Dacres. I wouldn't want him to think I was taking over his job.

CHAPLAIN: Leave well alone is what I say.

RUSS: But this man is creating havoc in the school.

CHAPLAIN: A move against Hendry is a move against the Head, who whether we like it or not, is the constituted authority.

[HENDRY *enters.*]

RUSS: Ah, Mr Hendry.

HENDRY: What is it?

RUSS: Have a look at this. Does it make sense to you?

HENDRY: What?

RUSS: This report.

HENDRY: What about it?

RUSS: Read.

HENDRY: What's wrong? I don't see anything wrong.

RUSS: 'He his'? H – I – S! 'He as not learn'?

HENDRY: Oh that, just a little slip of the pen. [*He attempts to correct it. Titters from the rest.*]

RUSS: A little slip, Mr Hendry? You slip on every report. As a teacher with some sort of responsibility to the students, I am going to take it upon myself to tell you that these reports will have to be done all over again. Here you are, sir. [*There is a long pause until* HENDRY, *red in the face, turns and walks out of the room, leaving* RUSS *with the reports.*] How could that fellow get in to teach?

JOE: The day he walked into this staff-room, I saw it as the beginning of the end.

[PAT *leaves in search of* HENDRY.]

CHAPLAIN: The man has done more harm than good. Mr Dacres, let me be the first to congratulate you. A few more people with your guts and determination on this staff, and things would really get moving. You have given me hope for the future. I am telling you before your face because I cannot play the hypocrite. [ROSCO *laughs and goes out.*] You are doing some excellent work. We are behind you. We have to join hands with Mr Dacres, don't you agree, Mr Josephs?

JOE: Isn't it too late?

CHAPLAIN: That's a very defeatist attitude, Mr Josephs.

JOE: No. Years ago, I used to try this, and try that. I too had dreams of a new Jerusalem. Look what I end up with, a desk next to Hopal Hendry.

CHAPLAIN: Hendry should go.

JOE: [*Stands and comes down to the* CHAPLAIN *who is to the right of* RUSS.] I agree in principle, but what happens when we get rid of Hendry, who do we get instead? [*To* RUSS] There's a never-ending stream of Hendrys yet to come. Yet I don't blame the man. It's not his fault he is here. We have to see him in terms of the breakdown of the social order and the dilemma in education, brought about by the concepts of the new social mobility.

CHAPLAIN: Words, words.

JOE: So when you attack Hendry [*pointing to* HENDRY's *chair*], you attack a greater dilemma. He is no isolated case. The man is a symbol of the decadence and decay that has come upon us since Independence. Fourteen years ago there would have been no place for Hendry in this school. Not as a teacher, not as student. It would have been unthinkable. He would be totally unacceptable. This school had a reputation and a tradition.

RUSS: A little corner for the elite and a few lucky blacks with pretension – that's all it was, Mr Josephs.

JOE: At least we had standards! What have you put in its place? The rabble I have to be teaching [*pointing to* HENDRY's *chair*], and some of the rabble I see teaching! People like you cry down the past, but if what I see happening around me today is any reflection of the future, then I say, 'Up the good old days'! Folks knew who they were, Mr Dacres; they knew their place, they were happier for it. Now the Philistines are in control. Listen to the modern-day garbage on the radio. Hopal Hendry to me is what reggae music is to Bach. Standards had to fall. Everything of value's been rejected. The English language is a perfect example.

RUSS: There is something to be said for the dialect, it's the language of the people.

JOE: I don't agree. This is an English-speaking country. Everything should be done to get the children to appreciate the English language. If Shakespeare is best in the language, then we continue with him. If Latin helps, then we do Latin.

RUSS: Nonsense. The dialect is more valid than Shakespeare.

JOE: This is not a pantomime, a cheap vaudeville show designed to titillate the vulgar appetites of the masses.

RUSS: The dialect is valid communication. As a teaching language, it should be encouraged.

JOE: You don't really mean that?

RUSS: I do. The curriculum has to be geared to the needs of the people. What does the country need to survive? French or agriculture? The time spent propping up the Eiffel Tower should be spent teaching agriculture.

JOE: You know, Mr Dacres, it's people like you who must take responsibility for people like Hendry. You are a contradiction. You go around the school shouting, 'Up with the people, help the sufferers, go down to the masses!' And when the masses get into power, you wonder how they ever got up there, and want to get rid of them. After twenty years, how do you think I feel to see things come to this? In a way, though, I know good sense will prevail. If not, we will be lost forever in the jungle of ignorance and vulgarity. Pray God I will not be around to see it happen! Excuse me! [JOE *strides out of the room.*]

CHAPLAIN: Well, well, well.

MICA: Somebody over-reacted. That man is totally against any sort of change. All he ever talks about are the good old days. Bloody colonialist!

CHAPLAIN: I think Mr Josephs goes back much further than colonialism. I see him as an Old Testament character.

MICA: The trouble with Mr Josephs is that he's caught between two worlds and living in none.

CHAPLAIN: And he's a snob, totally arrogant. He teaches his French with total disdain. I've heard him say that he has no intention of casting his pearls before swine. Mr Dacres ... [*He extends his hand to* RUSS. RUSS *ignores him as the bell goes.*]

MICA: Oh, I have a class.

RUSS: May I walk down with you, Mica?

MICA: Yes, please. [*They go out, leaving the* CHAPLAIN *with his hand still extended. He withdraws it, then goes out.*]

[HENDRY, *really furious, comes storming into the staff-room.* JOE *follows.*]

JOE: I know how you feel. The man embarrassed you, but relax.

HENDRY: Relax, Mr Josephs? Not the way I feel. Ooh! [*As he boils.*] If him all come in here now, I would take something an' lick him down. I will kick him an' go to court house an' pay for it.

JOE: That won't be necessary. See the man for what he is, a trouble-maker. There are people like him all over the place. Relax yourself. He is not the Headmaster here.

HENDRY: I come here before him, an' him going to leave me here.

JOE: Now you making sense.

HENDRY: I am going to tell him that, and I plan to talk loud when I talking, because I want him to hear. Who him think him is? God's gift to edication? What him think, that is him one know everything? I don't come here under false pretences. I come as a train' teacher. I fulfil all the requirements for this job. I come here highly recommended. I have a piece of paper at my yard that I can show. I arrive at the top of my class. All at college, is all B plus and A minus I use to get. And the Headmaster don't have no complaints about me so far, an' is eighteen months since me is here. If him had fault to find, him would find it already. If anybody work in this school, is me.

JOE: I know, I know. I had to defend you.

HENDRY: I am never absent. I am never late. My marks is always in on time.

JOE: I know. I came to your defence.

HENDRY: So if that Mr Dacres think that I am going to stand back an' let him snatch bread out mi mouth, then is going to be war in here. I work hard to reach where I reach, and nobody going to push me around.

Before that, I draw blood. Is liberty or death. Is a free country and I don't want no boss to slave-drive me. [*Enter* ROSCO.]

ROSCO: What's happening, fellers? Mr Hendry, how you head looking so square?

HENDRY: Mr Rosco, this is no time for jokes. Serious things going on.

ROSCO: Like what?

JOE: Crusader is over-stepping his mark, man.

ROSCO: I tell you already how to deal with that feller. Ignore him. Him soon burn himself out. What him really want is a girl. That man have too much energy.

HENDRY: From what I hear, him have a girl.

ROSCO: Who? McAdam?

HENDRY: No, a girl in 5B, the one with the big bosom. The one they call 'Hamper'. I think Wilhelmina Hermit is her real name.

ROSCO: Rumours, man.

HENDRY: Is so I hear. [ROSCO *sees* RUSS DACRES *approaching. He signals to* HENDRY.]

RUSS: Mr Callender.

ROSCO: What's happening, Mr Dacres? Sit down, nuh?

RUSS: [*Still standing*] You have any idea who should be teaching 4F at this moment?

ROSCO: 4F, 4F? We have a 4F? I don't think we have a 4F, you know, Mr Dacres.

RUSS: There is a 4F, Mr Callender. Next door to 4E where I was teaching a minute ago.

ROSCO: Brother Joe, any idea where the master timetable is? I don't believe there is a 4F at all. This man say so, but I don't think so.

RUSS: Yes, Mr Callender, and if I'm not mistaken, you should be with them now.

ROSCO: Me? No, sir.

RUSS: Yes sir. The class you walked out of a few minutes ago. That's 4F! Well, they're running riot all over the corridor.

ROSCO: Is 4F? I never know that. This school is too big.

RUSS: Anyway, I can't get a word in to my class, because of the noise from next door. I wonder if you could do something about it?

ROSCO: I am not going back up there until they learn to behave themselves. You know what a boy did to me up there, Joe? Mr Hendry, listen to this. A run the boy, what him name, out the class. Boy give me a whole heap o' trouble. Boy tell me say him not leaving, so A grab him an' push him outside. [*Acts it out with* DACRES.] The boy come back and start to make up a whole heap of noise 'bout freedom, justice, socialism, human rights, education code, United Nations Charter and process of participation, so A run him again. Boy hiss him teeth and wouldn't move, so me walk out. Until him apologise, I not going up there again.

RUSS: That's not the attitude.

ROSCO: Eh? [*Surprised.*]

RUSS: I teach those boys and I have no problems with them.

ROSCO: Well, master, you welcome to them.

RUSS: Running the boy out of the class doesn't solve the problem.

ROSCO: Mr Hendry, you have a cigarette? [HENDRY *is smoking.*]

HENDRY: Just this.

ROSCO: Give it to me then, nuh? [ROSCO *takes it.*]

RUSS: Your attitude is not helping to solve the problems of discipline in this school.

ROSCO: Discipline! [*Hiss.*] You see all the boy mi run out the class, is only one way to deal with that sort of discipline problem. I wish they would make me Headmaster, I know exactly what I would do. I would construct a Gun Court in the middle of the play field; and come Monday morning, right after Chapel, I would make the whole school gather right round the wire fence, then I would catch the boy and let the parson administer the last rites. Then I would tie up

the boy and call the cadets with the long guns and –
bang, bang, bang! Then you would see a little
discipline in this school. Boy, I wish they would make
me Headmaster!

RUSS: In the meantime, what are you going to do about
4F?

ROSCO: What you say? What am I going to do about 4F?
There is nothing I can do about 4F until they make
me Headmaster; nothing anybody can do. You know
what the 'F' stand for? I don't understand you all the
same, you know, Mr Dacres. You leave from upstairs
to come down here to worry about my 4F. I bet all
now your 4E running riot too. You really not serving
any purpose down here. I am not going back; and,
by the look of things, you not going back either, so
the two of us can stay here and rap. Mr Hendry, any
more cigarettes?

HENDRY: That was the last one.

ROSCO: Go buy some, and pass the race form for me; look
in mi desk. And on your way out pass by 4F and see
what going on.

RUSS: Are you going back to 4F or not? I would like to
continue my class.

ROSCO: In a minute.

RUSS: Why you boys keep up with this rass attitude all the
time? I just cannot take it, man.

ROSCO: Hold down, man. This is a church school. Suppose
the Bishop was to walk in here.

RUSS: As a pin drop, you walk out the class. You don't
give a damn for the students.

ROSCO: [*To* HENDRY] This is last week's race form, man.
Pick up a new one. Pass that for me all the same.

RUSS: You have no conscience.

ROSCO: Why you going on like that? Mind you get a heart
attack.

RUSS: Mr Callender!

ROSCO: Rosco, man. Bruck down the formalities.

RUSS: Mr Callender, about 4F?

ROSCO: Change the subject, nuh, man? What a man persistent!

RUSS: If you had any conscience, you would resign.

ROSCO: Finish the argument, nuh, man? Is a good thing me nuh married to you!

RUSS: Why don't you have a little responsi ... [*The bell goes.*]

ROSCO: [*Smiles*] Saved by the bell.

BLACK OUT

ACT TWO

SCENE THREE

[*The lights come up on* PAT *and the* CHAPLAIN *talking together in the staff-room*]

CHAPLAIN: I am totally upset, Mr Campbell. The man didn't even as a 'by your leave' extend me the courtesy. Next thing I hear is that a Welfare Society is started in the school, right under my nose, and after all, welfare is *my* type of work. People are my business; all my life, the welfare of people has been my concern. The man didn't even have the common decency to consult me.

PAT: He said he did ask you, but you didn't have the time.

CHAPLAIN: Not a word to me. I would have found the time. People are my business. He's making me out to be a liar. The man is trying to undermine my position and authority. Parents have been approaching me, wanting to know how it's going. I don't know what to say. I feel like a fool. Why is the man trying to embarrass me?

[RUSS *enters.*]

RUSS: Hello, sir. Mr Campbell.

[PAT *acknowledges him non-verbally. The* CHAPLAIN *beams and is most charming.*]

CHAPLAIN: Top of the world to you! [RUSS *collects a book and leaves.*] He didn't hear me. [PAT *shakes his head.*] Same thing with the Chapel. Worship is compulsory. It's a rule for the school. On Wednesday last, five boys from that Rastafarian element absented themselves from service, so I sought them out. All were from Dacres' class. Naturally I challenged him about it. Do you know what the man said? That he wonders whether a boy brought up in the Rastafarian tradition should be forced to attend a Church of England service. So I explained to him that Chapel is compulsory. Chapel is compulsory.

PAT: My main quarrel with the man, apart from his trying to destroy the Christian principles of the school and his general hanky-panky with fellow members of staff, is that the man is a racist, always giving off those black sounds.

CHAPLAIN: An attitude that is totally unnecessary and against the Christian principle of 'love thy neighbour', and totally against our national motto and the immortal words of our beloved Prime Minister – 'The word is love'. [*Enter* JOE.] Have you heard tha latest, Joe? Mr Campbell has been under attack on the grounds of colour, from guess who? [*Sticking his chin out towards* RUSS's *chair*.]

JOE: The man is a trouble-maker. Yes, I have heard him question your involvement.

PAT: My involvement?

JOE: You being an outsider.

PAT: I've been on this staff for two years, you are the people most able to judge. Haven't I been pulling my weight, contributing to the welfare of this country?

JOE: Pat, I've been on this staff for twenty years. In that time I've seen the Dacres of this world come and go, like footprints on the beach, the impression is temporary.

CHAPLAIN: Well said, eloquently expressed! [*Applauds.*] Dacres will burn himself out.

PAT: He is interfering more every day, if you ask me.

JOE: Dying embers always burn brightest before they fade.

CHAPLAIN: This man should have been a poet. Let me write that down. I must fit it into Sunday's sermon. 'Dying embers always burn brightest before they fade.'

PAT: Nonetheless, I think a report of his activities should be made to the Headmaster.

CHAPLAIN: No, man, heed the words of prophecy from the lips of Mr Josephs, poet, artist, linguist, musician, a man who has dedicated twenty years of his life to the cultural growth and expansion of young minds. The flash-in-the-pan miracle worker will burn himself out.

PAT: You know who has really suffered? Poor Mr Hendry, Hopal. Dacres sits on him daily. It's a bloody shame!

CHAPLAIN: Not a bad fellow, you know. Hopal tries hard, he's conscientious.

JOE: Right now he is on the verge of a nervous breakdown.

PAT: Dacres has completely undermined his confidence.

JOE: He has developed this nervous twitch. Have you seen it? [JOE *twitches*.]

CHAPLAIN: Poor fellow.

JOE: The students have picked it up now. All over the school you can see them. [*He twitches again*.]

CHAPLAIN: Poor boy needs a bit of sympathy. [*Enter* HENDRY.] Ah, Mr Hendry, we were just talking about you and that fly-by-night Dacres. We were saying that in the face of great adversity you have behaved like a true gentleman.

HENDRY: [*Twitches, and all his books fall to the floor.*] I tell you, my cup runneth over. My emotions are hard to be contained.

PAT: Mr Hendry, don't ever let him upset you. [*As he helps to pick up* HENDRY's *books.*]

CHAPLAIN: We are behind you my friend, totally. We know and appreciate your worth. [*As they seat* HENDRY *in the* CHAPLAIN's *chair.*]

JOE: That's what I have been telling him.

CHAPLAIN: We will have to stick together against that wicked man, a troublemaker with deep psychological problems. Long after he is gone you will still be with us.

HENDRY: Over the last number of months I have undergone a terrible strain. [*Twitches.*]

CHAPLAIN: Shame!

HENDRY: I go to bed at night and I wake up in the morning and my head does not touch the pillow, for I don't sleep a wink. [*Twitches.*]

PAT: Shame!

HENDRY: Trials and tribulations I know are in this world; but what I have done to deserve this, I don't know.

CHAPLAIN: Chin up, man, chin up.

HENDRY: It is heartwarming to know that some people on the staff, at least, are appreciative of my services.

CHAPLAIN: We are indeed.

PAT: And don't forget the Headmaster who loves you.

HENDRY: Yes, he is aware of the many things that has been tried by me to inoculate discipline and a sense of purpose into the children whose responsibility rests in my hands.

CHAPLAIN: And we love you too, as a friend and a brother. Don't we, gentlemen? Keep the faith and put your trust in Jesus.

[RUSS *is seen at the entrance. The group breaks up.* ROSCO *calls out to.* RUSS. *They talk at the Down Left entrance to the staff-room.*]

ROSCO: Hey, Mr Dacres! Is none of my business, right, but some serious rumours going around the school. I think you should try and put a stop to them.

RUSS: Mr Callender, they are what they are, you know – rumours.

ROSCO: But I …

RUSS: Anyway, thanks for bringing it to my attention.

[*He continues to the staff-room.* ROSCO *looks at him, then exit to the outside. Exeunt the* CHAPLAIN, JOE, HENDRY *and* RUSS *to class.* PAT *and* MICA *remain.*]

PAT: Miss McAdam. Mica. I must talk with you, as a friend.

MICA: Yes?

PAT: What's going on between Dacres and that girl in the fifth?

MICA: What girl?

PAT: The rumour is all over the school. What's her name? Wilhelmina Hermit? The way I heard it, she is your rival.

MICA: Augh!

PAT: You must have heard something. Snigger, snigger, snigger. One day it's Miss McAdam and Mr Dacres are doing a thing. Now it's Wilhelmina Hermit take away Miss McAdam's man. They have been seen together, in and out of school. I don't say hanky panky is going on, but it does look odd. It's not fair, involving you in this sort of scandal.

MICA: I don't believe it.

PAT: Somehow you have to squash these rumours. The things being said about you are most uncomplimentary.

MICA: Mr Campbell, I am an intelligent woman. The intelligent thing to do is to ignore it.

PAT: Maybe, but this thing with her is, I gather, really a passionate love affair.

CHAPLAIN: [*Entering*] Love affair? Who's having a love affair? Tell me about it. I bet it's not as interesting as what I just overheard from a couple of students.

MICA: I would ignore it.

CHAPLAIN: Naturally I dismissed it as rumour. I had to. One doesn't expect this sort of thing to happen in a respectable Church school, particularly when a supposedly respectable member of staff is involved, particularly one that goes on like he is the new Messiah.

PAT: Exactly.

MICA: Excuse me. [*Exit.*]

CHAPLAIN: She'll discover the truth. That man Dacres is a snake in the grass.

PAT: Carrying on with a schoolgirl is one thing, but ...

CHAPLAIN: Schoolgirl? What schoolgirl?

PAT: Wilhelmina Hermit.

CHAPLAIN: That wasn't what I heard. Hermit? No. It wasn't with a girl, it was with one of the boys.

PAT: What! One of the boys?

CHAPLAIN: So it's been rumoured. You know the boy, half-Chinese fellow, name's Lowe. Lowe in name, low in nature, low in stature. Feminine, wears sandals. I've always been suspicious of him.

PAT: Now you say it, certain things do come back. So what about this thing with him and the girl?

CHAPLAIN: It's very likely that he could be ... ahm ... ambidextrous.

PAT: It's not impossible.

CHAPLAIN: Wouldn't put anything past him. Something very strange about that man. He and the Lowe boy. The rumours are strong – gives him lunch money, buys his books. I've seen them together, a few days ago, under the mango tree, sitting very close, whispering, all very suspicious. All this do-gooding, rubbing the staff the wrong way, is obviously just a ploy to cover up some very dark secrets.

PAT: Man that age, not married, has to be suspicious.

CHAPLAIN: Doesn't live anywhere, I gather, half a house, back half. I've been making inquiries, not surprising he can't live some place decent. How can he, when he spends his money procuring? The man has to be stopped, sexually he is a maniac. Let him loose another six months in this school, we'll be having orgies in the Chapel. Such a shame really about the man, potentially a lovely person. What is he doing with his life, eh? What is he accomplishing for himself?

PAT: The point is, what action are we going to take? He must not be allowed to go unchecked.

CHAPLAIN: We have a moral right to society and the school. We have to move quickly, quietly and incisively. This scandal cannot get outside the school. What would people think?

PAT: After all, it's a Church school.

CHAPLAIN: Don't remind me. We will nip it in the bud.

PAT: The Headmaster has to know.

CHAPLAIN: He is well prepared. There has to be an emergency staff meeting at lunch time. Hopal, Joe, you, me, Callender.

PAT: Rosco?

CHAPLAIN: Let's find him. Dacres must have no time to prepare a defence. [*As they prepare to go out,* ROSCO *enters.*] Ah, Mr Callender.

ROSCO: Yes, Bishop?

CHAPLAIN: No time for jokes, man. I suppose you have heard?

ROSCO: No, tell me, nuh?

CHAPLAIN: Serious things are happening in the school, man.

ROSCO: Like what? They shoot the Headmaster?

CHAPLAIN: No such luck, but certain facts have come to light. It's serious! Our mutual friend, Mr Dacres, is not what he makes himself out to be.

ROSCO: Tell me more.

CHAPLAIN: I knew you'd be interested. In fact, the consensus of opinion so far is that he has got to go. Immediate expulsion.

ROSCO: Mr Dacres? Why?

CHAPLAIN: We have to be very hush-hush. The man could wreck the good name of the school. He is infecting the morals of student and staff alike. The man is a sex maniac.

ROSCO: Bishop!

CHAPLAIN: Yes, Mr Callender, we all know this, it is common knowledge. You didn't hear anything?

ROSCO: I have heard one or two rumours, yes, but you know me: I don't listen to rumours or spread gossip.

The devil is a wicked man, you know, Bishop: always finds work for idle hands.

MICA: [*Entering*] Where is the Headmaster?

PAT: What's happened, Mica?

MICA: Tell him I have no intention of teaching the dirty little prostitutes in 5B! [*She starts to pack.*] I am going home.

CHAPLAIN: Miss McAdam, what's happened?

MICA: And tell Mr Dacres he's very welcome to his little harem!

CHAPLAIN: What's happened to upset you?

MICA: Give me a lift home, Pat.

CHAPLAIN: You can't walk out on us, Miss McAdam.

MICA: You giving me a lift? [*As she is leaving.*]

CHAPLAIN: Mr Campbell, see what you can do. Try and bring her back. That man Dacres is going to wreck the school. [*Enter* JOE.] Mr Josephs, have you seen the Headmaster?

JOE: No.

CHAPLAIN: Serious things are happening. McAdam just walked out. The Headmaster has to be found. [*Exit.*]

ROSCO: You heard any of these rumours, Joe? About Dacres, McAdam and the girl Hermit?

JOE: I have heard rumblings.

ROSCO: Is one of them Pharisees that start the rumours. Jealousy, Joe. Jealousy. Any excuse to get rid of the man. Dacres is an idiot, leave himself wide open. The man is not mi friend, I hold no brief, but is a principle involved. The fellow means well, a little high-handed, but he get plenty benefits for the sufferers in the school. The girl Hermit is no more than another sufferer him trying to help. You people must learn the facts before you jump to conclusions.

JOE: What are the facts?

ROSCO: I see how Dacres operate. Once the Headmaster comes into it, him finish. We have to put in a word for him.

JOE: Excuse me. [*Exit to bathroom.*] Just going to wash my hands.

ROSCO: [*Almost to himself about* JOE] What a little … [*He hisses as the* CHAPLAIN *enters.*]

CHAPLAIN: No sign of the Headmaster. No sign. [*He is going out again as* HENDRY *is entering.*] Ah, Mr Hendry, just the man I wanted to see! Come with me. [HENDRY *is going with the* CHAPLAIN.]

ROSCO: Mr Hendry. [*Calling him back.* HENDRY *twitches as he goes after the* CHAPLAIN.] Come here. [HENDRY *returns as the* CHAPLAIN *re-enters.*]

CHAPLAIN: Hopal, stop wasting time, I'm in a hurry, we have to find the Head.

ROSCO: I feel you people must have some proof before you carry this thing to the Headmaster.

CHAPLAIN: You saw Miss McAdam and the state she was in. The facts speak.

ROSCO: What facts? Rumours!

CHAPLAIN: Come, Mr Hendry. [HENDRY *and the* CHAPLAIN *are going out as* PAT *enters from the opposite direction.*] Ah, here's Pat. Pat, any luck?

PAT: She's right here.

CHAPLAIN: Good. [PAT *waits by the door for* MICA. *She comes on almost immediately.*] Now tell me what happened?

MICA: It's just too embarrassing.

PAT: It's Dacres and the girl Hermit.

CHAPLAIN: Hermit? Oh yes, you did mention. Who is this girl? I don't know her. What does she look like?

HENDRY: Very tall, black with very big breasts. The students call her 'Hamper'.

CHAPLAIN: Big breasts. I should know her.

HENDRY: It is she they say that take away Mr Dacres from Miss McAdam.

CHAPLAIN: Augh … repeat that.

HENDRY: It is she they say …

CHAPLAIN: I heard you the first time.

PAT: I warned Mica about these rumours, but she thought the best thing was to ignore it. Mica, you better tell them. [*Enter* JOE *from bathroom.*]

MICA: Pat did warn me, but I ignored him. I left for my class and down the corridor I came upon a group of girls laughing, talking and carrying on like dirty little fishwives. I didn't hear what they were saying, but when I passed, there was a sort of hush. No sooner was I a little way off, there was the most disgusting raucous laughter.

CHAPLAIN: Psychological warfare.

MICA: I heard one say ... I'm sorry, I won't repeat it. I have no intention of allowing those dirty words to come from my lips.

CHAPLAIN: Oh no!

MICA: I was willing to ignore all that, but I couldn't ignore the lewd, dirty, suggestive drawing that greeted me on the blackboard.

PAT: Captions and all. Tell them about the captions, Mica.

CHAPLAIN: Yes, I would love to hear about these captions. What I would really love to see is the blackboard.

PAT: That's erased by now.

CHAPLAIN: The bold, barefaced, vicious, barbaric little sluts! They won't get away with it! Discipline must be maintained at all costs! They'll be expelled! If they get away with it, we can all pack up and leave.

MICA: It's them or me.

CHAPLAIN: They will be dealt with Mica. Of course this situation didn't come about by itself, it was obviously encouraged and nurtured by someone, and that someone, whoever he is, must be punished. That will be the Head's responsibility; but, I am telling you, if he does not take prompt action, I am prepared to go to the Bishop, and there will be hell to pay. This is after all a Church school. We cannot stand back and see fellow teachers subjected to this insulting, disgusting, disgraceful attack. It is humiliating. No, no, Mr Dacres has gone too far.

ROSCO: How Mr Dacres get into this?

CHAPLAIN: Who the hell do you think is responsible?

ROSCO: If you are going to try the man, at least give him a chance to defend himself.

CHAPLAIN: This is not a trial, Mr Callender. For the good of the school, we hope that it would never come to that. Hopefully, he will have the good sense to leave quietly.

ROSCO: How can you, of all people, condemn the man just so?

CHAPLAIN: Condemn him? I don't have to do that. Mr Dacres condemned himself by his actions and his utterances, and the headmaster, who represents the constituted authority in this school, will decide what action must be taken. We mustn't forget, Mr Callender, that the Head himself has been subject to insults and abuses from Mr Dacres. You yourself must have heard the vicious attacks against the constituted authority, and if you say you haven't, I will say you are a liar.

ROSCO: The man spoke nothing but the truth. The Headmaster is a shit, and the same goes for all of you.

CHAPLAIN: Now look here!

PAT: Who the hell do you ...

MICA: If you think I'm going to stay here and be insulted ...

HENDRY: Who do you think you are referring to?

ROSCO: Shut yuh mouth!

HENDRY: Speech is free. If I wish to express myself, I will express myself.

ROSCO: Go in the bathroom and pull the chain!

CHAPLAIN: It doesn't surprise me that a man like you would want to support a man like that. Ten chances to one, you'd do the same thing.

ROSCO: It would be an honour, Bishop, but if anybody was to say I'd follow in your footsteps, now that would be the insult!

CHAPLAIN: I treat you with the contempt you deserve.

ROSCO: And I disregard you.

JOE: Gentlemen, gentlemen. Let's not lose our intentions to petty squabbles and personal clashes. Now I actually haven't heard Mr Dacres attack the Head.

ROSCO: Thank you, Joe.

JOE: I have heard the rumours and I am willing to regard them as rumours.

ROSCO: Thank you, Joe.

JOE: I have no personal axe to grind.

MICA: None of us have.

CHAPLAIN: I don't see this as a personal matter.

PAT: Neither do I. Mr Hendry, do you?

HENDRY: It is not of my nature to bear grudge or carry feelings in my heart for another human being.

JOE: Good. Let's look at the matter objectively. Something bothers me and I must say it.

ROSCO: By all means, Joe.

JOE: As a member of staff who's been here for close on twenty years, my responsibility is to the school.

ROSCO: Hear, hear.

JOE: As teachers, we are dealing with young minds, easily influencable. We have to be careful how we mould those young minds. [*Pause. No one is certain on whose band waggon* JOE *rides.*] Mr Dacres has been here but for a short time. He has introduced certain things and brought about many changes.

ROSCO: For the better, hear, hear.

JOE: Now I'm all for change ...

ROSCO: Hear, hear.

JOE: But change has to be gradual.

CHAPLAIN: Hear, hear.

PAT: Hear, hear.

JOE: Any sudden upheaval must be traumatic.

ROSCO: In fact, Joe, change has to be so slow you never notice it.

JOE: Far from it, but you yourself must have noticed a certain unrest among the student body recently.

CHAPLAIN: A certain tension, yes.

PAT: I've noticed it. The students have been picking on

me, calling me names, openly questioning my relevance.

HENDRY: I agree with Pat. I go to my class and I cannot maintain any discipline.

ROSCO: But, Hendry, you never could. [HENDRY *picks up a ruler and threatens* ROSCO.]

CHAPLAIN: Gentlemen, let's keep it orderly.

ROSCO: Play with puppy ...

CHAPLAIN: Mr Josephs, you were saying?

JOE: Just that the state of unrest in the school was forcibly brought home to me yesterday, when I was approached by a student whose family has a long tradition in this school. This student expressed certain fears and anxieties about the activities of Mr Dacres.

CHAPLAIN: Go on.

JOE: In fact, he went on to suggest that Mr Dacres could be a communist.

CHAPLAIN: Oh my God!

ROSCO: Jesus Christ Joe, how you could say a thing like that?

CHAPLAIN: Hear him out, everybody gets a chance to speak. We must abide by the democratic process.

ROSCO: An intelligent man like you, Joe?

JOE: This student, a thinking student, simply expressed a view.

MICA: That's how the communists operate.

PAT: He's got a following and it's growing.

CHAPLAIN: At the same time, undermining and ridiculing the Head, making a mockery of the constituted authority. Creating disharmony in the staff-room. Contributing to the breakdown of discipline which can only lead to moral decadence and decay. At the same time, preaching racial intolerance, and when he comes in direct conflict with religious, moral and social principles that have served this country well, then I say this man is dangerous.

ROSCO: This is a joke. All you people mad.

CHAPLAIN: Next think we know it's chaos, confusion, total anarchy. There could be one in every school. Who knows where it could end, unless we put a stop to it now. Now all those in favour of an emergency staff meeting with the Head immediately, say 'Aye'.

[*All except* ROSCO *say* 'Aye'. RUSS *enters. There is a pause.*]

RUSS: I can't get a thing done in my class. The students on all sides of me are running wild. Is this school on holiday?

ROSCO: Now everybody been pressing charges behind the man's back. Right, see the man here, face to face, no more susu.

RUSS: I have a class.

ROSCO: What's happened? Everbody have lockjaw? Mr Hendry?

CHAPLAIN: This is not the time or place.

ROSCO: Come, Mr Hendry. You start the rumours.

HENDRY: I never start no rumours.

ROSCO: Is you I hear with the thing about Dacres and the girl Hermit.

HENDRY: I only repeat what I heard.

RUSS: And what's that, Mr Hendry?

HENDRY: I have nothing to say to you. You hypocrite!

RUSS: I beg your pardon.

HENDRY: Yes. You is a hypocrite, a fraud, a sneaking barefaced fraud, a impostor. Don't ask me about him and the girl Hermit. Ask any of the children in the school. They will tell you. 'Bout me start rumour. Look, nuh, man! [*Threatening to fight.*]

PAT: Yes, Mr Dacres, how would you describe your relationship with this girl?

RUSS: I don't have to explain anything to anyone. [*There is a general reaction to his arrogance.*]

MICA: I demand some explanation, Mr Dacres.

RUSS: I'll talk with you Mica, privately.

MICA: It is no longer a private matter, Mr Dacres, not after those disgusting drawings this morning.

HENDRY: I can bear witness to those drawings.

CHAPLAIN: What did they show, Mr Hendry?

HENDRY: A picture of Wilhelmina Hermit with a big stomach, and that man there kissing her and saying, 'Darling, darling', and in the background Miss McAdam is crying and saying, 'It is better to have loved and lost, than never to have loved at all'. That is what I saw.

MICA: Deliberately done to embarrass me!

RUSS: Come now, Mica, you know me well enough. At least you could have come to me directly. I am disappointed.

MICA: I know how I was made to feel.

RUSS: The girls responsible for the smutty drawings are mischief-makers, and should be treated as such. Mica … [As he takes her away to a quiet corner, the others strain to overhear.] Wilhelmina boards with an aunt. The aunt's man raped young Wilhelmina. The auntie accused her of trying to take away her man, and threw her out in the streets. Wilhelmina came to me for help when she discovered that she was pregnant. I found her lodgings and …

CHAPLAIN: Who pays for the lodgings?

RUSS: I do.

CHAPLAIN: Oh, so she is still in school and pregnant.

RUSS: She is still in school. [Pause.] I took her to a doctor and she had an abortion. [MICA recoils from him.]

CHAPLAIN: An abortion, Mr Dacres! [The others react. MICA rests her head on her desk.]

RUSS: Yes, Reverend Steele. An abortion.

CHAPLAIN: We must admire this Good Samaritan role. You say you paid for this abortion?

RUSS: Partially. Some came from the Welfare Fund.

CHAPLAIN: Just as well I didn't join your welfare society, as if I knew I was going to be party to abortion.

RUSS: What would you have me do? She is only fourteen, Chaplain.

CHAPLAIN: Very laudable, Mr Dacres, but we have to be realistic. You take responsibility for this girl. Does one take such responsibility upon oneself unless one is personally involved? Eh, Mr Campbell? [PAT *laughs nastily*.] Mr Hendry?

HENDRY: You think I born big so!

CHAPLAIN: Mr Josephs?

JOE: It is unbelievable.

CHAPLAIN: Mr Callender, you are a man of the world. Would you shoulder such awesome responsibility without personal involvement?

ROSCO: Don't judge the man by your own standards.

CHAPLAIN: [*To* RUSS] Consider your position, our position, the school's position. This is a Church school. Pray God the Bishop never hears about this. At this point I am not sure if this is a matter for the Board of Governors or the police.

RUSS: My conscience is clear.

CHAPLAIN: But I cannot be a party, Mr Dacres, to any situation where members of staff impute the reputation, my reputation, by being involved in an illegal act. Illegal in the eyes of God and the State. I have no option. I must resign. I will not, and cannot, be a party to it. You have put me in a most untenable position. I resign.

[*General chorus from the rest, except* ROSCO – 'Me too'. *They all start packing up to leave.*]

RUSS: That will not be necessary gentlemen. [*As he collects his things.*] My resignation will be with the Head within the hour. [*The* CHAPLAIN *immediately starts unpacking.*]

CHAPLAIN: I hope you don't see this as a personal matter, Mr Dacres. We have to protect the good name of the school. You may be sure that your good work will be carried on. I will personally look after the welfare myself. We do hope that you will find some success in your new sphere.

[*Exit* RUSS *Down Left to the outside.*]

HENDRY: Remember the stench we had here some months aback? It is finally gone. That reminds me, I have a friend, my class-mate, I must ring him and tell him that there is a vacancy here. [*As he goes to the telephone and starts to dial.*]

JOE: [*Quietly*] Oh my God, not another one of them!

CHAPLAIN: Ah Brother Joe, it is a great victory.

HENDRY: [*Leaves the phone and walks across to* JOE.] Brother Joe, you know what really got me about that man, brother Joe?

JOE: Mr Hendry, don't 'brother Joe' me. I am not your brother, and never will be.

HENDRY: [*He is stung by the retort, but he is no longer the weakling.*] Sticks and stones can break my bones but words cannot hurt me. [*He removes his books, etc. from* JOE'S *table, and plonks them down on the main table, sitting in* RUSS DACRES' *chair.*]

CHAPLAIN: Mr Josephs, after all the warmth of fellowship, the harmony of spirit that we shared. [JOE *stares at the* CHAPLAIN, *then sits and readies himself to leave. The* CHAPLAIN *turns to* MICA, *who is crying with head on table.*] This is a tough, hard world, Mica. People disappoint you. My conscience is clear. The matter is closed irrevocably. Now we must deal with the expulsions of the students involved.

ROSCO: How it go, Bishop, the shepherd and the sheep? [*To* JOE] One man let me down. [*As* JOE *goes out.*]

CHAPLAIN: Where were we? Ah yes, students to be expelled. The Head will want my recommendations. [*To* HENDRY] Wilhelmina Hermit? [HENDRY *nods.*] Definitely. The girls responsible for the smutty drawings? [HENDRY *nods.*] Maybe one should temper justice. Long suspensions? [HENDRY *shakes his head.*] No. Discipline must be maintained. [*The bell goes. Exit the* CHAPLAIN *to the Headmaster's door.* HENDRY *stretches, then yawns monstrously.* MICA *looks at him.*]

PAT: Come, Mica. [*Still sobbing, she follows him out.*]

[*The* CHAPLAIN *arrives at the Headmaster's door. He knocks and waits.* HENDRY, *in the staff-room, walks across to* ROSCO'S *desk, searches around till he finds a packet of cigarettes.* ROSCO *walks up to* HENDRY *and watches him.* HENDRY *lights the cigarette in a bold, larger-than-life way, tossing the burnt match on the floor. He blows cigarette smoke in* ROSCO'S *face. They face each other threateningly.* ROSCO *turns and walks away;* HENDRY *smiles and strides out arrogantly. The lights fade as music comes up.*]

Smile Orange

Smile Orange

Performed for the first time at the Barn Theatre, Kingston, Jamaica on 1 November 1971 with the following cast:

RINGO   – Carl Bradshaw
CYRIL (BUSBOY) – Harvel Peryer
JOE   – Stan Irons
O'KEEFE   – Vaughn Crosskill
MISS BRANDON – Grace McGhie

Directed by: Dennis Scott

The Setting

The scene is the Mocho Beach Hotel, a third-rate
establishment on the north coast of Jamaica. There are
three playing areas. In the centre is the small lobby, with
its semi-circular reception desk with switchboard and
telephone. We may imagine a window at its downstage
edge, through which the receptionist can see a small part
of the hotel driveway. A large poster and the trailing vine
dominate the walls. Left is o'KEEFE's office with telephone,
desk, chairs, shelf with a few books. Up Centre is the
entrance — an archway, through which can be seen the
insignia of the hotel painted on the wall of the
passageway. The whole thing has pretensions to good
taste, like the man himself — calendar, a print, loving-
cups, a first-aid box, a waste paper basket with the hotel's
insignia. A door left leads to the rest of the hotel.

Right Stage is the waiters' area, not the kitchen itself,
but the place where they meet to gossip, clean silver,
change clothes and so on. A swing door leads out at the
back to passageway that connects the three areas, while
down right there is an entrance from the back yard. A
window may be imagined in the front 'wall' of the stage
looking out on to the drive and gateway of the hotel. Two
stools, a table, a coat rack, a shelf with assorted pieces of
crockery complete the furnishings, along with a wall
phone. RINGO has added a number of Playboy-type pinups
stuck at random on the walls.

The playing areas can be arranged differently
depending on the shape and size of the stage and
auditorium. The waiters' area can be set Centre Stage
with the reception area Stage Right.

ACT ONE

SCENE ONE

[*At curtain time the hotel band can be heard playing an enthusiastic and off-key version of* 'Nobody's Business'. *Before the house lights dim* RINGO *hustles through the audience carrying a large airline bag. He pauses to check a handful of loose change, then moves on to disappear backstage. Immediately* CYRIL *lugs a huge new garbage bin in from the hotel yard on to the right area of the stage, while ...* MISS BRANDON *sashays on from the passageway into her area and begins to repair her makeup, while ...* JOE *slips onstage, changes his coat for a waiter's orange waistcoat, signs himself 'in' on the roster and goes out quickly, while ...* O'KEEFE, *crossing the central area, catches sight of* MISS BRANDON *studying herself in a hand mirror. He looks pointedly at his watch.* MISS BRANDON *stares at hers too, indicating smugly that it's not yet time for work.* O'KEEFE *bustles out, to reappear in his office, as* RINGO *appears, head and shoulders behind the set, telephone in hand, dialing. A jet plane is heard coming in to Montego Bay Airport and an airline announcement says:* 'MAY I HAVE YOUR ATTENTION PLEASE. EASTERN AIRLINES ANNOUNCES THE ARRIVAL OF FLIGHT 505 FROM WASHINGTON, NEWARK AND MIAMI NOW LANDING AT GATE NUMBER 7 ...' *while* ALL *freeze listening to the plane come down.*
The switchboard rings loudly. MISS BRANDON *seats herself, checks the time and condescends to answer the phone.*
JOE *chases* CYRIL *back to work.* O'KEEFE *settles down at his desk and the music fades.*]

MISS BRANDON: Mocho Beach Hotel. Good afternoon. May I help you?

RINGO: Yes. Listen now. Dis is Ringo. What happening, sweetness?

MISS BRANDON: Wrong number. [*She hangs up.*]

RINGO: Hello ... hello ... hello ... hello! [*During his 'hello' the telephone goes again and* MISS BRANDON *answers it.* RINGO *hunts in his pocket, finds a short, stiff wire and begins to pick the lock of the call box.*]

MISS BRANDON: Hello. Mocho Beach Hotel. Good afternoon. May I help you? ... What happen, Maisie? Can't see you, eh. [*Hiss.*] You call dis big job? Dis is no big ting. Di place like a morgue. Me see one or two dry-up looking white people but [*hiss*] is today dem say di season start proper. A group coming in dis evening. Di Assistant Manager boy jus' killing up himself. One piece of chaos! Guess wha' dem call him up here? Flap Flap. Yes. A local boy, coloured, married to a white woman. Is so all of dem stay, mi dear. She fluxy you see. Di boy live on pill. A was in him office di other day. You want to see pill box! ... Him nuh fresh wid me dis morning! His ass! Di boy trying to hinder mi progress. Him is nutten but a wart on di devil backside! [*Laughs.*] So what you doing wid yuhself? ... You lie! ... Jimmy! When you see him? ... Hold on a little. Mocho Beach Hotel. Good afternoon. May I help you?

RINGO: Yes, listen now. Dis is Ringo.

MISS BRANDON: Wrong number.

RINGO: Hol' on, what happen to Miss B? Mek A talk to her.

MISS BRANDON: There isn't a Miss B ...

RINGO: She not at the switchboard today?

MISS BRANDON: What number do you want?

RINGO: Don't dat is di Mocho Beach?

MISS BRANDON: Yes, it is.

RINGO: Well, den, dis is Ringo. You see my missis pass through dere yet?

MISS BRANDON: Who do you wish to speak to?

RINGO: Is who dat?

MISS BRANDON: This is Miss Brandon, front desk.

RINGO: Oh Brandon! So you is Miss B as well! All right, well, listen now, me is a waiter at di hotel. If you see my missis come looking for me, tell her dat A lef' di job and A gone to work in Port Antonio.

MISS BRANDON: Would you like to speak to someone in the kitchen?

RINGO: No, man, you just tell her dat. And hear me again, don't is today di season start?

MISS BRANDON: Yes, it is.

RINGO: Right. Tell di Maître D for me dat A got held up, but A'm on mi way. Tell him Ringo. All right, don't forget now, you know, and remember if you see mi missis come looking for me, A gone to work in Port Antonio. So what happen to di other Miss B?

MISS BRANDON: There is a call on the other line. I'll deliver your message.

RINGO: Jus' tell him Ringo, and another thing ... hello ... hello ... [*She has hung up on him.*] Is what wrong with dat girl?

[*After a moment* RINGO *disappears, still mildly abusing* MISS BRANDON.]

MISS BRANDON: Yes, Maisie ... [O'KEEFE *dials a number in his office, speaks inaudibly.*] So why Jimmy was asking for me? Him not mi boyfriend any longer, mi dear. I finish wid him — roun' three weeks now — little after me get di job up here. Everything have to change you know. Di boy was hindering mi progress, man ... Yes, him nuh did want di pearl for nutten! Hear me, anything dat drop into my lap have to come good. Is money I looking. Him have nutten to offer, mi love ... Hold on a little.

[*She answers another line.*]

Mocho Beach Hotel. Good afternoon. May I help you? ... I'm sorry, sir, but the Manager is in New York. Would you like to speak to the Assistant Manager? ... Will you hold, please? I am sorry, sir, but his extension is busy; would you hold, please? Hol' on a little again, Maisie. I have to check something.

O'KEEFE: Yes, doctor, oh it's nothing too serious ... same problem. I'm not sleeping too well. I know, doctor, but what with the new season starting today it would be impossible to take even a day's leave. Yes, doctor, it's just something to make me sleep ... I'll pick it up this afternoon ... Three, just before going to bed, and ahm, there is another matter that I want to discuss with you but it is a bit difficult over the telephone ... I'll come in next week ... Oh she's very well, lives in the sun, seems to be really enjoying it out here ... she's getting as ... hello?

MISS BRANDON: Hello. Hello.

O'KEEFE: Hello.

MISS BRANDON: Hello.

O'KEEFE: Hello. Oh blast! The blasted woman has cut me off again. Hello.

MISS BRANDON: Hello.

O'KEEFE: [*Jiggles the receiver*] Hello, operator ... operator ... ? Oh Jesus! Hello! [*He slams the phone down and leaves the office.*]

MISS BRANDON: Mocho Beach Hotel. May I help you? I think we got cut off sir, I'll connect you now. [*We hear the buzz in* O'KEEFE'*s office*] Where is di man? [*Hiss.*] Hello, there is no reply from his extension.

[O'KEEFE *appears in the archway centre.*]

... May I take a message and have him call you ... just a second, I see him coming through the lobby. Mr O'Keefe, call for you, sir. Take it on the white, please, sir.

O'KEEFE: Miss Brandon.

MISS BRANDON: Call for you, sir.

O'KEEFE: What happened to the call in my office? Why did you cut me off?

MISS BRANDON: I didn't cut you off, sir. There must be something wrong with the switchboard.

O'KEEFE: Possibly, possibly. Show me what you did when

the call came in. I was speaking on what line?

MISS BRANDON: This one, sir.

O'KEEFE: Two, right? And the call came in on?

MISS BRANDON: One, sir.

O'KEEFE: So what did you do? What button did you press?

MISS BRANDON: This one, sir.

O'KEEFE: No, Miss Brandon, that's not right. If you do that, then you are bound to cut me off. Tell me something, Miss Brandon, and I might have asked you this question before, is this the first time you are going to operate a switchboard? There is no need to look at me like that, it's not going to help the situation. The Telephone Company has been down here three times and there is nothing wrong with the switchboard. Every time you cut me off, every single time. We can't run a hotel like this, Miss Brandon.

MISS BRANDON: There is a call for you sir.

O'KEEFE: Who is it?

MISS BRANDON: I don't know, sir.

O'KEEFE: How many times do I have to tell you? Find out who it is before you put me on.

MISS BRANDON: Who may I say is calling? Mr Johnson, sir.

O'KEEFE: What is it about?

MISS BRANDON: Ahm ...

O'KEEFE: Give me the phone. [MISS BRANDON *gives it to him, then she turns her back ostentatiously and feeds chewing gum into her mouth.*]
Hello, O'Keefe, Assistant Manager, speaking ... yes ... the flight came in ... good, good ... so what's the problem? I don't understand you, man. Don't tell me rubbish! Whose responsibility is that? I didn't take on this job to play wet nurse to any lazy taxi driver, get that! If a man can't do his job than it's out. You had better find transportation for the guests and get them to the hotel. [*He hangs up.*]
The guests are on their way and not a thing's done.

MISS BRANDON: Mocho Beach Hotel.

O'KEEFE: Look now, Miss Brandon.

MISS BRANDON: Will you hold, please?

O'KEEFE: Miss Brandon, this business on the switchboard will have to get better, if not, we will simply have to think again. [*He is going, then returns.*] Mmm ... did you get through to the man about the boat?

MISS BRANDON: Not yet, sir.

O'KEEFE: But why not, Miss Brandon?

MISS BRANDON: His telephone is out of order, sir.

O'KEEFE: But Miss Brandon, there is always that possibility. So what? One telephone out of order is going to prevent fifty guests from having a good time. Initiative, Miss Brandon, that's what the job requires. Initiative! [MISS BRANDON *slams the phone back into its cradle.*]

We have a messenger, the boat is priority, and no personal calls through to me for the rest of the day. If GOD wants me I am out of town! Fifty guests on their way and not a thing arranged ... [*As he goes out.*]

MISS BRANDON: [*Muted to his back she swears at him.* JOE *enters pantry area.*]

Mocho Beach Hotel. Good afternoon. May I help you? ... What happen, Maisie? Something wrong wid di switchboard, mi love, we get cut off. I not staying in dis job, you know. Di Assistant Manager boy just bugging me. [*Hiss.*] Who him think him is? God? ... Look nuh, chile, A have to call you back, di switchboard just start busy up itself on me. All when A go to bed at night, all A can hear in mi head is 'paamp, paamp', A call you back. Mocho Beach Hotel. Good afternoon. I am sorry but Mr O'Keefe is not in at the moment. Can I take your number and ask him to call you back? ... Yes, Mrs O'Keefe. Will you hold, please?

[*She buzzes* O'KEEFE.]

O'KEEFE: Who is it, Miss Brandon?

MISS BRANDON: Telephone sir, personal!

O'KEEFE: When I said no personal calls I meant no personal calls.

MISS BRANDON: It's your wife, sir.

O'KEEFE: Ahm ... put her on. Hello. Yes, dear, oh not so bad ... busy. Oh blast, the lawnmower, it's still in the car. I haven't had a minute to scratch my head all morning. Is the gardener still there? Ask him to come back tomorrow, and, look, love, I won't be able to leave the hotel till late tonight, so if you would like to come and have supper here ...? You won't mind eating alone? That's all right then. I'll send a taxi for you 'round eight. Okay, dear, I'll see you later. Bye! [*Blows her several kisses.*]

[MISS BRANDON, *listening closely, can hardly believe her ears. She laughs raucously as the lights go down on the reception area and* O'KEEFE's *and come up full on the pantry.*]

[RINGO *appears at the back door of the pantry.* JOE *gets up to reach for a rag.* RINGO *puts down his bag quietly, grinning hugely, and snatches the stool away, so that* JOE *takes a fall when he settles back on to his seat.*]

JOE: Ringo!

RINGO: What's happening, Joe?

JOE: You come.

RINGO: A glad to see you, man. [*They do a fancy hand-shake.* RINGO *begins to change his clothes, shoes, and unpack cologne, rum, toilet articles from his bag.*]

JOE: Every day A looking for you but A can't see you. You looking well.

RINGO: You to.

JOE: A like di afro – soulful. [RINGO *scratches himself.*]

RINGO: Everything soulful now. [*Touching his fancy dark glasses.*]

JOE: Hey, we have a new Assistant Manager, if ice melt in di bowl is trouble. Is a coloured guy.

RINGO: Face card. [*Scratches himself again.*]

JOE: Married to a white woman. Him study everything 'bout knife an' fork, rum, food – di works, what to do, what not to do. Him strict like a bitch, but him nervous.

RINGO: As long as him don't mess wid my scene.

JOE: Watch him.

RINGO: You know how much bull come and go and leave me here. A glad to see you, boy.

JOE: Everybody asking – where Ringo, where Ringo – I know you would come.

RINGO: Di season couldn't start widout me. [*He scratches himself again.*]

JOE: I know dat. What happen, why you scratching so?

RINGO: Master, is a long story.

JOE: What happen?

RINGO: I don't know how I don't have no luck. [*Hiss.*] I was on mi way here … [*Continues scratching.*] Don't laugh, you know, sar?

JOE: No man.

RINGO: I was minding mi own business, you know, sar, when a little chick wave me down and beg me a lift. She fat, you see! So I decide to check her. Den she say 'Let me out', so I open di door – she don't budge. Den all of a sudden I hear her say, 'You see mi dying trial. Drive!' So further down di road me just park di car and tek her into di bush. She was all right, man – hot stuff – when all of a sudden me feel something start to tickle me in mi back [*scratches himself again*] and me see di chick start to go so [*imitates the girl scratching*] and me start go so. When A look roun' … Master!

JOE: Cowitch.

RINGO: Cowitch, yes! A put on mi clothes, and is den it start to scratch me. A thought A had it bad but you should have seen di chick! [*He imitates her again.*] Den, like a worse bad luck, me see a river across di road …

JOE: You go and bathe?

RINGO: A had to.

JOE: But dat nuh mek it worse?

RINGO: Is me you telling? Di thing almost kill me! A don't know how A don't have no luck. So look now, if anybody ask why A just come back, A want you to back me up, right? [*Scratches himself.*] Food poisoning.

JOE: Food poisoning?

RINGO: Yes.

JOE: Ringo, you is a bitch.

RINGO: [*Hisses and scratches himself*] This is di least of my problems. A should be here from yessiday, but me and my missis had problems. One bangarang! Di woman too jealous and love money, man. I don't know why I get involved wid her. If she come looking for me, you don't see me. A gone to work in Port Antonio. Di chick at di front desk suppose to be covering for me too. Is who she?

JOE: Di new operator.

RINGO: What happen to Miss B?

JOE: She get fired.

RINGO: Who fire her?

JOE: Di new Assistant Manager.

RINGO: What for?

JOE: I don't know, boy.

RINGO: And she was such a all right chick. What a girl did love her thing, sar!

JOE: Wha'!

RINGO: Master, I have to go collect mi silver.

JOE: I have everything under control for you.

[*He presents RINGO with his tray of silver.*]

RINGO: Me just going to put my busboy in charge. Where him is?

JOE: Di one from last year don't come back. A hear say him get a waiter work at New Yarmouth Hotel.

RINGO: Is di poor tourists I sorry for. What a boy was stupid, sah!

JOE: Di new one assign to you is not much better. Him and di chef get in bangarang every day.

[*Loud noise of pots and pans thrown.*]

RINGO: What's that?

[JOE *goes to look in the direction of the noise.*]

JOE: Is di chef.

RINGO: Him on di warpath already. [*More noises are heard.*] Is who dat him running down wid di frying pan?

JOE: Is your busboy.

RINGO: Is him dat? Duck, boy! ... [*More noises are heard.*] What a boy head look like a coconut, sah! Dat head going to be a real tourist attraction. [*Laughs.*] Hey, so how di season going so far?

JOE: A group from di States coming in today.

RINGO: What you saying to me?

JOE: Plenty pickings.

RINGO: Plenty pickings, yes. I only hope that my luck run right dis season. Last year wasn't so hot.

JOE: True.

RINGO: Hey, remember di blonde chick from Chicago?

JOE: Yes.

RINGO: I got a letter from her.

JOE: You lie.

[*Sound of cars arriving outside, doors slamming and the hotel band striking up their theme song* 'Jamaica, Jamaica'.]

RINGO: Not lying to you. She coming back.

JOE: When?

RINGO: She not certain but she coming back.

JOE: Back to the sun.

RINGO: An' ting. [*Gyrating his pelvic area.*]

[JOE *proceeds to the imginary window and looks out.*]

JOE: Hey, come look. You see what I see?

[RINGO *joins* JOE *looking through the imaginary window.*]

RINGO: Dem come. Is dem, yes.

JOE: See di guy – di new Assistant Manager.

RINGO: A don't see him.

JOE: See him there, man.

RINGO: Di guy wid di knock knee?

JOE: No, man, di coloured guy.

RINGO: Di guy wid di cigar … you lie!

JOE: Yes, man.

RINGO: What him wearing roun' him neck?

JOE: Is so him dress.

O'KEEFE: This way, madam. Welcome to Mocho Beach. Would you register over there and then you might care for a drink? Very good. Bell boy!

[*The hotel band is playing softly in the background.*]

RINGO: Look at him, nuh. You know what him look like to me?

JOE: No, what?

RINGO: Like a mulatto jackass looking over a whitewash fence. [*Both laugh.*]

JOE: But Ringo, dem guests is only old people.

RINGO: Is only old people, yes.

JOE: Look at dat one. Him look like di same man to me. Where him going again?

RINGO: Who dat?

JOE: You don't remember?

RINGO: What?

JOE: Last year, up in di dining room, I was serving di table, when all of a sudden A see dat man turn white. Him try to get up, den him crash down, crumple up. Him head hit di soup bowl. You should see di gungo peas fly!

RINGO: Him did dead?

JOE: No man, him never dead, just too much excitement – run up and down all day in the hot sun, tek picture and drink rum punch. Doctor had to come. It look like him, but A don't feel is him.

173

RINGO: Nah.

JOE: Dat chick don't look too bad. [MISS BRANDON *appears in her area and peers through the imaginary window at the guests arriving.*]

RINGO: Shame on you, man.

JOE: True.

RINGO: Di pickings slim.

JOE: Slim bad.

RINGO: Hey, look who peeping.

JOE: Who?

RINGO: Di new chick at the front desk.

JOE: She peeping out.

RINGO: Is man she peeping at.

JOE: Look how she looking.

RINGO: As you look on her you can tell dat she love man.

JOE: Look like she is another Miss Benson ... yes, yes.

RINGO: 'The world is saying yes'.

JOE: No man, fun and joke aside, dem people look like hospital cases, not hotel guests. If any of dem turkey-looking chicks ever hang on to you, you never get away.

[*Exit* MISS BRANDON.]

RINGO: But I know that from experience.

JOE: Oh yes, I forget one did hang on to you last year – Gladys, di chick from Georgia.

RINGO: Dat will never happen to me again.

JOE: I heard it was a hot romance.

RINGO: Nonsense! Is money I was looking.

JOE: That wasn't what I heard. It was love!

RINGO: You must be mad. I did feel so shame. I didn't want anybody to see me wid her.

JOE: Den what about the drama wid you and she at di airport?

RINGO: A did so want to see her go back A had to see her go on di plane man. Is two time she cancel di flight you know, and di third time, di plane delay. You should see her knocking back di rum and coconut water.

JOE: So what about when you grab her up for di goodbye kiss?

RINGO: Is she grab me up, grab me roun' mi neck. [*He grabs* JOE.] 'Ringo baby; Ringo doll, come up to di States!'

JOE: Take it easy, man, take it easy.

RINGO: 'Don't make me go back, Ringo baby, we had such a good time!' Jesus Christ, man, di woman carry on wid one thing! How she going to be lonely because is just she and her dog live up north. One piece of bawling and screaming. A embarrass! Di more A try to pull away from her, di more she hang on to me, till everybody at the airport start looking at me. Since dat day A don't go back to di airport, you know. If A'm leaving this country, A leaving by ship. To make matters worse, my missis' brothers was out dere dat day. You should see me trying to dodge dem. Dat kind of scene will never happen to me again. Di things a man have to go through to make a dollar, sometimes you shame of yuhself. What you laughing for? Everybody know say you was engaged to a white woman. Where is di diamond ring?

JOE: You keep out of my business.

RINGO: Is lie you telling 'bout diamond ring. You never get nutten.

JOE: You want to see it? [*He pushes his hand in his pocket, then pulls it out again and pushes it empty into* RINGO'*s face.*] Go 'way!

[RINGO *picks up a stool.* JOE *reaches for a knife. They threaten each other.*]
[*We hear the band outside playing* 'Jamaica, Jamaica'.]

RINGO: The band playing sweet music, boy.

[*The tension slackens. They cautiously put down the stool and the knife. They improvise some steps to the music, at the same time singing the odd phrase.*]

JOE *and* RINGO: [*singing*]
>Jamaica, Jamaica, beautiful Jamaica
>you swim all day, drink all night
>wake up in the morning
>and di sun is bright
>Jamaica, Jamaica, beautiful Jamaica
>you play all day, sleep at noon
>wake up in di evening
>to see di pretty moon
>Jamaica, Jamaica, beautiful Jamaica
>you go to bed at night and everything's all right,
>but you wake up wid di dawn
>and you find yuh money gone
>Jamaica, Jamaica, beautiful Jamaica –
>yeah, yeah, yeah.

[*The music fades,* RINGO *is at the imaginary window.*]

RINGO: Where dat one-foot man going? Him want to bruck di other foot doing di limbo?

JOE: Look at him beads.

RINGO: Is a white soul brother.

JOE: Him look like salt pork to me.

RINGO: Di only thing on him that will tan is di wooden foot.

JOE: Look at di Maître D. Dat smile bigger dan di one from last year.

RINGO: Is di biggest hypocrite in dis hotel.

JOE: Watch di bow. Chic-a-bow Maître D.

RINGO: Style! Dat bow should earn him at least ten dollars.

JOE: Him know who have di money. I never see a man could X-ray a handbag or a wallet so fast.

RINGO: Stop rough up di bell boy!

JOG: Is all right man. Is him best friend. Is a part dem playing.

RINGO: White people love to see black people bow down, you see!

JOE: I will touch di ground if I can find a dollar bill down dere.

RINGO: A will go further than dat. A will bury my head in di san'.

JOE: How low can you get?

RINGO: Try me, nuh? A will bend over backward and do it too. White people must pay dem way.

JOE: Dem must pay, yes. Look how long dem carrying us down.

RINGO: Exploit di exploiter – God laughs. [RINGO *laughs*.]

[*A commotion is heard offstage of a high-pitched female voice.* JOE *goes to the imaginary window*.]

JOE: Hey, hol' on. Who dat black lady boring in between di tourists? She look like your missis.

RINGO: My missis? Where?

JOE: Is your missis, yes.

RINGO: A gone. You don't see me. A don't come to work. Tell her dat car lick me down. Tell her anything. Tell her dat A dead.

JOE: Where you gone?

RINGO: Master, if she see me A double dead. A gone to Port Antonio.

[*Voices offstage raised in altercation.*]

JOE: Hey! Hey, Ringo! She and di Assistant Manager having words!

RINGO: Is bangarang in di hotel today. [*Pause.*]

JOE: Backside! She getting out on him. Him mus' be rude to her.

RINGO: She will cuss him. She's a bad woman. My God! Look! Her two brothers come wid her.

JOE: Relax, man. Things quietening down out there.

RINGO: Dat is what you think. Di Assistant Manager

directing dem to come around di back. A have to hide, but what a hell if dem back me up roun' dere.

JOE: Hide in di pastry shop.

RINGO: And di chef is about? She threaten to come and scandal me today. A can't go roun' di back, and A can't go roun' di front. You see what I see? Di Assistant Manager coming dis way. You don't see me. Is one chance A have. What about dat?
[*He indicates garbage bin.*]

[O'KEEFE *can be seen angrily crossing the stage along the passageway that leads from his office to the rest of the hotel.*]

JOE: Yes, man. I will cover for you. Get in fast. [RINGO *smells the garbage bin.*] It new, man, compliments of the season. [RINGO *ducks in but pops up almost immediately.*]

RINGO: Remember what A tell you. You don't see me. A gone to Port Antonio.

JOE: Di man coming! Duck! [JOE *covers him and sits on the bin cleaning his silver. He whistles a tune as* O'KEEFE *enters.*]

O'KEEFE: Who is Ringo?

JOE: Good evening, sir.

O'KEEFE: Ringo, who is he?

JOE: One of the waiters, sir.

O'KEEFE: Where is he?

JOE: Ahm, he's gone, ahm, he's round the back changing his clothes, sir.

O'KEEFE: Find him. Find him!

JOE: Yes, sir. Ahm, sir, I just remember, sir. He's in the dining-room.

[*Exit* O'KEEFE *swiftly.* JOE *sighs with relief.* RINGO *starts to get out of the garbage bin. There is a great crash offstage of a body falling, and* O'KEEFE*'s voice –* 'Blast! Blast!' JOE *rushes to the door and peeps out.*]

JOE: [*delightedly*] You sprain it, sir?
[*To* RINGO] Quick, get back in. Di man coming. Get in.

O'KEEFE: [*Enters, brandishing a banana-skin furiously*]
Who threw it there?

JOE: I don't eat banana, sir. Let me throw it away for you, sir.

O'KEEFE: Throwing banana-skin on the floor when there is a bin! This is damn rubbish! I want to meet the entire kitchen staff first thing in the morning. I could have broken my foot.

JOE: You sprain it, sir?

O'KEEFE: This sort of thing can't go on. We can't run a hotel like this. Everything out of place. Some strange woman up the front embarrassing the guests. Find Ringo!

JOE: A woman up the front asking for Ringo, sir?

O'KEEFE: I have to get them out of the lobby somehow.

JOE: Nobody didn't tell you, sir?

O'KEEFE: Tell me what?

JOE: About the woman, sir.

O'KEEFE: What about her?

JOE: You just seeing her for the first time, sir. She tell you that Ringo is her man? Is a mad woman, you know, sir. Next week she will come and ask for you, sir, say you owe her money. I know the woman, sir. Last week she ask for me. She mad, sir!

O'KEEFE: Jesus Christ!

JOE: The lady mad, sir. And two men come wid her? Dem crazy too. If you check with the other fellows they will tell you the same thing. I don't know why they don't keep that woman locked up. Every time they let her out.

O'KEEFE: Out from where?

JOE: Bellevue, sir.

O'KEEFE: Jesus! How am I going to get them out of the lobby?

JOE: I don't know what to tell you, sir, for she is a lady that will make up a lot of noise and go on bad.

O'KEEFE: Where is the security guard?

JOE: That might make matters worse, you know, sir.

What we always do, and the Manager before you, is to give her fifty cents or two dollars and tell her that Ringo gone to work in Port Antonio. She is a lady that walk everywhere she going, so by the time she walk to Port Antonio and come back the season is finished. Ringo don't know her. Him don't know her personally. You do what I say, sir. [O'KEEFE *puts his hand in his pockets and, half-limping, walks away.*] Remember to coax her, sir. Treat her gently. [JOE *taps on the bin.* RINGO *comes up.*]

RINGO: Boss. You is a boss.

JOE: Is so, me good, man. Coast clear.

RINGO: You are a bitch. Boy, you lie, you know. Is a good thing you and me is friend. If you ever tell a lie on me A wouldn't stand a chance.

JOE: [*Eyeing him speculatively*] Hey, di man coming back. Get back in. [RINGO *ducks in.* JOE *tiptoes to the door and enters as the Manager. He imitates the Manager as best he can, maybe he squeezes his nose together or picks up a glass and speaks into it.*] [*As Manager*] Now look here to me. What's your name? ... 'Joe sar' ... Look here, Joe, that story you told me about that man Ringo, it's a damn lie. The Bell Captain told me a different story altogether. I am not an idiot, you know. Now in future you don't try and cover up for anybody or you are both going to find yourselves out of a job. Who threw that banana peel there again? ... 'A will throw it away, sar' ... I will do it myself. There is a garbage bin there. What you think it's there for? – for garbage. Have I got to teach you how to use it? It's very simple. You take the cover off ... [JOE *walks up to the bin and takes the cover off.* RINGO *comes up terrified.*] A fool you!

RINGO: You mustn't do dem things, you know, man. [*Hiss.*] Feel mi heart. It going bup, bup, bup. I did know it was you all di time. For a big man you go on like a child, eh. Is a serious joke you just play, you know.

JOE: You must behave yuhself. Hey, look outside. Look

how him talking to her nice and patting her. Is you I
sorry for all di same when she reach Port Antonio
and come back.

RINGO: A have to get rid of her somehow. Di woman
roun' mi neck like a rockstone. A explain to her, you
know. A tell her dat di hotel business not as bright as
it used to be. Remember, years ago, when you want
to find me you had to follow a trail of dollar bills. If it
wasn't for di children A would get in trouble for her
already.

JOE: You are a scamp.

RINGO: I know dat. I don't need nobody to tell me dat. I
know I am a scamp. How else A going to survive?
How else A going to look after mi children? It cost
money, you know. Di woman is unconscionable.
What she think. Dat A work in a gold mine? Look on
di cost of a room, and look what we got. We have to
live off tips. And another thing, di boss man have a
black man out front as Assistant Manager. Di tourist
don't like dat, you know, and I don't blame dem.

JOE: And we is di one who suffer.

RINGO: You should see di room I furnish for di woman!
Things change and she have to get accustomed to it.
Look out dere – old people. We have to beat dem up
to get a tip.

JOE: Is di poorer class we getting now.

RINGO: When dem come. I don't blame dem all di same.
If I had to pay dat kind of money I wouldn't give no
tips.

JOE: Even Club Montego empty.

[MISS BRANDON *enters her area pleased with herself, dials a
number and waits impatiently for someone to answer.*]

RINGO: You lie! And down dere always full wid di best
chicks.

JOE: Is almost time to serve di food. I going to check my
station.

RINGO: Yeah, A soon come, A have to find my busboy.
When you go up, check if any chick look passable.
Dem might not be too bad from close up.

[*Exit* JOE. *The lights go down on the kitchen area and come up
on* MISS BRANDON *on the front desk. She is on the phone.*]

MISS BRANDON: Yes, mi dear. Not bad. A have some news
for you, chile. A wanted to phone you back from in di
evening, but up here was busy. Listen nuh, a man
nuh check me! Me was here, mi dear, and when me
look up to see a man trying to look down in mi
bosom. Yes ... a white man ... true, true. Me go on
like me never see him. Him ask me some sorta
foolishness 'bout if me think sun going shine
tomorrow. How me mus' know dat? Anyway, mi
dear, di man nuh start to check me, how since him
come to di hotel him been noticing me, say dat me is
one of di prettiest coloured girls him ever see ... him
want to take me out. Me had to tell him dat di staff is
not allowed to go out wid di guests...No, him not
bad looking, ... wait nuh, man ... Him suggest dat
we could meet outside, and as A said him not bad
looking, so A sorta agree ... wait nuh, man ... Mi
dear, when di man walk away, I almost dead wid
shock. Nuh one foot di man have! ... Yes ... is a
wooden-foot man! Me nuh know if is wood or cork.
Him mention something 'bout war, but me could
never imagine say him was a cripple. Mi dear, I don't
know. Me promise him to go out ... but ... all the
same you know I will see what him up to, one foot or
no one foot. Yes ... one foot man better than no
man. You know how long I been trying to get a
permanent visa to go to America? When I get what I
want, I dump him. A going to take him someplace
quiet. A don't want anybody see me. Yes, A will call
you tomorrow and tell you what happen.

[*Lights go down on* MISS BRANDON *and warm on* RINGO, *obviously in a hurry.*)

RINGO: Coconut! [*His name for the* BUSBOY]
[*Crosses to back door*] Nuts!
[CYRIL *the* BUSBOY *enters nervously, zipping up his pants.*]
Hurry up, man. Hurry up. What happen to you?
Come, man. Where you come from – St Mary? How
you look so foolish? Why you so lazy? Look on you.
You never see white people yet?
What happen, dem frighten you? Hurry up and serve
di guests. [*Thrusting the plate into his hands.*]

[*The* BUSBOY *who is really quite terrified makes a very fast exit.*]

Damn idiot they give me.

[*The* BUSBOY *is just offstage when we hear the most almighty crash.* RINGO *throws his hands in the air. The* BUSBOY *returns empty-handed.*]

What happen? What happen?

[NOTE: The BUSBOY *has a lisp – so all his* 's' *and* 'sh' *sounds will become* 'th' *sounds when spoken.*]

BUSBOY: Is buck A buck mi toe, sar. [*Massaging his toe.*]
RINGO: You clean it up yet?
BUSBOY: No, sar.
RINGO: What you waiting for? Clean it up.

[CYRIL *collides with* JOE *in the swing door.* JOE *is carrying a plate with steak and potatoes.*]

JOE: What happen out dere?
RINGO: Nuh di idiot.
JOE: Me almos' bruck mi foot. [*Hiss*] Di big-belly white
man say di steak raw.

RINGO: Give it to di cook mek him bu'n it up, man.

JOE: Me not serving dem people at number 5 again, you know.

RINGO: What happen?

JOE: Me go to di man, nice and polite like, and ask him, 'What can I bring for you this evening, sir?' You know what di man say to me?

RINGO: No.

JOE: Him say me mus' bring everything.

RINGO: Everything on di menu?

JOE: Yes, everything. So me try and explain to him dat if him have di fish den him can't have di steak. Is a choice. Di man look on me and tell me dat him come on a package and everything inclusive, as if me know what dat mean.

[CYRIL *sidles in with tray and goes to the bin, removes the lid carefully, then finds his hands are too full to do anything else. He reconsiders.*]

Him mention to him wife dat him out to get him money's worth. Him ask her if she hungry, she say no. Him say dat don't matter, she have to eat. So me jus' pile up di food on di plate. Now him tell me 'bout di steak raw.

RINGO: Is full di man belly full, man.

JOE: Full, yes. But him still out dere eating.

[*During the above dialogue* CYRIL *has replaced the lid, put down the tray, opened the bin and dropped everything in triumphantly and with a great clatter. They stare at him as he drops the tray. Apologetically he retrieves it and goes out cautiously. They watch him go. Then* JOE *crosses to the bin and retrieves the knife and fork.*]

Di res' mash up.

RINGO: That's why we can't find the silver.

JOE: I don't know what wrong wid dem tourist people. Is

definitely di poorer class we getting now. Everything
wrong. I know dat all like dat package tour man not
giving no tips.

RINGO: Give tips what? A woman asking me a whole heap
a question, whole heap a fool-fool question, like what
is the population of dis country.

JOE: Must be somewhere in di region of three or four
million.

RINGO: Me tell her six.

JOE: Nutten not wrong wid dat. Give or take a million
what difference it make. Anything you tell dem, dem
believe. Dem stupid.

RINGO: A guy in my station – Winnie di Pooh, him say
him name – all him sing is 'Jamaica, Jamaica,
beautiful Jamaica'. Di rum punch gone to him head.
Him happy. Mek him sing. Him soon lose all him
money. Hey, who's di chick sitting alone by di piano?

JOE: Di black one?

RINGO: No, man. Who's she anyway?

JOE: Di new social director. Say she on managerial staff.

RINGO: If is me she waiting on to serve her, she goin'
starve to death. Is di other chick A talking about. Di
white one wid di long blonde hair, young. She never
arrive wid di group?

JOE: I don't know who she is.

RINGO: Look interesting. A going to check it.
[BUSBOY *enters again.*] You finish cleaning up di mess
you make outside?

BUSBOY: Yes, sar.

JOE: A soon come. A have to go and look about dis raw
steak.
[*Exit* JOE]

RINGO: Di place clean?

BUSBOY: Yes, sar.

RINGO: What?

BUSBOY: Yes, sar.

RINGO: Relax, man. How you look so frighten? Di white
people not going to eat you, you know. Listen to me

now. Dere is one or two things dat I have to bring to yuh attention. I been watching you in di dining-room. Listen to me, and listen good. I don't talk more dan once. Stand up good, man. Now di first thing: fix yuh clothes, man. If you going to work wid me, den you have to look better dan dat. You not only have to look better [*sniffs*], you have to smell better dan dat. Understand?

BUSBOY: Yes, sar.

RINGO: You ever hear 'bout a thing call deodorant?

BUSBOY: No, sar.

RINGO: Give me a dollar.

BUSBOY: A don't have any money, sar.

RINGO: All right, I will buy it for you. You owe me a dollar. Now look, I want you to pay attention to di table. As di man finish eat, A want you to take up di plate. You understand what A mean?

BUSBOY: Yes, sar.

RINGO: A going to show you something. Sit down. Sit down! Now, you are di guest and I is di waiter. The first thing is when you put in di plate. You see where my hand is?

BUSBOY: Yes, sar.

RINGO: Don't do it like that. If you do it like that you see what will happen?

BUSBOY: No, sar; no, sar.

RINGO: Nose gone under arm. B.O. Dat's what A mean.

BUSBOY: Yes, sar.

RINGO: Now try it. [*They change places.*] Straighten up yuhself man. Mek A see yuh face.

BUSBOY: Yes, sar.

RINGO: Smile. Smile.

BUSBOY: Yes, sar.

RINGO: Jesus Christ, man, you can't be a waiter if you can't smile.

BUSBOY: Yes.

RINGO: Master smile. Straighten up yuh head. Tell me something, what you use to do before?

BUSBOY: Before what, sar?

RINGO: Before you come to di hotel.

BUSBOY: A use to be chopping sugar cane in di country, sar.

RINGO: What? [RINGO *mimics the* BUSBOY'*s lisp*] Chopping sugar cane in di ... Master, you going to be in plenty trouble if people can't hear what you saying. Straighten up, [*Mimics* BUSBOY *again*] Chopping cane ... Tell me something, you know any Big Boy joke? [*The* BUSBOY'*s face explodes in a big grin.*] Oh, A see, you is a dirty-joke man. You playing fool to catch wise. What did Big Boy say to di teacher? [*Big grin again.*] Tell me, nuh.

BUSBOY: Me nuh know, sar.

RINGO: What A going do wid you? Tell me? Report you to di Manager and tell him dat you have no use?

BUSBOY: No, sar. [*He is frightened.*]

RINGO: No, A wouldn't do dat. You know why?

BUSBOY: No, sar.

RINGO: Because A like you. You are a nice boy. You have any sisters?

BUSBOY: Yes, sar. Five.

RINGO: Any of dem older dan you?

BUSBOY: No, sar, me is di bigges' one.

RINGO: How much brothers you have?

BUSBOY: Six, sar.

RINGO: Any of dem working?

BUSBOY: No, sar.

RINGO: You have a tie-tongue?

BUSBOY: Yes, sar.

RINGO: What am I going to do wid you? Di only thing dat might save you is if di tourists find di tie-tongue to be a native attraction. Yuh mother an' father work?

BUSBOY: Me nuh have no father, sar.

RINGO: So yuh mother expecting you to help wid di children?

BUSBOY: Yes, sar, she depending on me.

RINGO: If you use yuh head an' smart you can make

plenty money in di hotel, but you have to follow what I say, and I am a 'C' man. You know what dat mean?

BUSBOY: You work on a ship.

RINGO: No, 'C' – 'C' as in rooster. You know what A mean now?

BUSBOY: Yes, sar.

RINGO: You is a man dat like woman?

BUSBOY: Sometime, sar.

RINGO: How you mean sometime? A man mus' like chicks all di time. [RINGO *rubs him on the leg. He jumps.*]

BUSBOY: Don't do dat, sar.

RINGO: What happen, you never like dat?

BUSBOY: No, sar.

RINGO: I was testing you. You don't dig dat scene?

BUSBOY: No, sar.

RINGO: Cool, den. Now look, most of di girls dat come to di hotel don't come for sunshine, beach and all dem things. You know what dem come for?

BUSBOY: No, sar.

RINGO: How you mean you don't know? What you know? You know what girls like most of all?

BUSBOY: No, sar.

RINGO: You have a girl?

BUSBOY: Sometime, sar.

RINGO: How you mean sometime? You have a girlfriend? Anybody have any children for you?

BUSBOY: No, sar! [*With incredulity.*]

RINGO: Tell me: you like girls, though, cause if is not like dat, your scene finish wid me. You will have to go across to Willie. Him will look after you. You like girls?

BUSBOY: Yes, sar. Yes, sar.

RINGO: All right, now occasionally…Tell me something, you well blessed?

BUSBOY: Sometimes, sar.

RINGO: How you mean sometimes? If a man is well blessed it mus' be all di time. Wait now, you know what A mean when A ask if you well blessed?

BUSBOY: Yes, sar. Yes, sar.

RINGO: You well blessed?

BUSBOY: Sometimes, sar.

RINGO: You think you are a donkey? Only a donkey would be allowed to say that him well blessed sometimes an' other time him is not.

BUSBOY: But donkey can't talk, sar.

RINGO: You know, you right. You not so foolish, you know. But anyway, listen good to me. Occasionally a few girls will come to di hotel, and dem going to want everything wid a Jamaican flavour, right? I will spot dem. I know dem. Dem going to want a man. You have to take dem out, let dem drink two liquor. You don't drink.

BUSBOY: Sometimes, sar.

RINGO: No. You don't drink. You give dem a half bottle of white rum to drink [*claps his hands*]. You take dem to Mass Jim place, or down by di beach, and lick out.

BUSBOY: Yes, sar.

RINGO: You understan' dat?

BUSBOY: Yes, sar.

RINGO: You have knee-pad?

BUSBOY: No, sar.

RINGO: [*Laughs*] You ever try and do anything on di sand yet?

BUSBOY: No, sar.

RINGO: You will have to try it or you can't work here.

BUSBOY: All right, sar. You will show me?

RINGO: No. I can't show you. You must be mad. You will have to get yuhself together, and, most important, you have to charge dem. Yes, you have to charge dem. Not directly, but you have to make dem pay, right? Give dem a sob story. Tell dem dat yuh mother dead, or dat bailiff threaten to take away yuh things, or dat yuh baby sick in di hospital. You have to work dem over, and if you work dem good, you busy every night. And don't forget how yuh poor mother wid di whole heap of children in di country depending on you. Dat is a good story to give dem. If you find any wid plenty money you pass dem over to me. You understand?

BUSBOY: Yes, sar, but what happen between di time you pick dem out for me, and me lick out down at di beach?

RINGO: You have to make contact. You have to chat dem up.

BUSBOY: How me do dat?

RINGO: Simple, simple. Sit down again, mek A show you. Imagine you is di girl an' me is di waiter. Dis is a follow-up to what A was showing you earlier. I should've been a teacher. Step by step. Now, you have to use yuh brains. Before you check di chick you have to make certain dat she is alone. I don't make mistake, but you have to check for yuhself. All right, you is di guest and you having soup.

[RINGO *hands him an empty bowl with a spoon.*]

BUSBOY: Where is di soup?

RINGO: Imagine, man! What happen, you don't have any imagination? [RINGO *demonstrates.*] Like this. Now you do it. Dat's better. So I come up to you. 'Enjoy the soup, madam?'

BUSBOY: Eh?

RINGO: Yes. You playing a part, like in a show, so just play it natural. Let me tell you dis as a fact. If you is a black man and you can't play a part, you going starve to death. Dat is di first thing you have to learn – to play a part. A going to try it again. 'Enjoy the soup, madam?'

BUSBOY: Oh, a lady ask me to get her some water. [*Getting up to go.*]

RINGO: [RINGO *pulls him back*] Relax, man, answer me, 'Yeth [RINGO *picks up the* BUSBOY's *lisp, then corrects himself*], yes, thank you'.

BUSBOY: Yes, thank you.

RINGO: Good, good. Now for di tricky part. When you pop di question, two things you have to watch, dat di Manager not nearby, and dat you keep yuh voice down. Now watch me again. 'Enjoy the soup, Madam?'

BUSBOY: Yes, thank you.

RINGO: 'You look lovely tonight, madam. Would you like to see some Jamaican night spots?' [BUSBOY *is busy trying to catch a mosquito that is buzzing by his ankle.*] You hear me?

BUSBOY: No, what you say?

RINGO: Forget it. Give di lady her water.

BUSBOY: Me never hear what you say.

RINGO: You ask her if she want to see some Jamaican night spots, because she lonely. When she say yes, you agree to meet her outside di gate. Den is Jim place, or down di beach ...

BUSBOY: An' lick out!

RINGO: Right, now I will be di guest. Take up di tray, I am di lady. Go off a little bit an' den come in. [RINGO *starts playing the role of the lady.* BUSBOY *approaches.* RINGO *smiles.*] Smile, nuh man? Remember di Big Boy joke. [*He does.*] Dat's better. Now try an' date me.

BUSBOY: Dis is di dinner, ma'am.

RINGO: A don't hear what you say, and remember di arm pit.
[*He sniffs.*]

BUSBOY: Dis is di dinner, ma'am.

RINGO: Yes.

BUSBOY: Hope you enjoy di dinner, ma'am.

RINGO: A can't hear you, but anyway, good. Yes.

BUSBOY: Dinner, ma'am, enjoy di dinner?

RINGO: What you say? If you can take me out to dinner? You have di scene all wrong. You mus' tell me dat di dinner nice. I will tell you yes. Listen, nuh, what you doing can't work. Try and speak up. A losing mi temper and mi patience now. Everything wrong wid you. Try it, man. Last time, last chance. Remember di arm pit. Come in.

BUSBOY: Here is di dinner, ma'am.

RINGO: Easy. A left out something. Listerine is another thing A have to get for you. Action! Dat mean come in. Test me – arms, mouth, knee-pad. Speak up!

BUSBOY: Dinner.

RINGO: Yes, I enjoyed it very much.

BUSBUY: Can I take you out to a night club tonight, ma'am [*Touching* RINGO.]

RINGO: You skid! You skid! You can't touch di woman! Suppose she don't like you? You want to get both of us in trouble? If di woman report you, is assualt dem charge you with! Is jail dat, you know. You can't touch dem. You must know how to say it. You know what, I give up. You is of no use to me. You is a failure. You know what dat mean? You no good!

BUSBOY: Give me another chance, sar. A nervous, you know, sar.

RINGO: Nerves don't reach you yet.

BUSBOY: Another chance.

RINGO: Tek two weeks and watch me.

BUSBOY: Remember mi mother in di country, sar.

RINGO: [*Pauses, reflects.*] All right, but one more skid and you gone.

BUSBOY: Sit down! [*Very aggressively.* RINGO *looks at him.*] Sar … Enjoy di soup, ma'am?

RINGO: Yes, of course. Dat's better, dat's better.

BUSBOY: Enjoying your stay here?

RINGO: Boss! Now whisper. Quiet for di next line.

BUSBOY: You look lovely tonight, madam, would you care to see some Jamaican night spots? [*With strong pelvic movement.*]

RINGO: But of course. Boss! To find you A going have to follow a trail of dollar bills. Only one thing need to finish you up now. Now listen, you hear how I talk to you roun' di back – Jamaican?

BUSBOY: Yes, sar.

RINGO: Well, roun' di front is different business. You have to check an' hear which country dem come from by di way dem talk. You have English, American and Canadian. Forget about di English, dem too mean. Di American and di Canadian accent is almost di same. Concentrate on di American, and it will do for di Canadian.

BUSBOY: Yes, sar.

RINGO: No more a dat 'yeth thar' [RINGO *mimics the* BUSBOY]. Nobody talk like that. When di American going to say Saturday, him say 'Saterde ... Saterde' Check it? Say it.

BUSBOY: Therde.

RINGO: Saterde.

BUSBOY: Therde.

RINGO: Yeah. [*Despairingly*]

BUSBOY: Yeah!

RINGO: Yeah! [*Hopefully*]

BUSBOY: Yeah!

RINGO: You cotton-picking son of a gun! [*Eagerly*]

BUSBOY: You cotton-picking son of a gun!

RINGO: Sock it to me, sweetness!

BUSBOY: Sock it to me, sweetness! [*Pause*]

RINGO: Forget about di twang, play it natural. I going upstairs now to select a girl for you to tackle. Di blonde by di piano is mine. Don't forget now, smile! [BUSBOY *smiles*] Seen!

[RINGO *leaves through the swing door.* CYRIL *stands a moment, on the verge of a new life-style. Then* ...]

BUSBOY: Seen! [*He rushes off through the back door.*]

MISS BRANDON: [*Framed in her archway, stares down the corridor.*] Goodnight, Mrs O'Keefe. [*Pause.*] White bitch! [*Moves to her desk*] A wonder where *she* going now.

JOE: [*Rushes into the pantry. The band is playing brightly, a little off-key as usual. They will continue to play until the house lights are up and the audience gets up to stretch its legs.*] Ringo! [*No *answer.* JOE *dials the reception area.*] Miss Brandon?

MISS BRANDON: Yes? [*Applying lipstick, the phone cradled in her shoulder.*]

JOE: Joe here. Ringo pass you by the desk?

MISS BRANDON: No, none of the kitchen staff up here.

JOE: If you see him, tell him A looking for him.

MISS BRANDON: [*Smugly*] Just going off duty, sorry. [*She hangs up.*]

JOE: Him in trouble dis time for true. [*The* BUSBOY *enters, hiding a small bag behind him.*] Where is Ringo?

BUSBOY: I don't know, sar.

JOE: Well, you better find him. Tell him dat di blonde chick by di piano is Mrs O'Keefe.

BUSBOY: Mrs O'Keefe? Di Assistant Manager wife?

JOE: Yes! [*The* BUSBOY *turns to rush off.* JOE *swings him round again.*] What you have there?

BUSBOY: Is mi knee-pad, sar.

JOE: Knee-pad! You in dis racket too? What you doing?

BUSBOY: A jus' changing mi clothes, sar.

JOE: Where you going?

BUSBOY: A goin' home, sar.

[MISS BRANDON's *switchboard begins to ring. She eyes it contemptuously, snatches up her bag, and goes out swinging.*]

JOE: You too lie! You think A never see you in di dining room tonight making contact. That is your funeral! Better try di club and warn yuh boss. [*Exit fast.*]

BUSBOY: Yes, sar. [*But he can't resist a final look at his hair, and he hasn't tried the deodorant yet.*]

O'KEEFE: [*Enters* MISS BRANDON's *area angrily and fast. The phone stops ringing.*] Miss Brandon! Miss Brandon! [*Uses the P.A. mike on the desk*] Mrs O'Keefe, Mrs O'Keefe. Paging Mrs O'Keefe. Will Mrs O'Keefe kindly come to the lobby? Miss Brandon. Miss Brandon.

[*The* BUSBOY *sprays with deodorant hesitantly. Then with delight smells his armpits.*]

O'KEEFE: Mrs O'Keefe. Mrs O'Keefe!

[*The* BUSBOY *begins to smile and smile and as the lights fade he is spraying himself from head to toe.*]

ACT TWO

[*The band has been playing* 'Island In The Sun'. *The stage is dark. For a moment, crickets and night sounds can be heard. The band welcomes in a new day with a raucous version of* 'Rookombine'.

JOE *hurries in from the backyard bearing a basket from the florist's, with a card attached. He signs himself in, goes out through the swing door, reappears in* MISS BRANDON'S *area, leaves the flowers on her desk, notices an envelope there, takes it, leaves, reappears in* O'KEEFE'S *office where he leaves the envelope, and retraces his steps down the corridor to disappear in the direction of the dining room, while …*

CYRIL, *the* BUSBOY, *signs himself in and heads for the dining room backstage, while …*

MISS BRANDON *enters, takes her place, sees the flowers, puts them in a vase, smiles over the card. The phone rings. She checks the time, and reluctantly picks up the receiver.*]

MISS BRANDON: Mocho Beach Hotel. Good morning. Can I help you? What happen, Maisie? … No, man, A have to see you to talk. A feel A'm on to something … Yes, we went out. You know di club we went to di night? … Him have money – like dirt! Him mus' be 'bout forty … No, we never dance, just drinks. You forget is one foot di man have? Me never want anybody see me wid him. People chat too much. Him all right though. Tell me everything 'bout himself. How him lose di foot an' everything. Yes. Vietnam. Him come home an' find him wife shacking up wid another man. When him ask her 'bout it, she say if him did expect her to live like a nun. Woman too wicked! Tears almost come to him eye while him was telling me. A feel sorry for him, you see? Is one of di reasons why him come on holiday. Him say dat me is

di nicest thing dat happen to him in a long while.
Yes, A tell you I'm on to something.

[O'KEEFE *passes noisily*. MISS BRANDON *eyes him, and
remembers something* ...]

Guess who me see down at di club last night? Flap
Flap wife! When you see who she was wid! You know
di little twis' head cocky boy dem have here? Dem
call him Ringo. Yes, nuh him! Little hurry-come-up
boy! You want to see him. One piece a rub up! It look
like Flap Flap not doing him homework.

[O'KEEFE *in his office reads the note and takes a tranquiliser*.]

Anyway, hear me, I don't want to put mi mouth in
nobody business. So look, A want you to see di man.
Him little bit and twis' up, but him worship di
ground me walk on. Him don't have to do a thing.
What A tell you? I want to go to America and it don't
matter. [*Hiss*] Di bed business? If push come to shove,
me jus' shut mi eye and do it. Di man have di money
and I want to go ... [O'KEEFE *buzzes the reception area*.]
Hold on a minute ... Yes, Mister O'Keefe, the line to
the kitchen is out of order, sir. I'll send a message
down to him ... Yes chile, bangarang here today!

[MISS BRANDON *buzzes the pantry phone*. JOE *answers*.]

JOE: [*Eagerly*] Ringo?
MISS BRANDON: Front desk, please.

[JOE *leaves through the swing door*. MISS BRANDON *scribbles on
her pad, folds the note*. CYRIL, *the* BUSBOY, *enters the pantry
dreamily, carrying his knee pads*.]

[*On the phone again to Maisie*] Flap Flap want to see
Ringo. Di woman shouldn't really do him dat all di

same. Not wid a waiter. And you want to see her pass
through here last night. She come and ask me to get
her husband on di phone, never even tell me howdy.
… She don't chat to me, mi dear. All I know is if she
try to show off on me, I jus' let her know dat Ringo
couldn't be my yard boy.

[JOE *enters the central area.* MISS BRANDON *hands him the note.*
JOE *eyes her legs. He fiddles with a flower for his buttonhole.*]

What? Oh, you want to see di man. Den you nuh can
pass by later. We going out dis evening. [O'KEEFE
enters, stares at JOE, *who sidles out.*] Mi dear, all flowers
arrive dis morning. [O'KEEFE *puts papers on* MISS
BRANDON's *desk, and stares at her for a moment, then leaves.*]
A have a little work to do, so A see you later.

[*The lights come up on the kitchen area.* RINGO *enters. There is
a plaster on his forehead.*]

RINGO: Hey, young boy, you see Joe?
BUSBOY: Morning, sar. Him looking for you, sar. Him give
me a message to give you last night.
RINGO: Find him for me. Hey come here, how you got on
wid di chick last night?
BUSBOY: Not bad, sar. [*With much pleasure.*]
RINGO: You raise money?
BUSBOY: Not yet, sar.
RINGO: Dis thing don't go on credit, you know. Lend me
ten dollars.
BUSBOY: A don't get any money yet, sar. [*Enter* JOE.]
JOE: Ringo, where you was, man?
RINGO: I'm in a spot. Lend me ten dollars.
JOE: How ten dollars going to help you? Your young boy
never give you di message last night?
RINGO: No.
JOE: You never give him di message?
BUSBOY: A never see him, sar.

RINGO: You must have ten dollars, man. [*Pointing to the plaster on his forehead*] Look what happen to me last night? Mi missis never buy di story. I should know better than to think she would believe A gone to work in Port Antonio. She and her two brothers back me up and tek away every cent A had. Is bitch today if A don't give her another ten dollars. I in trouble!

JOE: You really in trouble. Di Assistant Manager want to see you. About three messages come since morning.

RINGO: What for?

JOE: You too careless, man.

RINGO: What happen?

JOE: Di chick you took out last night, you know is who?

RINGO: No.

JOE: She never tell you whose wife she is?

RINGO: No.

JOE: She have long blonde hair? Had on a blue frock and talk wid a funny accent?

RINGO: She talk funny, you see? A couldn't understand a word she say.

JOE: Is di Assistant Manager wife. [*Pause.*]

RINGO: Dat all right.

JOE: You tell him dat.

RINGO: You making joke?

JOE: Look on mi face.

RINGO: Jesus Christ, you lie!

JOE: Me is a big man.

RINGO: Don't do me dat. She couldn't say something to me. Him want to see me?

JOE: Yes.

RINGO: Him know, him see me, him trail me. You cover me?

JOE: A wanted to cover you, yes, but I never know where to cover.

RINGO: Him can't know, unless him trail me or somebody tell him. Nobody saw me. Wait, A wonder if is di Afro chick at di front desk. Me see her up at di club, she and a one-foot man. Di same one-foot man dat came in yesterday. One of di guests. Dat's against di hotel rule. I will mek her lose di work if is she. Den you want to see her caressing di wooden foot. Is mus' she, man; nobody else never see me.

JOE: Di whole hotel talking 'bout it.

RINGO: You couldn't tell me?

JOE: Me never know. Me tell yuh busboy to find you.

RINGO: Why you never find me?

JOE: Me look everywhere for you.

RINGO: Hold on, man. It don't necessarily mean dat di man want to see me 'bout di woman. Di only thing to do now is to check wid di woman herself. A have to check wid her. Yes. A have to find out if di little Afro chick at di front desk grounds or if she sheg up. A going to ask her to phone di woman.

JOE: I don't trust dat girl.

RINGO: I have her card, man. I have to find out how much di man know. As a matter of fact, what I put on him wife last night, him can't fire me. If him fire me, A jus' take up residence in him house. I can't lose di work. Di phone working?

JOE: It go an' come.

RINGO: I going to talk to her. A soon come.
[*To the* BUSBOY] Go and look after di breakfast things!

[RINGO *goes across to the front desk.*]

JOE: [*Shouts to the* BUSBOY] You don't hear what di man say?

[*The* BUSBOY *scampers out.*]

RINGO: Hi, Miss B. [MISS BRANDON *ignores him and reaches for the phone.*] A saw you last night with a nice-looking guy. Nice. Look, I know you are new here, so you might not know what is what, but is against regulations to go out wid di guests. People get in trouble for it already. But me is grounds. I will cover for you. Any little favour, jus' ask me, like taking a message up to him room, check me. You can depend on me, all right? Now look, you grounds. [*Putting his hand through his Afro hair – she does likewise with hers.*] A see you grounds. A want you to do me a favour. Get dis number for me. You know is who to. Flap Flap wife. [*He takes a flower from the vase, kisses it and hands it to her.*] I will take it in di kitchen. [*She dials as* RINGO *leaves for the kitchen.*]

[*The phone in the pantry rings.* JOE *reaches for it, but* RINGO *is first.*]

RINGO: She grounds. Hello.
MISS BRANDON: Can I speak with Mrs O'Keefe? [*She listens to conversation.*]
RINGO: She getting her. Hello. Michelle? Hello, ah, ahh ha, ha ... Ringo, Ringo, yes, yes. Ringo from di hotel ... You never tell me dat you was married. [*To* JOE] I can't understand a word she saying ... Is when I got down here dis morning dat I got to realise dat my boss – Flap Flap – and you ... [*To* JOE] She not understanding a word I saying either, you know ... He won't like it if he hears about last night. A don't want him to know. Him say anything to you 'bout last night? [*He speaks very slowly.*] Him don't say anything to you 'bout last night? Is all right den. Di taxi got a puncture, oh, oh, and I was only helping you to change di tyre. You are di greatest! Right, A want you to cover me. Look, A want to make dat scene again. Yeah, listen, nuh, you enjoy it?

[*He gives the phone to* JOE, *who listens to the reply.* O'KEEFE *passes through* MISS BRANDON's *area, pausing at her desk. She shakes with laughter, covering the phone and eyeing him.*] Yeah, yeah, all right, all right. A see you ... later. [*He hangs up.*] Boss! She cover me, man.

[MISS BRANDON *hastily dials Maisie, and though we can't hear what she is saying, it is clear that she is passing on the gossip as usual.*]

RINGO: Dat covered, A hope. A wonder what him want to see me for.

JOE: Maybe somebody report you.

RINGO: Nobody never fresh wid me last night. I going to face di music. What time you have?

JOE: 9.30.

RINGO: A mus' raise ten dollars by ten. Di woman coming for it.

JOE: I bruck.

RINGO: Depending on what Flap Flap want to see me for, A might be able to hit him for the ten dollars. Him wouldn't know mi mother dead from last year.

JOE: How much more you hope to make off di poor old lady? She worth more to you dead dan alive.

RINGO: So life go. Me have to settle wid her today ... Oh Jesus!

JOE: What now?

RINGO: Last night when dem back me up A promise to find jobs for the brothers. Any jobs up here?

JOE: What dem can do?

RINGO: Bruck shop. What else? Is two old criminals.

JOE: Dem would make good studs.

RINGO: What! How I get myself in all dem spots. If is not one thing is another.

JOE: Hold on!

RINGO: What?

JOE: Any of dem can swim?

RINGO: A don't think so, why?

JOE: Di lifeguard for di pool walk off di job, and I don't see di pool attendant come back. A hear him gone to America.

RINGO: If dem can swim maybe dem can raise a little work by di pool. I don't want dem to work here all di same, but what to do. A going find out if dem can swim. Even if dem can't swim, no big t'ing, we nuh

can fix dem up wid papers? Recommendation not
hard to get.

JOE: You don't have to be able to swim to be a lifeguard at
a hotel.

RINGO: Nobody ever drown in di pool yet.

JOE: No, sah.

RINGO: No big t'ing den. All di boys have to do is oil up
dem self an' play di part. [*Poses like a lifeguard.*]

JOE: Yes. Di American tourists can swim, man. Is only
Jamaicans afraid of water.

RINGO: You can swim?

JOE: No, sah! What 'bout you?

RINGO: Like a fish.

[RINGO *does a few fancy strokes in the air with his hands.*]

JOE: You too lie.

RINGO: I am a boss!

[JOE *grabs his hands behind his back into an arm-lock.*]

JOE: Tell me di truth.

[RINGO *continues to say he can swim until the pain becomes too
much — he cries out that he can't.*]

RINGO: You play too rough, man.

JOE: An' you tell too much lie.

[RINGO *nurses his hands and hisses.*]

JOE: You wait till di Manager back you up dis morning!

RINGO: A wonder what him want me for. A going check
wid him. If is nutten too serious, A knock him for a
ten dollar, den get mi missis brothers a job, an' all mi
problems solve. Boss!

JOE: Him strict, you know. Him going to need papers for
dem jobs.

RINGO: No big t'ing! Where my young boy? Hey, 'Nuts', come here.

BUSBOY: Yes, sar.

RINGO: Come here. You know Bongo Man?

BUSBOY: Bongo Man, sar?

RINGO: Yes, man. Di big black guy dat wear di dark glasses. Him work wid di black chile dat have di goat race for di tourists.

BUSBOY: Oh yes, sar.

RINGO: Check wid him for me. Ask him if dem having crab race tonight, then come back an' tell me. An' one more thing, what your girlfriend name again?

BUSBOY: Miss Gladys, sar.

RINGO: Now you going ask her to do you a favour. First of all, check if she planning to go to di crab race. If she not planning to go, then you have to inveigle her to go. Then you ask her to place two bets on two crabs for you. But I will check you an' tell you more about it. Just check wid Bongo Man for a start. Seen? [JOE begins to peel an orange.]

BUSBOY: Seen!

RINGO: And [puts his fingers to his lips saying], 'Mum's the word.' [Exit BUSBOY.]

JOE: Ringo!

RINGO: A soon come.

JOE: No, come here.

RINGO: What happen?

JOE: Take it easy.

RINGO: What happen?

JOE: Leave di crab race alone. You don't know what di Manager want to see you for yet, an' you mixing up yuhself in more worries.

RINGO: Cool yuhself.

JOE: No, listen to me, man. Is a black man running di show, you know.

RINGO: You afraid of him?

JOE: No, but is not like say is a white man who don't
know what going on.

RINGO: Dat's where you wrong. White man know more
racket dan black man. What little I know, who you
think I learn it from?

JOE: Di new Manager good too. Him know every little
racket dat go on in di hotel, you know. So cool it!
Study him first.

RINGO: How him going to catch me? Crab foot can bruck
by accident, you know.

JOE: Hear what I say, cool it!

RINGO: A see you later. I going to face di music. [*As he goes.*]

[*The band is playing the end of some song.* RINGO *returns. He's had
an idea. The following sequence occurs like an elaborate ritual.*
RINGO *takes the orange and knife from* JOE, *and cuts the fruit. He
places it on a saucer. The knife on the shelf is smeared so he spits on it
and wipes it shiny on his jacket, then adds it to the orange. He turns
to go.* JOE *catches on, stops him, blows the dust off a tray, places plate
and knife on the tray and sends* RINGO *on his way through the swing
door. Before leaving also,* JOE *buzzes* MISS BRANDON *and tells her
what's happening. As* RINGO *passes down the corridor,* MISS
BRANDON *calls him in, pats his hair into place, straightens his jacket,
puts the flower he gave her on the tray beside the orange before
leaving the stage. A moment later, as the music and laughter from the
poolside fade,* RINGO *knocks on* O'KEEFE's *door and sticks his head in.*
O'KEEFE, *deep in paperwork, ignores him.* RINGO *frowns, ducks out.
He knocks again.*]

RINGO: Mister O'Keefe! [*His hand appears round the door,
holding the tray aloft like an offering.*]

O'KEEFE: [*Glances up.*] Come in.

[RINGO *enters.* O'KEEFE *moves his papers.* RINGO *places the tray
down with a flourish.*]

RINGO: Ringo Smith, sir.

O'KEEFE: One moment, Smith. [RINGO *waits, smiling*

205

innocently.] First thing, Smith, what happened to you on Tuesday? Beginning of the season and you were late. What's the excuse?

RINGO: I am sorry, sir, but I was sick, sir. Food poisoning, sir.

O'KEEFE: You have a doctor's certificate?

RINGO: Well, no, sir. Di last time dat I had a complaint like this, sir [*scratching himself*], di doctor put me on two weeks' leave, sir, but as di season was just starting up again, sir, and A didn't want to miss it, sir, and since I wasn't feeling too bad, sir — it still troubling me a little bit, you know, sir? [*scratching himself*] — nonetheless, I thought I would try and come out, sir. I'm all right really, sir. I am sorry I was a little bit late, sir.

O'KEEFE: Cut the sir!

RINGO: What, sir?

O'KEEFE: The other thing, Smith, and I don't want to beat about the bush for I don't have the time, I had a report about you this morning. I don't like it, and I don't want it to happen again as long as I am at Mocho Beach. I am not going to put up with this sort of nonsense.

RINGO: What I do, sir?

O'KEEFE: As far as I am concerned, anybody who does that sort of thing is out!

RINGO: What I do, sir?

O'KEEFE: Grow up, man, grow up. What happened in the dining room last night?

RINGO: What, sir?

O'KEEFE: Why didn't you serve Miss Thomas?

RINGO: Which Miss Thomas, sir? Who is she, sir?

O'KEEFE: The new Social Director. Here we are. [*Picking up a letter.*] The lady threatened to resign. I have no idea what is going to happen yet, but it's serious. [*Looking at her letter.*] She says here that she went along to the dining room and waited for over an hour before she was served. She says she was deliberately ignored for over an hour. I have a report here from the bell captain that says you were on Station Two, and that you were responsible for serving her.

RINGO: Deliberately, sir? Why would I do that, sir? I don't even know her. What she look like, sir?

O'KEEFE: One black face in a room, you can't miss her, man.

RINGO: You see my dying trial! People going mek I lose my work now. I serve her, you know, sir.

O'KEEFE: After one hour?

RINGO: I was busy serving di tourists.

O'KEEFE: The hotel is only a quarter full.

RINGO: Is my fault to come out when I know I wasn't so well. I try mi best to look after di guests.

O'KEEFE: Look, Smith, I know what goes on, so don't try an' bullshit me! I know you waiters. You don't like to serve black people.

RINGO: I am a black man too, you know, sir, an' there is no one to me like my black brother an' sister. I am very conscious, very conscious. At di same time, I don't differentiate. I love white people too … black man, white man, coolie man, chiney man – we is all God's children. We all have to live as brothers, an' I try, you know, sir, but every time mi own black man let me down. What you say is true, you know, sir. I know most of the waiters don't like to serve black people, but there is a reason for it, you know, sir. Di minute a waiter see a black man or a black lady enter a dining room, him frighten, him heart start to go 'bup, bup'. Him 'fraid straight away, him nervous.

O'KEEFE: Why is this, Smith? [RINGO *stalls for a moment, then tenderly offers the orange.* O'KEEFE's *face softens a little.*] Have a seat.

RINGO: [*Under his breath*] Why is this? Di black people who come to di hotel treat waiters like dirt, like you still cutting dem garden up in di hills, an' if you don't serve him right away him say you snob him, an' him is di first man to report you, you know, sir. I 'fraid o' dem too, you know, sir. Dat's why di waiters in any hotel avoid dem. As a Manager I feel proud of you, you know, sir, for I see you as one of my own. [O'KEEFE *chokes on the orange.*] You have to get to realise these facts. There is plenty prejudice among black people an' if you don't realise it, sir, every time a black man come into the hotel, you going to fire a waiter. Dem don't respect us, you know, sir; call us boy an' gas something or other. If a man don't respect you, you can't respect him back, sir. Di waiter try, for most a dem conscious, but a party will come in from Kingston, and because you know dat them will report you, you jump roun' fast, sir, and you give them the best service, an' also you looking a good tip. [O'KEEFE *reaches for a cigar, then looks around for his lighter.* RINGO *beats him to it and offers him a light.* RINGO *then pockets the lighter.*] I work for tips, you know, sir. Is it we live off, so we have to work for it.

O'KEEFE: Lighter, Smith.

RINGO: Lighter? Oh yes? [*Returns it.*] So you give di man from Kingston a good service, sir, an' when him done, if him don't report you an' say you rude, him give you ten cents. What ten cents can do, sar? So next time you see him, you avoid him for you don't want to lose di work. You see di position, sir? Is bad enough when a white man call you boy an' den give you a dollar, but when you own black man call you so an' give you ten cents, plus report you? [MISS BRANDON *enters her area and buzzes* O'KEEFE'*s office.*] [*Pause*]

O'KEEFE: I am here to run a hotel Smith, not to ... [*Telephone rings.* O'KEEFE *answers.*] O'Keefe, Assistant Manager speaking ... Yes, ask her to come up and see me. [*He hangs up.*] Just don't let it happen again. I'll have to apologise to Miss Thomas. We'll forget about it this time.

RINGO: But I explained the position to you, sir. I know them.

O'KEEFE: It's okay, Smith.

RINGO: All right, sir. [*He is going, but returns.*] Ahm, I wonder if I could ask you a favour?

O'KEEFE: You'll have to come back later, Smith. There is a lady coming up to see me.

RINGO: It won't take a second, you know, sir.

O'KEEFE: Yes, what is it?

RINGO: I hear there is going to be a vacancy for a lifeguard at di pool. I know somebody wid plenty experience in dat line.

O'KEEFE: Ask him to come and see me.

RINGO: All right, sir. And, sir, I know somebody else who could work as di pool attendant, you know, sir.

O'KEEFE: Ask him to come and see me too.

RINGO: All right, sir. Thank you, sir. [RINGO *turns to go, then returns. He has forgotten the tray and the remains of the orange. He collects them, then empties* O'KEEFE'*s ash tray, dusting off any little specks of dust etc. from the desk.* O'KEEFE *watches him for a moment and then their eyes meet.*] Ahm, sir, I wonder if you could lend me ten dollars, sir?

O'KEEFE: I don't lend money, Smith!

RINGO: Well, you see, sir, it is to fill the prescription for the food poisoning. It is still troubling me a little, an' seeing as how I don't want to miss the hotel work, being as how we busy like, if I get the medicine today, I would feel better.

O'KEEFE: [*Totally swamped by* RINGO'*s verbiage, goes into his pocket for the money. He hands* RINGO *a ten-dollar note.*] Let me have it back.

RINGO: Have it back? Oh yes! [RINGO, *leaving, makes a face at* O'KEEFE'*s back.* JOE *meets* RINGO *along the passageway.*]

JOE: You got it?

RINGO: Got it? What you think? You think I'm an ass? You think I come to town last week or what? [*He shows him the money. With much jubilation they proceed to* MISS BRANDON'*s desk.* RINGO *shows her the money.*] Your boy. [*The jubilation continues as the lights go down on them slapping palms. The lights go out.*]

[*One day later. The band is playing.* JOE *is dusting in the corridor outside the swing door.* RINGO *is at the pantry window.*]

RINGO: Mi missis' brothers get di jobs after all.

JOE: Me see dem. Dem nervous, though.

RINGO: Me had to talk to dem, tell dem to relax. Dem just not playing di part right. I was by di pool a while ago and a man was up on di diving-board. You want to see di boys, particularly di one playing di lifeguard part. See di man on di diving-board here, an' see di lifeguard. [*He acts it out.*] Is when di man dive in you want to see di tension. It wasn't 'till di man surface again dat me see di boy relax a little.

JOE: Dem look good, though.

RINGO: You want to see di chicks looking at dem. They have to learn to play di part better dan dat. All di same is none of my business now. Di problems I had to get di recommendations! They even have papers to show that they win 'cross-di-harbour swim in Kingston. [JOE *laughs.*]

BUSBOY: [*Entering*] Here, Missa Joe! Di lady at di front desk say dat a man leave dis letter for you, sir. [*He gives it to him.*] And Missa Ringo, di lady say that she want to see di rest of mi family, sar.

RINGO: Which lady?

BUSBOY: Miss Gladys, sir.

RINGO: Oh, your chick. Den take her, nuh.

BUSBOY: All right, sar.

JOE: Pete, Pete, Pete, oh hell! Hey, Ringo, check dis. [*Giving the letter to* RINGO]

RINGO: You get money. Is a chick?

JOE: No, check dis. [RINGO *takes the letter and reads.*]

RINGO: You are a gentleman. [*To* JOE] Who? You? No, man, you is no gentleman, you is a black man. Who is dis guy Pete?

JOE: Is some guy A met yessiday, a little white man. A met him on di road. Him was having a little problem wid him car, di jack wasn't working, and A helped him change di tyre.

RINGO: And him sen' you ten dollars?

JOE: Him offer me a dollar at di time, but as it was no big t'ing A did, me tell him don't bother.

RINGO: After you refuse di dollar him sen' you ten! Him is a faggot. Him looking something.

JOE: Rubbish.

RINGO: Man don't give away money like that. Is something him want.

JOE: I help di guy because him was in a spot. No big t'ing! What happen, you can't do something for a man sometime without having to get something back?

RINGO: Something wrong. [*Reading letter*] You are a gentleman. See you next year. Mmm, the man planning for you.

JOE: I not talking to you, man.

RINGO: Di Yankee man pay him way. Him don't want you to do anything for him for nutten.

JOE: I ask you a question a while ago and you never answer me. You don't feel that sometime you can do something for another without getting something back?

RINGO: Yes, but not you. Di way you love tips?

JOE: In di hotel is different business. Business is business.

RINGO: You not keeping di ten dollars then?

JOE: Yes.

RINGO: See what A mean.

JOE: What?

RINGO: If you did it for love as you say, you would give it back.

JOE: I don't know where to find him.

RINGO: Give it to me then. [*He snatches it.*]

JOE: Give me mi money. [*They fight for it, until* JOE *gets it back.*] Di way I bruck it going to come in handy.

RINGO: You don't want to invest it on di crabs tonight? You can't lose on di orange and di red because everything else under handicap.

JOE: If dem catch you, you salt.

RINGO: Where is mi young boy? [*Calling the* BUSBOY] Coconut! Coconut!

BUSBOY: Sar.

RINGO: Come here, man. [*To* JOE] You not betting?

JOE: Go on, nuh?

RINGO: All of it?

JOE: Might as well. [*Enter* BUSBOY.]

BUSBOY: Sar.

RINGO: Where you was?

BUSBOY: I was getting a rum punch for Missa Winnie, sar.

RINGO: Who?

BUSBOY: Di jokify man, sar.

RINGO: Come here.

BUSBOY: Sar?

RINGO: You line up Gladys for tonight?

BUSBOY: Yes, sar.

RINGO: See di money here. She mus' bet on di red crab an' di orange crab. What A say?

BUSBOY: Di red crab an' di orange crab, sar.

RINGO: [*He signals him to go.*] An' get her by herself. I know how you stupid.

BUSBOY: It all right, sar. [*He goes.*]

[MISS BRANDON, *on her way down the corridor, answers the phone, buzzes the pantry and goes out again.*]

JOE: Hey, Ringo, you certain it going to work?

RINGO: Can't fail. Big pay day tonight. [*The kitchen telephone goes.* RINGO *answers.*] Hello, kitchen. What happen, guy? Say what? Doris? Doris who? ... Oh, dat Doris! Di maid up at room service ... Hot romance? ... She and di one-foot man? What you saying to me? You lie! I thought it was di Afro chick at di front desk controlling him ... so what role him playing? [MISS BRANDON's *phone rings again. She hurries in to take the call.*] Hey Joe, come listen to dis. A hot story, man.

MISS BRANDON: Mocho Beach ... What happen, chile?

JOE: I can't hear nutten.

MISS BRANDON: Not bad. Me get a present from him. A bikini.

RINGO: You can see fat Doris in a bikini! Why him buy it for her?

MISS BRANDON: I was thinking maybe he wanted us to go for a swim.

RINGO: What you mean? Him ask her to teach him to dance, dress in di bikini?

MISS BRANDON: A thought it was a bit funny him wanting me to teach him to dance dress like dat.

RINGO: What kind of dance?

MISS BRANDON: Me ask him if it was Reggae but him say no. Nuh some rude dance him see at di club di other night.

RINGO: Tell me more. Nuh bump an' grind dat?

MISS BRANDON: True! You know I wouldn't hide nutten from you.

RINGO: Dat weird.

MISS BRANDON: I put it on but I wouldn't do di dance.

RINGO: She do it, man. Woman will do anything as long as di price is right. Is true all di same. Doris proud. She not doing dem things. You know how long I making after her?

MISS BRANDON: Of course you know I don't shave my t'ing. You should see di man eye! I determine though, you know, chile, I going to America, and I don't care how I go. One thing I tell you, I not giving away my pearl for nutten. Is all I have. It have to work for me.

RINGO: I wonder what else him lose beside di foot.

MISS BRANDON: Is di same thing I was thinking.

RINGO: Him offer her ring too? What kind of ring?

MISS BRANDON: Not a thing happening till it on mi finger, mi dear.

RINGO: Is a trap, yes. To do di nastiness.

MISS BRANDON: Oh, his head, it not so bad, mi dear.

RINGO: She lick him over him head wid a bottle. Boss!

MISS BRANDON: Him slip in di bathroom, mi dear.

RINGO: Mek him tell people dat, man. She should buss him head.

MISS BRANDON: Hold on, a call coming in. Hello, Mocho Beach Hotel. Hold, please.

RINGO: Keep me in touch. [*He hangs up.*]

JOE: What happen? I never hear a thing.

RINGO: One piece o' scandal! You know di one-foot man? [*The telephone rings.* RINGO *answers.*]
Hello, kitchen. What happen, Bongo Man? All right, give me a minute, I'll be right there. [*He hangs up.*] I soon come.

JOE: So tell me what happen.

RINGO: When I come back.

JOE: I'm coming wid you, man. [*The two leave very quickly.*]

MISS BRANDON: Later, den. I will keep you in touch.

[*In the dark we hear the crab race. Then lights warm slowly.* MISS BRANDON, *with back to us, is on the phone. One day later.*]

JOE: [*Off*] Ringo! [*He enters from the yard, signs in, goes out towards the dining-room.*]

MISS BRANDON: I am telling you, chile, things happening fast. [*She displays ring.*] I don't know what it is … It look like diamond, yes. Him going to Ocho Rios to see some friend of his later today, then we meeting later to make di final arrangements. When I get to America it will be a different business … I will send for you. Why not? I writing di resignation today. I want to get out of dis country so bad, chile. I see you later, all right.

JOE: [*Off*] Hey, young boy, come here.

BUSBOY: [*Off*] A soon come, sar.

JOE: Come now!

[JOE *re-enters the pantry. He means business. He sits, and puts his feet up on the other stool, as* BUSBOY *enters.*]

JOE: Come here, man. What happen last night? Ringo win anything on di crabs?

BUSBOY: Yes, sar. Plenty, sar.

JOE: Where it is?

BUSBOY: Missa Ringo have it, sar.

JOE: Where him is? Find him for me. [*The* BUSBOY *goes out one way and* RINGO *comes in another.*]

RINGO: What's happening, Joe?

JOE: Give me my winnings.

RINGO: I don't win nutten.

JOE: You too lie!

RINGO: No, honest to God, everything crash.

JOE: Your busboy tell me different.

RINGO: The boy is an idiot, man.

JOE: Don't try an' fool me.

RINGO: I wouldn't do dat. I lose everything. I don't know what happen. I don't see how di crabs never come in. What I thinking is dat Bongo Man double-cross me, or one of di other waiters playing di game too. Boy, A sorry. Yuh ten dollar gone, and my thirty gone too, an' is borrow I borrow it.

JOE: Let me see yuh pocket. [*He reaches for* RINGO'S *pocket.*]

RINGO: Go 'way. Slip, yuh fool. You want to see it? Look! [*Very slowly he pulls all the money out.*] Money like dirt.

JOE: Let me see it.

RINGO: Hold on. Is fifty you getting.

JOE: Fifty? And you have thousands.

RINGO: Thousands what? Check dis.

JOE: I suppose to get more. Give me another ten. If not, I going to talk.

RINGO: [*Hiss*] Tek dat.

JOE: Cool.

[*Screams are heard.*]

RINGO: What's that?

[MISS BRANDON *runs to her imaginary window.* RINGO *and*

JOE *move more slowly to theirs. The* BUSBOY *comes racing down the corridor towards* MISS BRANDON.]

BUSBOY: Get di Manager!

MISS BRANDON: What happen?

BUSBOY: A man dead outside.

MISS BRANDON: A white man? [*She leaves quickly in the direction of the pool.*] Where's di Manager?

RINGO: [*Appears near front desk.*] What's happening, what's dat noise?

BUSBOY: You see di Manager? A man dead outside.

RINGO: Let me through. [*The* BUSBOY *is again alone. He goes to the switchboard and looks at the instrument, then starts to fiddle with it.*]

JOE: [*Entering the reception area*] Leave it!

BUSBOY: How you get di Manager?

JOE: What's all dat noise outside?

BUSBOY: A man dead. A man drown.

JOE: You lie! [*He leaves immediately in the direction of the screams. As he does so, the telephone rings. The* BUSBOY *looks at the telephone. He doesn't know what to do. He goes in the direction of the scream.*]

BUSBOY: Miss B, Miss B, phone ringing. [*There is no reply from her. The phone continues to ring. The* BUSBOY *disappears down the corridor, then bursts into* O'KEEFE'S *office.* O'KEEFE *is trying to get* MISS BRANDON *on the phone.*]

O'KEEFE: Out!

BUSBOY: But, sar ...

O'KEEFE: Out, and knock! [BUSBOY *goes out, then knocks.*] Come in. What is it?

BUSBOY: Serious things happening down at di pool, you know, sar. A man drown.

O'KEEFE: [*Picks up the phone*] Hello, hello! Operator! Operator?

BUSBOY: She not there, sar. She gone to look on di dead man.

O'KEEFE: Dead? Who is dead?

BUSBOY: That is what A came to tell you sar. Down by di pool.

O'KEEFE: Oh my God! [*He splits.*]

[MISS BRANDON *enters her area frantically and buzzes* O'KEEFE's *office.*]

MISS BRANDON: Where's di man?

[*As* O'KEEFE *runs out, his phone is ringing. The* BUSBOY *eyes the instrument, then lunges for it and picks it upside down as* MISS BRANDON *slams down the receiver and runs out again. The* BUSBOY *puts down the receiver, takes a sip of* O'KEEFE's *water, and runs out too.*]

O'KEEFE: [*On the phone in the reception area.*] Mocho Beach Hotel, O'Keefe, Assistant Manager, speaking. Get me an ambulance right away. Yes! And a doctor too! [MISS BRANDON *runs in.*] Where were you?

MISS BRANDON: [*Buzzing the pantry*] Ringo, Ringo, where are ...

[*The* BUSBOY *is in the pantry eating a banana. He throws the skin on the floor. The phone rings. He leaps to answer it. At that moment* MISS BRANDON *hangs up, for staggering into her area to lean against the desk, wearing only trousers but carrying his shirt, and soaking wet, is* RINGO. *Trailing him is* JOE, *who carries* RINGO's *shoes.*]

O'KEEFE: You okay, Smith?

RINGO: Yes, sir. [*Very dazed.*]

O'KEEFE: You have a change of clothes?

RINGO: Yes, sir.

O'KEEFE: Well, get changed.

RINGO: Okay, sir.

O'KEEFE: I'll come and see you in a minute. You certain you feel okay?

RINGO: Yes, sir. [O'KEEFE *goes out.*]

JOE: You okay, Ringo?

RINGO: Yes. I going to take off these wet clothes. [*They go out.*]

[O'KEEFE *gets the first-aid kit from his office.* MISS BRANDON *telephones the ambulance again.* BUSBOY, *in the pantry, picks up the banana peel thoughtfully and puts it in the bin. He eyes the bottle of rum on the shelf.* JOE *and* RINGO *enter the pantry.* BUSBOY *moves guiltily away from the bottle.* O'KEEFE *gives* MISS BRANDON *the kit, and both rush off on their errand of mercy to the poolside.*]

JOE: Young boy, sit down. [*Both very shaken.*] You saw what happen outside?

BUSBOY: Yes, sar.

RINGO: Hold on, young boy. A soon come.

JOE: Hey, Ringo!

RINGO: Hmm?

JOE: Dis thing is going to have serious repercussion, you know.

RINGO: I don't get over di shock yet, you know. I still shaking. What you say happen, young boy?

BUSBOY: I was outside, sar, when A saw Missa Winnie looking very serious. You know how him always jokify? Well this morning him was looking very serious. Him face look like something was bothering him, an' him had a bottle in him hand drinking from.

RINGO: Di whisky bottle?

JOE: Him drink too much, man.

RINGO: Dat is why I don't drink. •

JOE: I hear dat Winnie went to di bar last night and order a bottle of Scotch, but as you know di bar is cash, and Winnie had no money to pay.

BUSBOY: Missa Winnie lose plenty money on di crabs last night.

JOE: Who say so?

BUSBOY: That is what I hear, sar. I hear dat him lose all him money. Him bet all him money on di yellow crab, and every time him lose is di more money him put on di next race, till him lose everything.

JOE: Di barman should never credit him di whisky.

RINGO: Dat is what I say too.

BUSBOY: When I saw him early this morning him was drunk. I see him walking like this wid di bottle in him hand. [BUSBOY *acts it out*.] I didn't pay him much attention till I saw him by di swimming pool. When him get close to di pool, di lifeguard start to watch him. Everywhere him go, I see di lifeguard eyes watching him.

RINGO: Anybody else was by di pool?

BUSBOY: No, sar, jus' Missa Winnie, di lifeguard, di man dat clean out di pool, an' me, sar.

RINGO: All right, go on.

BUSBOY: All of a sudden, sar, I see when Missa Winnie slip and drop in di water. I see when Missa Man-Man, di lifeguard, see him, an' him get nervous, an' I see him look on di other big man dat look after di pool – Missa Jimmy him name, sar?

RINGO: Go on, man.

BUSBOY: And I hear Missa Man-Man call to Missa Jimmy and Missa Jimmy say 'what?' an' Missa Man-Man point into di pool on Missa Winnie who was coming up for di second time, sar. Missa Man-Man an' Missa Jimmy start to do like this, sar. [*He imitates their panic.*] An' den Missa Jimmy jump in di water, but from di way him handle himself it never look like him could swim, sar. Him hands just going like this, sar. [*He acts out Jimmy in distress.*]

RINGO: Why you never jump in?

BUSBOY: Me can't swim, sar. Missa Jimmy couldn't get to Missa Winnie who was now coming up for di third time. Next thing me see was when Missa Jimmy start to go down and come up, and then Missa Man-Man throw in a piece of rope, and Missa Jimmy grab on to it, and him start to pull. Him mek a big pull and Missa Man-Man slip and drop into di water too, sar. An' den me scream out and run for di Manager.

RINGO: You should scream out earlier.

BUSBOY: Mi foot and mi mout' was paralysed, sar.

JOE: Hear me now, dis thing going to have serious repercussion, you know.

RINGO: I don't see what can come out of it.

JOE: Don't chat rubbish, you hear. If it wasn't for you, all this would never happen.

RINGO: At least I jumped in and tried to save them.

JOE: What good dat do, when they dead long time? Anyway, it was just style you was pulling, for you can't swim. So just shut yuh mouth. Is your fault. You should never have got dem di jobs if you knew they couldn't swim.

RINGO: Is you suggest it to me.

JOE: Don't involve me.

RINGO: You in it, so don't try and back out now.

JOE: Look, Master, don't let me get mad! I know what's going to happen when di news get out. It going to give di hotel a bad name. Nobody coming here again. It mash up. I warned you. I'm tired of talking to you. Now look what you make happen?

RINGO: Is you tell me 'bout di jobs.

JOE: Is you ask me. How was I to know it was for two land sharks? Master, I don't know nutten 'bout it. I will put my head on di block. Master, I have my children. If I lose dis work, you going to take care of dem? Tell me? You sheg up everything, man! If you never fix di crab race last night, di man wouldn't lose him money and have to get drunk, and so slip into di pool. See di money there. I don't want it. Take it! Take it!

RINGO: Why all di fuss? Dat's why black people will never get anywhere. We don't stick together. We will try and make a little get out, but as soon as something goes wrong, a little slip-up, we start nyam up each other.

JOE: A little slip-up! Dat's what you call it? Look how far di man come from to drown.

RINGO: Dat's not my fault. Me never tell him to get drunk. Him lose a little money, so what? No big t'ing!

JOE: Is a big thing to me, for if dis news ever get out, di hotel going to close down.

RINGO: Listen to me, man.

JOE: I don't want to hear nutten more from you, for my mind decide. If I ever see where I going to lose dis job … Hunh.

RINGO: All of us lose out if anybody talk.

JOE: No, you know.

RINGO: Stop yuh noise, an' listen to me. As I see it, is only di three of us know di full facts, and if any of us talk, all of us in trouble and I don't see how dat going to benefit me, or you, or you.

JOE: Hold on a little.

RINGO: Hear what I have to say, man. Now everybody see when I jump in di pool.

JOE: Is slip you slip, man.

RINGO: No matter. I jump in. I risk mi life. I risk my life to save di tourist. You hear how people was congratulating me, how me brave. You listen to what di tourists were saying? Di fact dat a man had to jump in and save me too, no big thing. If me never get a cramp me would save everybody. You is di only two dat know me can't swim, so all you have to do is spread it roun' di hotel dat 'Ringo risk him life to save di tourist an' pool attendant'. Two twos you hear it over di radio. Next thing you know you see it in di newspaper. Is a great selling card. Next time dem giving out medal for bravery my name will be on di list. As far as di world is concerned, 'Ringo is a hero'. What I say – 'Hero'. All when di Manager come back and hear di story, is promotion dat, you know. Head Waiter, then Dining-Room Captain. When me get into dem high position, I jus' bring you up wid me. Eh, sweet boy? You can see yuhself as a waiter?

BUSBOY: Yes, sar.

RINGO: So all you have to do is keep yuh mouth shut 'bout what really happen and shout out 'Ringo risk him life to save di people'. People believe anything you tell dem, you know. After me get di promotion, you know, Joe, any little racket you want to run, me nuh jus' turn mi eye? What you say? A talking sense?

JOE: It sound all right, but what about di Assistant Manager? They going to have big investigation into what happen.

RINGO: Dat is true. Even if him find out di truth, what him going to do? Him can't do nutten. Him reputation at stake. Is him employ di boys. When it get down to di nitty-gritty is each man for himself. Everybody protecting him own things. If is not money, is power. Is two things I sorry 'bout, though. One, dat di white man dead – him wasn't a bad guy – and two, dat di other brother never drown too. [*Laughs.*] So, young boy, when anybody ask you what happen today, what you going to say?

BUSBOY: Dat you risk yuh life, sar.

RINGO: Seen. I going finish change mi clothes.

JOE: You hear what di man say?

BUSBOY: Seen.

JOE: You don't have any work to do? You don't get di promotion yet, you know [*as he chases him out*].

LIGHTS OUT

[*The ambulance is heard departing. Lights warm on* MISS BRANDON *entering as phone rings. It is the next day. The* BUSBOY *is lazing in the pantry.*]

MISS BRANDON: Mocho Beach Hotel. What happen, Maisie? ... No, him suppose to be in Ocho Rios. Where you see him? ... Where? Airport? A call you back. [*She pushes a button and the phone rings in the kitchen.*]

BUSBOY: Hello, kitchen.

MISS BRANDON: Is Ringo there?

BUSBOY: No, him not here now.

MISS BRANDON: Who is that?

BUSBOY: This is Cyril. Di busboy.

MISS BRANDON: Could you do me a favour? Come up to the front desk.

[*The* BUSBOY *hangs up, deodorises himself, checks the mirror, and then goes in the direction of the front desk. As he leaves the stage sound effects come up.*]

EASTERN AIRLINES ANNOUNCES THE DEPARTURE OF FLIGHT 505 TO WASHINGTON, NEWARK AND CHICAGO.

[*The* ASSISTANT MANAGER *and the* BUSBOY *meet in* MISS BRANDON's *area.*]

O'KEEFE: Did you see what happened by the pool this morning?

BUSBOY: Yes, sar. Missa Ringo risk him life to save di tourist.

O'KEEFE: [*Smiles*] Where is he now?

BUSBOY: Him roun' di back, sar. [O'KEEFE *turns to go.*] Talking to a reporter, sar. [O'KEEFE *freezes in his tracks. Smiles.*]

O'KEEFE: Tell him, tell him I'd like to see him when he has a moment! [*Heads back to his office.*]

BUSBOY: Yes, ma'am?

MISS BRANDON: Look, I want you to do me a favour. I want you to check room 57. Tell me if you see any suitcases or luggage or anything.

BUSBOY: Fifty-seven?

MISS BRANDON: As quick as possible. [BUSBOY *goes.*]
[*On telephone*] Good morning. Is that Eastern Airlines? Could you check and tell me if you have a Mister Gerald O'Brien booked on the flight to Newark this morning? Yes, I'll hold.

RINGO: [*Entering the pantry*] Hey Joe, you want orange?

JOE: Mmm.

RINGO: Everything cool, man. Di Assistant Manager just back me up roun' di corner. You want to see how him pat pat me up. Newspaper coming down to get mi story. You hear what him say – di hotel won't forget what I do. Him jus' waiting for di big Manager to come back to arrange a promotion for me. [*He bites on the orange. They eat.* BUSBOY *enters* MISS BRANDON's *area.*]

BUSBOY: Nobody there, ma'am. No suitcases or anything.

MISS BRANDON: Thank you.

BUSBOY: I can do anything else for you, ma'am? [*In an over-friendly manner.*]

[MISS BRANDON *picks up the vase after him. The* BUSBOY *leaves quickly. Sound effects of airline announcement.*]

EASTERN AIRLINES ANNOUNCES THE DEPARTURE OF FLIGHT 505 TO NEWARK AND CHICAGO BOARDING AT GATE 5.

[*The* BUSBOY *re-enters the pantry.*]

RINGO: Di orange sweet, boy. Eh, young boy? You want orange?

[*The band strikes up* 'Jamaica, Jamaica' *on a sad, haunting note.*]

BUSBOY: Me don't eat orange, sar.

RINGO: Where you come from?

BUSBOY: Clarendon, sar.

RINGO: Oh. So why you don't eat orange?

BUSBOY: Dem say it will rotten out mi balls, sar.

RINGO: [*Laughs, mimicking the* BUSBOY's *lisp*] Who say so?

BUSBOY: So me hear, sar.

RINGO: And you believe it?

BUSBOY: Yes, sar.

RINGO: You hear dat, Joe? Eat di orange, man.

BUSBOY: No, sar.

RINGO: I would like to know who start all dem rumours.

JOE: Mus' be di man who own di orange tree.

RINGO: Yes. Dem things start from slavery days. Wicked!

JOE: Eat di orange, man.

BUSBOY: No, sar.

RINGO: Hold him, Joe. [*They make a grab for the* BUSBOY *to force the orange down his throat. He protests, 'No, sar, no, sar!'*]

BUSBOY: Okay, peel that ripe one for me. [*They release him to get the ripe orange and he scampers away outside. They laugh and relax, sucking on their oranges.*]

RINGO: Stupid! Him will learn.

MISS BRANDON: Hello, hello, Eastern? Eastern?

[*We hear the airline announcement*]

EASTERN AIRLINES ANNOUNCES THE DEPARTURE OF FLIGHT 505 TO NEWARK WASHINGTON AND CHICAGO NOW BOARDING AT GATE NUMBER 5. THIS IS THE FINAL CALL.

O'KEEFE: [*On phone*] Miss Brandon, Miss Brandon! [*But she is waiting so intently for the airline to answer her call she doesn't even hear him. The* BUSBOY *is at the door again.* O'KEEFE *hangs up wearily.*]

[*The band plays its song very sadly.* CYRIL *comes slowly in.* RINGO *holds out the orange, not even looking at the boy.* CYRIL *stares at it, fascinated. He reaches for it very slowly.* JOE *watches him. A jet roars over. All are frozen in tableau till it has passed. Then* MISS BRANDON *knows she has lost. She hangs up with a sharp click.* O'KEEFE *leans back slowly in his chair.* CYRIL *takes the orange.* RINGO *and* JOE *laugh softly.* CYRIL *begins hesitantly to peel the orange. The band plays softly. The lights dim and go out.*]

In the Castle of my Skin

George Lamming

A boy grows up on a small Caribbean island in the 1930s: a personal, partly autobiographical record of adolescence and, at the same time, a record of the pattern of life during a period of rapid social change. The record is earthy, funny, tender, the bright joys of youth contrasted with the darker undertones of helplessness.

First published more than quarter of a century ago, and quickly established as a classic, George Lamming's first novel won both awards and acclaim. 'Its poetic, imaginative writing has never been surpassed.'

Tribune

'One is back in the world of Huckleberry Finn. . . . Mr Lamming catches the myth-dissolving mind of boyhood.'
The New Statesman

'Humour, pride, poetry and violence are the qualities that blend in this haphazard yet deeply coherent book.'
The Observer

'There is not a stock figure in the story. Nor is there a trace of the bitter recrimination that stifles many similar books.'
The Sunday Times

'A rich and memorable feat of imaginative interpretation.'
The Spectator

Not for sale in the United States of America, Canada and the Philippine Islands.

Drumbeat 3
ISBN 0 582 64267 1

Ways of Sunlight

Samuel Selvon

In these short stories, some set in the Caribbean, some in London, we meet a variety of characters such as Ma Procop, who goes to extraordinary lengths to protect her mango tree; Eraser the bus conductor who loves his bus as a sailor does his ship; Algernon who convinces the English he is an expert on cricket; Small Change who finally wears out the patience of London Transport; and four Jamaican boys who bring obeah to defeat a rapacious London landlady.

When *Ways of Sunlight* was first published, it won high praise from the critics:

'A delightful book. For humour, sprightliness and downright exuberance at being alive, Mr Selvon's people are positively Neapolitan.'

The Sunday Times

'Samuel Selvon brings out well the colour and individuality of life in the West Indies and paints an even livelier picture of exiled West Indians living in London.'

The Guardian

'Mr Selvon writes naturally in dialogue, he never lets the pace sag, and he suggests a scene with a telling economy of means.'

Times Literary Supplement

Drumbeat   4
ISBN 0 582 64261 2

A Brighter Sun

Samuel Selvon

Tiger is sixteen. According to custom among the East Indians of Chaguanas, it is time to prove himself a man, to marry a girl he has never seen, to set up his own home, found his own family and earn his own living. Urmilla, his child-bride, shy and bewildered, is equally anxious to prove herself a woman, a wife and a mother.

The setting for this sensitive novel is Trinidad in the years of the second world war, a period of change as intense and far-reaching for Trinidad as the years of his maturing are for Tiger.

Samuel Selvon, himself an Indian from Trinidad, wrote *A Brighter Sun*, his first novel, in 1952; it is now established as a classic.

Drumbeat   5
ISBN 0 582 64265 5

The Lonely Londoners

Samuel Selvon

In the hopeful aftermath of the war they flocked to the Mother Country: waves of West Indians looking for a prosperous new future and finding instead a cool reception, bone-chilling weather and bleak prospects. Yet friendships flourish among these lonely Londoners and they learn to survive, and even to love their London.

Samuel Selvon's classic novel about immigrants in the 1950s is rich in characters such as Galahad who never feels the cold, Big City who dreams of fame and fortune, Harris who likes to play ladeda, Moses who hates his own soft heart, and the Captain who has a way with women.

'Delightful . . . an entertaining read and accurately portrays the climate in Britain in the 1950s when immigration and racism were nascent issues.'

West Africa

'A vernacular comedy of pathos.'

The Guardian

'Classic, award-winning novel about those pioneers of the West Indian "invasion" who found London a glitter-city full of human problems.'

The Evening News

Drumbeat 6
ISBN 0 582 64264 7

Edufa

Efua T. Sutherland

For a successful, modern, educated Ghanaian, Edufa is surprisingly insecure. He has partially deserted the values of the African society into which he was born, and in his passion for status and prestige he is driven to barter his beloved wife's life against loss of these privileges. But he is not prepared for the day of reckoning . . .

This early play by Efua T. Sutherland, first published in 1967, shows the playwright's command of tragic drama as well as her sympathetic understanding of human failings and frailties.

'Ms Sutherland has risen above colour, place and time in this play to deal wholly with people. (She) has used classical techniques in an unclassical way. The chorus . . . becomes part of the action. She makes use of a prologue, in (which) the wistful poetry which pervades the whole play is introduced. Dramatically sound . . . worthy of production.'

Rhodesia Herald

Drumbeat 11
ISBN 0 582 64272 8

The Marriage of Anansewa

Efua T. Sutherland

Ananse the cunning spider man is the hero of countless Ghanaian legends. In this play, which the author calls a 'story-telling drama', Ananse hits upon a get-rich-quick scheme of breathtaking simplicity. He will betroth his beautiful daughter Anansewa simultaneously to several rich chiefs and pocket the cheques the prospective bridegrooms send to seal the engagement.

But alas for Ananse! He is caught in his own web of deceit when all four chiefs, eager to see the bride, announce their imminent arrival. The only solution is for Anansewa to die . . .

Drumbeat 17
ISBN 0 582 64260 4

Anowa

Ama Ata Aidoo

Anowa is based upon a nineteenth-century Ghanaian legend about a girl who defies her parents' wishes to marry the man of her choice but then does not live happily ever after. Ama Ata Aidoo first heard the story from her mother in the form of a song and, in turning it into a play, has given it her own interpretation.

'Ama Ata Aidoo has a gift for the sparse economical language of sadness and despair and for the gaiety, rollicking boisterousness and acid wit of comedy, satire, irony and parody.'

African Literature Today 8

Drumbeat 19
ISBN 0 582 64269 8

The Dilemma of a Ghost

Ama Ata Aidoo

Ama Ata Aidoo's first play focuses on the marriage of a Ghanaian and his American bride who soon find themselves at loggerheads with his deeply traditional family.

'*Dilemma of a Ghost* is the most thoughtful thing that has come out of the modern Ghanaian theatre to date. In technical and verbal mastery it is superior to any other Ghanaian play.'

Perspectives of African Literature

'The whole play is obviously much influenced by Greek drama . . . Miss Aidoo is very sensitive to language, and employs it cunningly to suggest the nature of her characters.'

Protest and Conflict in African Literature

Drumbeat 27
ISBN 0 582 78529 4

The Dragon Can't Dance

Earl Lovelace

All the year round Aldrick lives in the Calvary Hill slums of Port of Spain, waiting for the two days of Carnival, when he will parade and dance in pride and triumph in his resplendent Dragon costume. But this year is different. How can he prevent seventeen-year-old Sylvia from selling herself to rich, middle-aged Mr Guy for the sake of a Carnival costume?

Aldrick and Sylvia are just two of the colourful characters in this brilliant novel by the author of *While Gods Are Falling*.

'This novel is a landmark, not in the West Indian, but in the contemporary novel.... Nowhere have I seen more of the realities of a whole country disciplined into one imaginative volume.'

C. L. R. James in Race Today Review

'A tough, sharply written book which rewards careful reading.'

Trinidad Express

Drumbeat 26
ISBN 0 582 64231 0